FOLKTALES OF MAYOTTE, AN AFRICAN ISLAND

Folktales of Mayotte,
an African Island

From research by Claude Allibert, Noel Gueunier, and Sophie Blanchy

Lee Haring

https://www.openbookpublishers.com

©2023 Lee Haring

World Oral Literature Series, vol. 10 | ISSN: 2050-7933 (Print); 2054-362X (Online)

ISBN Paperback: 978–1-80511–004-0

ISBN Hardback: 978–1-80511–005-7

ISBN Digital (PDF): 978–1-80511–006-4

ISBN Digital ebook (EPUB): 978–1-80511–007-1

ISBN XML: 978–1-80511–009-5

ISBN HTML: 978–1-80511–010-1

DOI: 10.11647/OBP.0315

Cover image: Mayotte (2016). Foto by Martine at https://bit.ly/3odGEZL.
Cover design by Margarita Louka

Contents

Foreword

Mark Turin

Folktales of Mayotte is the tenth publication in the World Oral Literature series and the second monograph by Lee Haring that our partnership with Open Book Publishers has seen into press. Now running for a decade, the series was designed to preserve and promote the oral literatures of Indigenous people by publishing materials on endangered traditions in innovative, responsive, ethical and culturally-appropriate ways. Situated at the intersection of anthropology, folklore, linguistics and information studies, the study of oral genres is an exciting and fast-developing field, but one with few publishing outlets.

Haring's 2013 publication in our series, *How to Read a Folktale*, offered the first English translation of Ibonia, a captivating tale of old Madagascar.[1] Containing African-style praise poetry for the hero replete with Indonesian-style riddles and poems, Ibonia elevates the form of folktale to epic proportions and in so doing, asserts the power of the ancestors in resistance to European colonial settlers. With Haring as our guide, through the lens of Ibonia, readers are invited to rethink the very nature of folktales, and the author's expert analysis raises fundamental intellectual questions that engage with anthropological theory as well as literary criticism.

Building on the success of this earlier monograph, and through a long professional career devoted to the careful study and analysis of folklore and verbal arts, in *Folktales of Mayotte* Haring sets himself a particularly curious challenge — a conceit more than a constraint — to offer a contextually rich and vivid description of an oral tradition that he has never witnessed. That Haring succeeds in realizing this ambitious goal is a testament to the sophistication of his analysis and the enormous comparative knowledge of folklore on which the author is able to draw.

   https://doi.org/10.11647/OBP.0315.04

This book provides a compelling story about folktales in Mayotte, an island in the Indian Ocean about 1,000 miles east of the African coast, through the perspective of the oeuvre of three French ethnographers who worked there in the 1970s and 1980s: Claude Allibert, Noël Gueunier and Sophie Blanchy. Focusing on the storytellers and their oral performances, Haring makes a strong case for the value and utility of such an approach — which he charmingly refers to as 'a relatively polite kind of eavesdropping' — by effectively showcasing the verbal dexterity of Mayotte storytellers and the impressive narrative techniques and ancient symbols on which they draw.

A multicultural island neglected by the French colonial regime, Mayotte has a folktale repertoire that links it to Madagascar through many common threads. The cultural hybridity of Mayotte is particularly distinctive, with a repertoire of verbal arts that draw from and have been transmitted from Persia, India, Europe and Africa. The storytellers themselves take inspiration from the widely divergent traditions of their island, blending elements of the past with objects from everyday life in creative and engaging ways. As Haring so elegantly puts it, the stories from this underrepresented island 'amount to a network of the metaphors traditional to Mayotte.' The author asks us to consider a deceptively simple question: how much can a reader at a distance expect to appreciate these translated stories from Mayotte? Thanks to Lee Haring, the answer is: a great deal.

Dr Mark Turin
Director, World Oral Literature Project
Institute for Critical Indigenous Studies
University of British Columbia

Vancouver, Canada
January 2023

Endnotes

1   Lee Haring, *How to Read a Folktale: The 'Ibonia' Epic from Madagascar* (Cambridge: Open Book Publishers, 2013). https://doi.org/10.11647/OBP.0034.

Preface

I Am a Stranger There Myself

This book is about storytellers and their oral performances of folktales in Mayotte, an island lying in the Indian Ocean about 1,000 miles east of the African coast. The book is built on a constraint: I have not witnessed the performances I discuss; in fact I have never been to Mayotte. Within that constraint, I indulge a whim. I use books by three French ethnographers of the 1970s–80s to imagine the oral performances. My whim follows the 'law' devised by the Oulipo group in Paris: 'A text written according to a constraint describes the constraint'.[1] I ask, what can we comprehend about an oral art without witnessing it in person? Numerous critics of Homer and succeeding classical authors have answered: quite a lot. Imagining a performance — which I practice and recommend — does not replace the physical presence of a storyteller, but like reading the script of a play, it urges us to see the performance of oral literature as a kind of theater. Storytellers in Mayotte are skillful at blending different traditions and using the past to deal with the present. The books celebrate their skills. I invite you to try this relatively polite kind of eavesdropping with me.

All three ethnographers were well prepared to transmit Mayotte's culture to the West and tell us why audiences like these stories; each had a distinct purpose. Claude Allibert, while teaching in a *lycée* (secondary school), looked to folktales to preserve traces of Mayotte's early history. He found many. Noël Gueunier, teaching anthropology in the University of Madagascar not far away, and interested in the uses of Malagasy language, collected scores of tales in Kibushi, Mayotte's dialect of that language. He also recorded people's continual switching between Kibushi and a second language, Shimaore, which is

  https://doi.org/10.11647/OBP.0315.05

related to the Swahili spoken in Kenya and Tanzania. They inherited their bilingualism from the converging cultures in Mayotte's history. Sophie Blanchy's devoted attention to female storytellers reveals their mastery of the narrative art. All three collectors show their hundreds of storytellers commanding an impressive range of narrative techniques employing symbols from the past, with which they comment on their present. I am grateful to the three collectors for translation permission, for allowing me to paraphrase their notes and comments, and most of all for saving me from embarrassing mistakes.

Obligatory Background Information

Mayotte, I have learned, is smaller than Africa's smallest country (Seychelles) and more multicultural than most. Historically, although no longer politically, it is one of the four Comoro Islands, an archipelago lying between Madagascar and East Africa, which used to be France's most neglected colony. The other three are Grande Comore (Ngazidja), Mohéli (Mwali), and Anjouan (Ndzuwani). Mayotte's population of 288,926 (in 2021) comprises people whose culture is an amalgam created by African, Arab, European and Malagasy settlers. The folktale repertoire connects Mayotte to Madagascar; they share many tales, which have ancient roots. The early Malagasy originated in what is now Indonesia and settled in the Comoros at least as early as the tenth century, maybe earlier. Then Arabs and Persians came into east Africa, in enough numbers to intermarry with Bantu Africans and convert people to Islam. That mix formed the foundation of Swahili culture. Some say that the history of the Comoros archipelago goes back to the era of King Solomon; anyway, it is never separate from the history of Madagascar. How complicated that mix can look to a newcomer is formidably stated by the anthropologist Paul Ottino.

> Malagasy ideas and conceptions, whether comprised in myths and wondertales or in historical legends, must be systematically brought together with the Indian and Muslim religious, philosophical, and political representations that, from the 13th century on, converged across India on the Malay peninsula and the Insulindian archipelago, at the same time as Islam and the Bantu world were encountering each other on the shores of the east coast of Africa, producing what were to become Swahili civilization and culture.[2]

The models for Mayotte were hybrid from birth.

History forced people together; their convergence brought forth creativity. People brought to Mayotte tales that had been transmitted from Persia, India, Europe and Africa. Also, life in Mayotte from its early days has been dominated by Islam. In the twelfth century, the Shirazi, a group originating in Persia, mixed with and married Africans, and began evangelizing, which they continued to do as they migrated to the Comoros and other offshore islands. Traces of Persian, even of Indonesian culture are evident in some of the tales. In response to the conversion, African identity and customs went underground. That is where folklore resides. But the tales collected in the 1970s–80s tell us that in earlier times, those Islamized Africans did not discard African values; they added new characters and plots to the stories they already knew. Islam does not dominate the texture of the folktales in this book, though it saturates people's lives. Few of the tales feature Islamic priests, for instance, as principal characters. When they do, they slander them. Islam has survived in Mayotte not by drowning out popular beliefs, but by living side by side with them.[3] Some tales can be read as Islamic allegory about a believer's relation to God: 'Under the pretext of a plot strongly rooted in the daily life of women of Mayotte (says Blanchy), these tales also carry a message of a spiritual order'.[4] Blending diverse images is one thing the storytellers are very good at. Their creativity shows when they draw the plots and characters they have learned from other storytellers and point them at their present social situation.

Mayotte is now an overseas *département* of France, like Martinique and Guadeloupe. It has always been loyal to the metropole. In the 1970s, when some of these tales were being collected, it refused to join the independence movement of the other Comoros. A story in "Chapter 2" shows how hot the issue was in the villages. At that time, Mayotte was classified as a 'territorial collectivity'; in 2011 the loyalists finally got their wish to be an overseas *département*. Every week now, French people arrive from the metropole permanently or temporarily, adding their own linguistic and cultural heritage to the local network. Some see Mayotte as a less expensive Réunion (another Indian Ocean *département*, 900 miles away). Also arriving are illegal immigrants from Anjouan and the other Comoros, seeking work. If the immigrants do not perish on the way from overloading and bad weather, they will be blamed for a rise in crime and evicted from their homes. Now this African-Malagasy island is obliged to pretend to be part of France (5000 miles away), to use France's manufactured products and currency, and to leave behind the village traditions sampled in this book. With its economy and finances linked ever more closely with Europe, Mayotte sees French capital being used for exploitation rather than development. The gap between villagers and settlers increases. The tales translated in this book speak from a village life that was already passing in the 1970s–80s.[5]

The narrators draw from their island's widely divergent traditions. Their creativity lies in a highly developed capacity for combining the new and the old. Their art is to blend what they remember from other storytellers with settings and objects from everyday life. It is a capacity cast in theoretical terms by the critic Julia Kristeva: 'the text is doubly oriented, towards the signifying system in which it is produced (the language, and the language of a specific era and society), and towards the social process in which it participates by virtue of being a discourse'.[6] In practical terms, the translations by our three collectors show performers skilled in entertaining their audiences while they deal critically with issues like colonial power, marriage and the need for secrecy. Taken together, their stories amount to a network of the metaphors traditional to Mayotte. Storytellers in Mayotte choose tales from the past that are somehow relevant to their present. Sometimes the choice is conscious, sometimes calling it a choice is my interpretive move. Each of the following chapters will discuss the findings of one collector.

Endnotes

1   Jacques Roubaud, 'Introduction: The *Oulipo* and Combinatorial Art', in *Oulipo Compendium*, ed. Harry Mathews and Alastair Brotchie (London: Atlas Press, 1998), p. 42.

2   Paul Ottino, *L'étrangère intime: essai d'anthropologie de la civilisation de l'ancien Madagascar* (Paris: Éditions des Archives Contemporains, 1986), p. 576. Claude Allibert follows up Ottino's directive in *Mayotte: plaque tournante et microcosme de l'océan indien occidental* (Paris: Éditions Anthropos, 1984).

3   Along with collecting folktales, Sophie Blanchy has closely observed Islam in the daily life of the 1980s: *La vie quotidienne à Mayotte* (Paris: L'Harmattan, 1993), pp. 180–96.

4   'Lignée féminine et valeurs islamiques à travers quelques contes de Mayotte (Comores)' (Saint-Denis: Université de la Réunion, 1986), pp. 136–46.

5   Sources of information on Mayotte today include: Michael Lambek, *Knowledge and Practice in Mayotte: Local Discourses of Islam, Sorcery, and Spirit Possession*. Toronto: University of Toronto Press, 1993. Dan Golembeski, 'Mayotte: France's New Overseas Department in the Indian Ocean', *The French Review*, 85, 3 (February 2012), pp. 440–57. https://www.jstor.org/stable/41346263. Claude-Valentin Marie, Didier Breton, Maude Crouzet, 'More than half of all adults living in Mayotte were born elsewhere'. *Population and Societies*, 560 (November 2018). Nina Sahraoui, 'Constructions of Undeservingness around the Figure of the Undocumented Pregnant Woman in the French Department of Mayotte'. *Social Policy and Society*, 20, 3 (July 2021), 475–86. https://doi.org/10.1017/S1474746421000038. Iris Derœux, 'Mayotte: Four key dates to explain the migratory tensions on the French department. Events in the recent history of the archipelago shed light on the current difficulty in curbing illegal immigration'. *Le Monde*, 27 August 2022. https://www.lemonde.fr/en/les-decodeurs/article/2022/08/27/mayotte-four-key-dates-to-explain-the-migratory-tensions-on-the-french-department_5994998_8.html. Rémi Armand Tchokothe, 'How Can Literary Works Help Us to Understand the Politics of Migration?' LT Video Publication. https://doi.org/10.21036/LTPUB10756.

6   Julia Kristeva, *Desire in Language: A Semiotic Approach to Literature and Art*, ed. Leon S. Roudiez (New York: Columbia University Press, 1980), p. 332.

A Note on the Text

All translations are mine, from the texts and translations of the collectors.

The storytellers' words appear throughout in Small Caps, to distinguish them both from my words in the main text and from the words of the three French ethnographers, which are given as ordinary quotations. Square brackets are used to indicate my words within a quote. Parentheses are used to indicate a speaker's interpolation into his or her own speaking.

Information for folklorists is conveyed in footnotes. Taylor Hein's index gives each tale a title; identifies the narrator, date, and place of collecting; points out significant motifs in the tale as found in Stith Thompson's *Motif-Index of Folk Literature*; indicates its type, according to H.-J. Uther's *Types of International Folktales*; and shows the volume and page numbers in the source. It takes the place of the update to my *Malagasy Tale Index* that Noël Gueunier once wished for, in a letter to me.

This index can be found online in the Additional Resources section: https://www.openbookpublishers.com/books/10.11647/ obp.0315#resources. It can also be downloaded directly at: https://hdl. handle.net/20.500.12434/7488670a.

1. Mayotte Is Ours

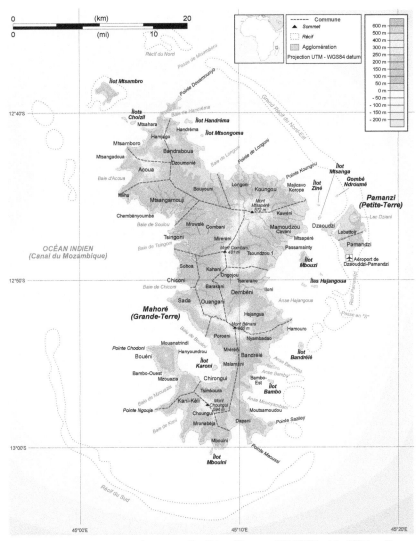

Fig. 1 Mayotte topographic map. By Rémi Kaupp, CC BY-SA 4.0, Wikimedia Commons, https://upload.wikimedia.org/wikipedia/commons/f/f1/Mayotte_topographic_map-fr.svg

    https://doi.org/10.11647/OBP.0315.01

'Although in the morning I was the *maître* [teacher], in our long afternoon and evening meetings they became my *mafundi* [teachers]'. This is how Claude Allibert recalls the rhythm of authority between himself and the schoolboys he was teaching, during his two-year posting to Mayotte (1973–1975). To convey the flavor of their exchanges, he switches between French and Kibushi, the Mayotte dialect of Malagasy. Throughout, he names nearly all his informants, most of whom are male. Others are probably persons he visited on non-school days. Trilinguals like Mohamed el Anrif, who lived in the Kibushi-speaking village of Mzoizia, told his tale in Shimaore (old Comoran), and sometimes used words from coastal African Swahili. Switching codes was normal; the new game between Allibert and the schoolboys was switching authority. His translations are clear and simple. Although Kibushi and French do not agree on things like word order and the sequence of verb tenses, the disagreement does not obscure narrative movement. The pieces sound traditional, and on examination the symbols are too.

Through his pages, storytelling in 1970s Mayotte looks like a politics of cultural survival. When Allibert arrived in September 1973, the Comoro Islands had not yet declared independence. During his two years training students to be proper citizens of a French dependency, they must have wondered about their future. Going to the French school, shouldn't some expect to become leaders in an independent Mayotte? Their tales draw on the past for content and style, but they also allude to the precarious present. Often, they seem to be referring to situations their home audiences would recognize.

Claiming the Place

Imagine being one of those students. You are asked for stories of the past. Semiconsciously you set a cultural strategy in motion. You are aware of differences of status, age and ethnicity, so the interview situation determines what stories you bring out to tell. You can rely on your hearer's knowledge, or his ignorance. Your story can give him a history lesson, but you don't want to lead towards a political discussion. The nearest choice might be a story you have heard about a certain place. That points to the past; it is the kind of thing newcomers should hear. A dozen or more of Claude Allibert's narrators made that choice. Whether intentionally or not, they tell stories about particular places asserting the Mahorais, not the French, are the owners of the colonized island.

Fig. 2 Fisherman in lagoon. By Pierrick Lizot, CC BY-SA 4.0, Wikimedia Commons, https://commons.wikimedia.org/wiki/File:P%C3%AAche_dans_le_lagon_de_Mayotte.jpg

Sufiana Ali, for one, told a little story explaining why the island of Pamandzi (or Pamanzi) has that name. A visitor would already know that it holds Mayotte's airport; formerly it held the capital, Dzaoudzi. It bore its name long before the arrival of the French, but, says the legend;

SOME COMORANS LEFT PAMANDZI AND WENT TO THE BIG PLACE [MADAGASCAR]. A FEW MONTHS LATER, THE FRENCH ALSO BEGAN TO SUFFER. ONE AFTER ANOTHER WENT TO SETTLE AT THE BIG PLACE. WHEN THE MEN WERE ASKED, "WHY'D YOU COME HERE?" [THEY SAID] "THERE'S NOTHING TO EAT THERE!" BUT THE COMORANS, WHO DIDN'T SPEAK GOOD FRENCH, WOULD SAY, "PAS MANGER" (NO EATS). TWO YEARS LATER, WITH LOTS OF WORK, THE CRISIS ENDED AND THE PEOPLE CAME BACK TO PAMANDZI. THAT'S THE NAME THAT STAYED ON THIS PLACE.[1]

It is the kind of legend that gets quoted in Lonely Planet travel guides — told as true, set in the world we know. In the United States, figures like Paul Bunyan and Pocahontas are legendary because stories are told about them. Sufiana Ali, knowing what his interviewer represented, chooses a story about economic depression and recovery, incidentally making the point that colonized people had better speak good French. His interview situation seems to have determined that choice, or strategy.

It is a strategy I first noticed far from Mayotte, in the 1970s. Not long after Kenya's independence, I visited Kisii, in the west. Local people learned quickly that I was interested in old stories; they probably assumed I was either a Christian missionary or a leftover government spy, and they welcomed me cordially. One of their pieces resembled the Mayotte stories in being about ownership of the land. It said that the Gusii (that is the adjective) prophet Sakagwa, also known as Eliamwamu, foretold the coming of British settlers sixty years before. (Kenyans have the habit of referring to white people as Europeans.)

> THERE WAS ALSO A MAN CALLED ELIAMWAMU, WHO WAS AN OLD PROPHET. HE PROPHESIED THAT THE EUROPEANS WILL CAME [SIC], BUT MOST OF THE KISIIS USED TO DESPISE IT BECAUSE THEY THOUGHT THAT HE WAS JUST JOKING. HE WAS TRYING TO TELL THEM THAT THERE WILL COME SOME PEOPLE WHO ARE WHITE, AND THEN THEY WILL SETTLE IN OUR LAND HERE — BEFORE THEY CAME. AND ALSO THERE WAS A SECOND MAN, A WITCH DOCTOR SAMWEL NYAMAO. THIS MAN ALSO WAS TRYING TO TELL THEM THE SAME STORIES. BUT MOST OF THE KISIIS DID NOT BELIEVE THEM [...] WHEN THE PEOPLE THOUGHT THAT IT WAS NOT TRUE — BUT WHEN THE EUROPEANS CAME, THEY [SAW] THAT THEY HAD BUILT [...] HOUSES WHICH LOOKED LIKE MUSHROOMS [THIS WAS SAKAGWA'S PROPHECY], AND THEN THE PROPHECY OF SAKAGWA BECAME TRUE.[2]

If Sakagwa's prophecies are mightier than the foreigner's gun, the lesson is that people in Kisii are a force to be reckoned with. Such situations of unequal power (as my late collaborator David Samper once wrote to me privately) engender expressions 'fashioned from the combination of divergent cultural forms, images, goods, and meanings appropriated from a variety of different countries, cultures, and ethnicities'. The narrators in this book practice that method.

The legends continually assert ownership of the land.[3] Here are two brothers, Muzidalifa and Asani Yusuf, instructing their instructor about bilingualism in their island. We notice their schoolbook style.

> FORMERLY, BEFORE OTHER NATIONS ARRIVED, THERE WERE PEOPLE LIVING IN MAYOTTE WHO SPOKE TWO DIALECTS, ONE CLOSE TO MALAGASY LANGUAGE AND THE OTHER TO SWAHILI. THE PEOPLE OF MAYOTTE LIVED ON THIS ISLAND NOT KNOWING ABOUT FOREIGNERS. ONE FINE DAY A VILLAGE CHIEF MKOLO LEARNED IN A DREAM THAT FOREIGNERS WOULD BE ARRIVING ON THE ISLAND SOON. NEXT

DAY AT DAWN HE BROUGHT HIS FELLOW CITIZENS TOGETHER AND TOLD THEM HIS
DREAM. THEN HE PROPOSED THAT THEY SHOULD MOVE THEIR ISLAND, SO AS TO
GET RID OF THESE PEOPLE. AFTER HIS SPEECH HE SENT YOUNG MEN INTO ALL THE
VILLAGES TO ALERT THE INHABITANTS AND ASK THEIR HELP. THE MESSENGERS
TOLD THE CHIEFS TO APPEAR BEFORE THE DREAMER WITH ALL THEIR BOATS AND
STRONG ROPES. A DAY WAS SET, AND ON THAT DAY ALL THE MEN SET OFF BEHIND
MKOLO GOING TOWARDS THE SEA. THEY STOPPED NEAR A POINT AND PUT A
HOLE IN IT. THEN THEY PUT THE ROPES INTO THE HOLE AND FASTENED THEM TO
THE BOATS. AT THE SIGNAL, EVERYONE BEGAN TO ROW. BUT THE EFFORTS WERE
VAIN, THE ISLAND DIDN'T MOVE. THE MEN WERE TIRED AND WENT BACK TO THEIR
VILLAGE. SINCE THAT DAY, THAT POINT IS CALLED BWÉ FORO, PIERCED ROCK.[4]

The immovable home island still shows the scar caused by the threat of
invasion; resistance is remembered and honored.

Yes, the story is a tourist item explaining the origin of a name, but
consider the futile effort chief Mkolo demands of his men: they are
to move their home away from foreigners. When the chief's dream
accurately foresees the future, the threat of invasion requires instant
compliance with its message. Any audience will see the hopelessness
of his scheme. Probably the men with the ropes saw it too. The
contradiction between aspiration and visible reality is enough to keep
the story alive. Maybe some people laugh at it, but the legend asserts,
'Mayotte is ours'.

Some of the history narrated in the place legends is bloody. The
narrator Mwananku Saindu takes his listener back to the time when the
French were seizing Dzaoudzi (the capital on Pamanzi), and Bwana
Madi, who ruled from 1817 to 1829, was unable to prevent them. He
was attacked by his people. Willing to sacrifice himself for his land, he
ordered them to kill him, but only at sea. If he were killed on land, he
said, Mayotte would never grow. But they violated his command and
killed him on a mountain. Furious at seeing his blood drying in the
sun, the king cursed Mayotte with drought and poverty. The narrator's
gloomy closing line brings the past into the present: THE BLOODY ROCK
HAS REMAINED RED UNTIL NOW, IN A PLACE NAMED RED ROCKS (*MAUÉ
MAKUDRU*).[5] How useful the legend is: it explains why people in the
present are not well-off.

Other place legends are flavored with morality and strange gods.
Reinforcing the theme of resistance without the bloodshed, Haruna
Rachidi tells of villagers so quarrelsome that their chief decided to
divide them into three clusters. One moves to the islet Mbara and tries

to displace it by rowing it away (we've heard that before); the local god, angry, kills them. The second group tries to sweeten the river by throwing in masses of sugar (a local crop). The god of beauty, angry, kills them too, leaving only the third group. Thus all those who left the village were killed by the anger of the gods. AND SINCE THAT OLD EVENT, THE *ILOT* OF MBARA AND THE RIVER OF BEAUTY HAVE BECOME *ZIARA*, [PLACES TO] PRAY AND WORSHIP GOD.[6] Another narrator, Waldati Omar, moralistically portrays a gluttonous daughter who is about to eat the biggest of the family's squashes, until her parents tell her it's a *démon*. Paying no attention, she rolls it down to the river, then to the sea, where the *démon* drowns and eats her.[7] *Mali ya mjiga huliwa na wendza âkili*, says the proverb: the fool's fortune gets eaten by the clever ones.[8] It's hard to miss the implications for an island dominated by a foreign power.

Another legend of violating an interdiction, says narrator Ahmed Atumani,

IS A WELL-KNOWN STORY IN THE WHOLE ISLAND, BECAUSE SAZILÉ IS KIND OF A SACRED PLACE. LONG AGO THERE WAS A KING WHO HAD A VILLAGE. ALL THE PEOPLE THERE LED A HAPPY LIFE WITH NEVER A CARE. THE KING WAS CHARITABLE AND LOVED HIS PEOPLE. THERE WAS A VERY PRETTY GIRL, WHO WAS LOVED BY THE PRINCE FROM ANOTHER VILLAGE. ONE DAY THE YOUNG PRINCE CAME TO ASK HER FATHER FOR THE PRINCESS'S HAND, AND SOON THE MARRIAGE WAS ARRANGED. AS THE KING HAD ONLY ONE DAUGHTER, HE INVITED ALL OF MAYOTTE FOR A BIG CEREMONY. THE GREAT DAY ARRIVED AND THE CELEBRATION BEGAN. TWENTY OXEN WERE KILLED.

At this point the narrator inserts an ethnographic detail for the interviewer: in Mayotte, the bridegroom is escorted, crossing through the village and dancing, to the house the bride's father has built. Then he goes into legend for the origin of a place name, and of a feature a visitor might notice.

THE KING WANTED TO SATISFY THIS CUSTOM, BUT HE DIDN'T WANT HIS SON-IN-LAW TO WALK ON THE GROUND. THEY SPREAD RICE ON HIS PATH, FROM THE PALACE TO THE END OF THE VILLAGE. NOW, EVERYBODY IN MAYOTTE KNOWS THAT WALKING ON FOOD, ESPECIALLY RICE, IS FORBIDDEN BY GOD. SO, THE ALMIGHTY BECAME ANGRY AND THE VILLAGE WAS FLOODED BY AN EXTRAORDINARY HIGH SEA. THE NUPTIAL PROCESSION WAS BROKEN OFF AND MANY PEOPLE COULD NOT BE SAVED. THE RICE WAS IMMEDIATELY TRANSFORMED INTO WHITE SAND. THAT'S WHY TODAY WE SEE WHITE SAND IN THE MIDDLE OF THE SEA AT THAT PLACE. THE FEW PEOPLE WHO COULD REACH MUTSAMUDU, OR THE BAMBO COAST AT MBWINI, WENT THERE TO TELL THEIR STORY AND TALK ABOUT THE LIFE THEY LED

AND MISSED. THAT'S WHY THEY SAY *SAZILÉ*, "IN THOSE DAYS." SINCE THEN THAT
REGION IS CALLED SAZILÉ. THERE ARE SPIRITS LIVING THERE. THEY FORBID THAT
WORD TO BE PRONOUNCED WHEN YOU GO BY THERE, BECAUSE THAT RECALLS THE
EVENT, AND THEY PUNISH WHOEVER DARES TO DO THAT.[9]

Fig. 3 White Sand. By VillageHero, CC BY-SA 2.0, Wikimedia Commons, https://
upload.wikimedia.org/wikipedia/commons/5/53/Sable_Blanche_%28Mayo
tte%29_%2831357582336%29.jpg

Other versions of the same plot confirm how well-known the story is.
One names the village, Majumeuni, and even the girl, Layraza; in an
Anjouan version, where the violation is using milk for bodily hygiene,
the result is the same: the visitor is shown the ruins. For Claude Allibert,
the value of such orally transmitted narratives is their record of the past.
This one, he says, might be historical memory of a tidal wave after a
cyclone. Farther back, in Mayotte's earliest history, he writes, 'It is very
probable that vestiges of India and Malaysia exist in certain tales', prior
to the Bantu, Swahili, even Persian contributions.[10] While the place
legends are local, and their concerns are of the 1970s, their fervent
proprietorship, their clinging to tradition, can be heard in every other
story in this book.

Tricksters

Students understood what M. Allibert was asking them for. Narrating
a places legend is pretty straightforward. One performs it without

flourishes. The schoolboy *fundi* is more of a performer when he entertains his instructor. Why not offer him funny stories? Africa and Madagascar have bequeathed many trickster stories to Mayotte. Tortoise, for example, made his ponderous way from East Africa to Mayotte, where he triumphs over the ridicule of everybody around. The chief of a drought-ridden village, says Anli Ibrahim, makes a futile trip to find water, then learns the secret. On his return, he calls together all the birds and sends them to the place, carrying an axe and a pot. They are to plant the axe in the tree and repeat an incomprehensible magical song.

> Niregé patsu crain wano rakusin maji namukalatcha, magiao namukalakatcha,
> Niregé mabu crain wano rakusin maji namukalatcha, magiao namukalakatcha,
>   Hi mambo hi namukalakatcha

We do not have the tune, but those weird words are a charm, in a modified kind of Swahili. They mean 'Big tree-trunk, Take the axe, take the pot, and bring back water'. It is no wonder that neither Crow nor Turtledove can repeat them. Tortoise happens to hear about the quest and offers to go. He successfully sings the song and plants the axe in the tree; water gushes out, everybody is happy, and he is rewarded with money. 'From that day on, he was named Gnamba Mali, and the stream is still running in the village'.[11] The stream is still there; Gnamba means Tortoise; therefore the story must be true — just as the hole in Bwé Foro confirms the story of its immovability. But the legend is a parody of myth: not only does trickster conquer ridicule, but his classic heroic deed earns him his real name. If trickster in a colonized island wins out like this, he could, in some eyes, be typifying the colonized 'native'.

Tortoise is not Mayotte's only East African animal trickster. One accomplished narrator, Bwanali Said, tells of an unlikely friendship between Porcupine and trickster Hare. After an epidemic kills all the game animals — which might be a topical reference — the two make a contract to plant banana trees. Hare violates their contract by convincing Porcupine to plant upside down, so his trees yield nothing while Hare gets many bananas.[12] Bwanali Said uses that tale to lead off a string of six pieces starring a well-known human trickster, who deserves a digression.

Bwanawasi

Bwanawasi is the folktale name for the distinguished poet Abu-Nawās, of the court of the ninth-century Abbasid Calif Haroun al-Rasheed. As acclaimed for his poetry on love and sex as he was notorious for homosexuality and drinking, Abu-Nawās played a politically oppositional role through issuing satires to convey his prejudice against Arabs. Thus, he became the ancestor of insurgents. In the *Arabian Nights*, we find a fictionalized version of him with clairvoyant powers, which make up for his scandal-mongering. He also escapes punishment for his homosexual carousing by reframing his plight in poetry, as a folktale character might escape by singing a song. Later oral fictions make him into al-Rasheed's jester. His fame spread in stories in Ethiopia, Egypt and (coming back towards Mayotte) among Swahili people on the Kenya coast. In tales from Grande Comore, he has been seen as a knight errant fighting on behalf of the people. There he is called *Buwaswia*, a creolized version of his name, which adds the title 'son of wisdom'.[13] Bwanawasi exists in variant forms. So do the tales about him, which audiences recognize as traditional. Equally traditional is this narrator's way of sequencing the pieces so that the trickster will triumph. As he becomes further and further off-color, he seems more and more confident of getting laughs with his theme of taking power by deceiving people. And as we shall see later, even imams can be fakes.

The account of him that Bwanali Said presents to M. Allibert looks like the well-rehearsed performance of a mature artist. One day, he begins, some villagers wanted to organize a *daira*. Strictly, that is a circle of adepts repeating the names of God to the point of ecstasy, but (as we shall see in the comedy routine in the next chapter) a *daira* can be just a big religious gathering. The trickster's robe, hat, and holy book are parts of his disguise.

THEY WANTED TO KILL AN OX. PEOPLE ALL OVER KNEW THEY WANTED TO KILL AN OX. BWANAWASI TOOK HIS, KILLED IT, AND SKINNED IT SO IT DIDN'T GET SPOILED. HE SOLD THE MEAT AND STUFFED IT WITH STRAW TILL IT GOT ITS SHAPE. THEN HE STOOD IT UP AND TIED IT NEAR THE VILLAGE. NEXT HE WENT TO THE KING AND SAID, "I HAVE AN OX I CAN SELL YOU. BUT BE VERY CAREFUL, IT'S VERY WILD. GO GET IT ONLY AT NIGHT". THE KING GAVE HIM THE MONEY AND HE LEFT. THAT HAPPENED IN THE MORNING. BWANAWASI WALKED A LONG TIME. THAT EVENING

THE VILLAGERS WENT TO GET THE OX. AS SOON AS THEY PULLED THE ROPE, THE
OX FELL OVER. THEY WENT QUICK TO THE PALACE AND TOLD THE KING WHAT
HAPPENED. THE KING ORDERED THEM TO CHASE HIM. FIVE MEN STARTED OUT ON
THE CHASE.

THEY WALKED ALL NIGHT. IN ALL THE VILLAGES THEY WENT THROUGH, THEY
ASKED IF BWANAWASI WAS THERE. THEY TOLD THEM "NO" AND THEY KEPT GOING.
FINALLY THEY REACHED THE PLACE WHERE BWANAWASI WAS. THEY FOUND HIM
DRESSED IN A *KURTA* AND A *KUFI* AND HOLDING A QUR'ANIC BOOK. THEY DIDN'T
RECOGNIZE HIM. BWANAWASI ASKED, "WHO ARE YOU AND WHERE ARE YOU
FROM?" THEY TOLD HIM THEIR STORY. HE TOLD THEM HE WOULD GIVE THEM
SOMETHING TO EAT AND THEY WOULD SLEEP IN THE MOSQUE. THE STRANGERS-
VISITORS AGREED, THEY ATE, THEN WENT TO SLEEP.

BWANAWASI TOOK SOME PAPAYA AND ROASTED IT TO LOOK LIKE EXCREMENT,
THEN HE PUT IT BETWEEN THEIR LEGS. IN THE MORNING WHEN THEY AWOKE, THEY
SAW THE PAPAYA AND THOUGHT THEY HAD POLLUTED THE MOSQUE, SO THEY FLED
TOWARDS THE VILLAGE.

For his next number, Bwanali Said inverts an episode found in many
folktales. Finding an old lady, Bwanawasi offers to harvest her field, but
violates hospitality by eating her sugar-cane, then burning the field,
and devouring her food while she is out. Then he puts her plates and
pots in the bed she has offered him, knowing she will be fooled into
beating it and destroying her crockery. In Malagasy storytelling, putting
something into the bed to enable your escape is a favorite trick.[14]

Fig. 4 Mosque in Mtsapere. By franek2, CC BY-SA 3.0, Wikimedia Commons,
https://upload.wikimedia.org/wikipedia/commons/4/4c/Mosquée_de_
Mtsapéré_-_panoramio.jpg

Bwanawasi is not content with dishonoring one old lady. Knowing how much women like perfume, knowing equally that eating raw sweet potatoes will cause him to break wind, he farts into a pocket flask and closes it up. Then he buys some perfume, which he sprinkles on some women at a dance. When they want more of it, he takes them into a certain house and throws in the flask, which breaks and asphyxiates the women. Was M. Allibert laughing yet? If not, Bwanali Said sets Bwanawasi up more outrageously, for a defeat after all his successes. He finds a village stricken by an epidemic. He tells the women they can escape it by sitting on the little point sticking out of the water near the shore. That is his penis. They all fall for the trick until one smart old lady sticks it with a needle. Defeated, Bwanawasi flees.

But he is a trickster. His defeat must be followed by a success, which Bwanali Said gives him in his final trick. As effectual and familiar as the others, this one will award him with high rank.

AFTER THAT LAST MISDEED, BWANAWASI LEFT. BY THEN EVERYBODY KNEW THERE WAS A MAN AROUND THERE CALLED BWANAWASI, WHO HAD TO BE ARRESTED. IN THE VILLAGE HE WENT TO, THERE WAS ONE MAN WHO KNEW HIM. WHEN HE GOT THERE, THE MAN SAW HIM AND WENT TO TELL THE KING. THE KING CALLED HIM TO THE PALACE AND ASKED HIM, "ARE YOU BWANAWASI?" HE SAID YES. THE KING ORDERED HIM PUT INTO A SACK AND THROWN INTO THE SEA. FORTUNATELY THE WATER WAS LOW. THE KING'S SERVANTS LEFT HIM ON THE SAND AND WENT BACK TO THE PALACE. THEN BWANAWASI HEARD A HERDSMAN GOING OUT TO PASTURE WITH HIS HERD. HE STARTED YELLING, "NO, I WON'T MARRY HER! I WILL NEVER MARRY HER! YOU WANT ME TO MARRY THE KING'S DAUGHTER, BUT I WON'T! YOU CAN THROW ME INTO THE SEA!"

THE HERDSMAN HEARD WHAT BWANAWASI WAS SAYING, SO HE LET HIM OUT AND GOT INTO THE SACK IN HIS PLACE. BWANAWASI CLOSED THE SACK UP TIGHT AND WENT OFF WITH THE HERD. HE WENT AND SOLD IT, THEN WENT BACK TO THE PALACE SAYING, "KING, O KING! I'M COMING FROM THE SEA. THE KING OF THE SEA IS INVITING YOU, 'CAUSE HE'S ORGANIZING A *GRAND MARIAGE*. HE TOLD ME TO COME AND SAY HE'S INVITING YOU, AND YOU HAVE TO GO WITH ME. THERE'S BIG FUN IN THE SEA, EVERYBODY IS HAPPY."

HE TOLD EVERY PERSON TO ATTACH A STONE TO HIS FOOT, SO AS TO GET DOWN TO THE KINGDOM OF THE SEA FASTER. WHEN THEY GOT TO THE REEF, HE HAD THEM LEAN OVER [THE RAIL] AND TOLD THEM TO LISTEN TO THE ORCHESTRA. THAT WAS THE SOUND THE SEA MAKES ON THE CORAL. HE MADE THEM JUMP OVERBOARD ONE AFTER ANOTHER.

AS ONLY THE KING'S DAUGHTER WAS LEFT, HE GAVE HER THE CHOICE TO MARRY HIM OR JOIN HER FAMILY. SHE AGREED TO MARRY HIM, AND HE WENT

BACK TO THE KING'S PALACE, AND THE DAUGHTER BECAME HIS WIFE. THEY LIVED
HAPPY AND HAD MANY CHILDREN.[15]

Material as familiar as that last trick is surefire; we'll meet it again.
Stringing the tricks together, Bwanali Said follows what African and
Comoran narrators often do, to alternate success and setback. Sooner
or later, the trickster's successful trick will be followed by a successful
trick against him by his dupe. Sometimes that final defeat succeeds,
sometimes not.[16]

Bwanawasi triumphs again in a piece told by Hasani Miradji. Having
no taste for forced labor (who has, in a plantation society?) and being
unafraid of punishment, he refuses to help dig the king's well. Once
it is finished, he comes back to drink the water, playing a little drum.
Music, the king's soldier guards tell him, will not get him permission
to drink, but he convinces them that what he is drinking is honey, and
shares it with them. As his price for giving them a second helping, they
agree to be fastened, and he gets to drink his fill. To punish him, the
angry king offers his daughter to any captor of Bwanawasi. Tortoise
offers, successfully trapping the trickster by playing Tarbaby — that
is, he covers his shell with sticky stuff, as in the oft-reprinted African
American tale.[17] Bwanawasi escapes decapitation by playing sage:

IN THE MORNING THE KING LED THE TRICKSTER TO THE SQUARE WHERE CRIMINALS
WERE PUNISHED. "I'D LIKE TO DIE", SAID BWANAWASI, "BUT WHEN YOU CUT OFF
THE HEAD OF A *MATABA* [SUPERNATURAL], THERE'S ALWAYS A PRETTY GIRL NEXT
TO HIM". SO THE KING PUT HIS DAUGHTER NEXT TO HIM. THE CROWD SHOUTED,
"DEATH TO THE PHONY *MATABA*!" WHEN THE BIG *ODA* OPENED, THAT SMART
GUY DUCKED, AND THE AXE FELL ON THE KING'S DAUGHTER. THE KING DROPPED
DEAD. THE SOLDIERS WAITED FOR THE ORDER TO GRAB THE TRICKSTER, BUT THE
DEAD KING COULDN'T SPEAK, HE HAD ALREADY GONE TO JOIN HIS DAUGHTER. SO
BWANAWASI TOOK POWER.[18]

All trickster tales are about reversing power relations.

Bwanali Said's sequence shows his skill in drawing pieces from
Mayotte's repertoire to make his point: victory must belong to the
powerless. In theoretical terms, he deftly manages the dialectic between
tradition — conventions of African-Malagasy storytelling — and
situation, the moment of being asked to perform. The West African
narrator does it too: 'he must question himself at every instant, choose
from his repertoire the action appropriate to the lesson he wants to

get across'.[19] What was 'tradition' in a village society of 1970s Mayotte, where the 'situation' was the imminence of town life? Bwanali Said's traditional-sounding performance speaks against Europeanization in favor of a loyalty to Mayotte's blend of African, Malagasy, and European discourse. That blend is the island's history of creolization.

Making and Breaking Friendship

Tricksters have friends but not for long. In the African-Malagasy narrative tradition, deceit between friends is ridiculed as often as power is reversed. Ahmed Atumani, who gave M. Allibert the legend of that sacred place Sazilé and four other pieces, holds up trickster Hare. When his friend Porcupine begins to choke on a piece of meat stuck in his throat, Hare, in an ostensible attempt to sustain the friendship, goes to fetch water. His quest is delayed by a sequence of progressively lucky bargains, distractingly amusing. In the end Hare leaves Porcupine to choke. So much for the friendship.[20] When interdependence is destroyed, a fundamental social value is being questioned. Trickster tales do look like social criticism.

In another unlikely friendship, Hare first asks a dupe his name. 'ME? MY NAME IS HEDGEHOG! AND YOU?' 'ME? MY NAME IS STRANGER [*VAZAHA*]!' lies the hare. Since *vazaha*, the key word in the story, means both stranger and European, using it alludes to the presence of foreigners (who equally might be Arabs or Indians). When the two friends reach a village and ask for hospitality, a servant brings food 'FOR STRANGERS, THAT'S WHAT THE CHIEF SAID'. As counteraction, Hedgehog puts on Hare's clothes, goes out and eats all the sweet potatoes. Wait for their effect. After coming back and graciously returning the clothes, he goes to sleep. Then when the villagers accuse 'strangers' of destroying their fields, Hedgehog says, 'THEY'RE TALKING ABOUT *VAZAHA*, THAT MUST BE YOU!' The trickster's violation has a consequence. The chief, seeing Hare's muddy clothes, accuses him and immediately sides with Hedgehog: 'HOW MANY WHACKS YOU WANT US TO GIVE HIM?' 'NOT MANY', he replies, 'SAY TWO HUNDRED'. As his escape trick Hare sets a test: 'HAVE US DRINK SOMETHING THAT'LL MAKE US VOMIT'. Hare throws up the rice he ate; when Hedgehog throws up the sweet potatoes, that gets him three hundred whacks. Doesn't that end the friendship? No, Fasuru Isufa is not finished. He follows the African rule: tell trickster stories in strings.

Hare and Hedgehog are still friends; they keep swapping tricks. Meeting some smiths in the road, Hedgehog plays master: 'IF YOU SEE A HARE BEHIND ME CARRYING BELLOWS, I GIVE THEM TO YOU'. The smiths pull off Hare's ears despite his protests, and he counteracts with the same trick: boys pull out Hedgehog's quills as he yells in pain. But he counteracts by prompting some hunters to catch Hare and kill him while Hedgehog looks on. His pleasure is curtailed, and the string of episodes ends, when a pack of dogs attack and kill him. To signal his tale is done, Fasuru Isufa ends with a moral: 'THE ONE WHO HASN'T REACHED THE OTHER SHORE MUST NOT MAKE FUN OF THE ONE WHO'S DROWNING'.[21]

A formal note: the alternation of success and setback in Fasuru Isufa's story is like that climactic moment in Bwanali Said's series of deceptions when the trickster's success is followed with a counter-trick that defeats him. A textbook example of that sequencing, from Grande Comore: Cock and Hare each will plant a field. When Cock has a good harvest and Hare a bad one, and Hare proposes they exchange, all they exchange is more tricks. Cock finds he got nothing in the deal, so in revenge he hides his head and deceptively smears red coloring on his neck. Seeing him, Hare — duller than usual — goes home, takes a sharp knife, and cuts off his own head.[22] Again, the final defeat kills off the trickster. As a narrator, Bwanali Said learned to imitate performances he had heard and he doubtlessly absorbed these patterns. He would have got to practice in recitation in the Qur'an school. Successful reciters get recognition, the boys for their trickster repertoire, the girls for their readiness for the grandmother role.

The breaking-of-friendship pattern isn't all laughs; it can be parodied (as can almost everything else in Mahorais culture). For Mohamed Chakir, the trickster is a *ginnaru* or *djinn*,[23] who pretends to be an animal helping the dupe Sabuyama. A *djinn*, like a *lolo* or a *dyab*, is a useful supernatural for the storyteller. When this *ginnaru's* serviceable soldiers clear a field in five minutes, Sabuyama is charmed: 'WHAT A GOOD GINNARU YOU ARE'. That kind of reply ought to come from a wise counselor: 'DON'T SAY ANYTHING YET, WAIT FOR THE END'.[24] The *ginnaru* keeps repeating the advice, and the audience keeps hearing it as ironic, until the soldiers destroy the field and kill Sabuyama and his family. We might have known 'THAT PLACE WAS INHABITED BY VERY WICKED DEVILS', as Mohamed Chakir comments at the end.[25] Or that his neighbors are sometimes unreliable, or that there are foreigners in his island who are quite capable of deceitful speech. A trickster *ginnaru* simultaneously personifies serious and playful attitudes. Ambiguity and play are a weapon of the powerless, laughing through their resistance and accommodation. It doesn't hurt when they laugh.

The Plain Style for Parody

If Claude Allibert's tales sometimes read like schoolroom reports, we should not be surprised. Other narrators — African, Malagasy — conventionally open and close their pieces with fixed-phrase formulas, but these schoolboy narrators don't use those. Maybe they were omitted in translating, but more probably it's the narrator's choice. The resulting style resembles those crime stories in French newspapers that are called *faits divers*, news in brief ('Just the facts, ma'am'.) When Mohamed el Anrif is asked for a story, he reports it soberly in plain style.

> A MAN WAS WEAVING A ROPE. HE HAD TO GO OUT TO THE COUNTRY TO GET LEAVES. HE DRIED THEM IN THE SUN. HE NOTICED THAT AMONG THE LEAVES HE CUT, THERE WAS ONE THAT WASN'T DRYING OUT. EVERY MORNING HE WENT WITH THE VILLAGERS TO THE COUNTRY. ON HIS RETURN HE FOUND HIS MEAL READY. HE WONDERED WHO DID THAT. "IT CAN ONLY BE A WOMAN!" HE SAID TO HIMSELF.
>
> THAT WENT ON THREE TO FOUR DAYS. THEN HE HID AND PRETENDED TO LEAVE, TO SEE WHO WAS DOING THAT WORK. HE HID IN THE HOUSE. HE GATHERED LEAVES UNDER THE BED. THEN HE SAW ONE LEAF SHAKE AND BECOME A BEAUTIFUL WOMAN. THAT BEAUTIFUL WOMAN WASN'T FROM THE VILLAGE. HE SAW THE WOMAN DRAW WATER, MAKE THE BED, PREPARE THE MEAL. AT THE MOMENT WHEN SHE WAS GOING TO TRANSFORM HERSELF BACK INTO A LEAF, THE MAN PROPOSED MARRIAGE TO HER. SHE ACCEPTED, BUT TOLD HIM HE COULD NOT GO AGAINST HER CONDITIONS. HE MUST KEEP HIS WIFE'S SECRET.

Every sentence moves the narrative one step ahead, never decorating it, never digressing.

> THE KING OF THE TOWN, WHO HAD AN UGLY WIFE, FOUND SOMETHING WRONG WITH A POOR PEASANT HAVING A PRETTIER WIFE THAN HIS OWN. HE SUMMONED HIM. THE MAN TOLD IT WAS A WOMAN HE FOUND DURING A TRIP. THE KING DIDN'T WANT TO BELIEVE HIM. THEN THE MAN CONFESSED HIS STORY.
>
> THE KING SENT HIS SON, TO TELL THE WOMAN [HE KNEW] SHE WAS A LEAF OF DATE-PALM. THEN THE WOMAN SHOWED HER HORNS, HER TAIL AND HER LONG HAIR, AND HER EYES GOT RED. SHE WAS A *DJINNI*. AS SHE HAD MARRIED CHILDREN

ALL OVER THE PLACE, SHE BEGAN SINGING TO CALL THEM, "KUMLALA KUETU,
DATE-PALM CHILDREN, YOU ARE ASLEEP, COME, YOU ARE FROM DATE-PALMS". THE
CHILDREN ANSWERED "AÉÉ", YES. THE DJINNI BEGAN TURNING, GOING AROUND
THE YARD, REPEATED HER SONG THREE TIMES, AND THE CHILDREN CAME. THEY
ALL SANG TOGETHER, MOVED OFF TOGETHER, WENT OUT TO THE COUNTRY AND
TURNED INTO DATE-PALMS.[26]

The eerie transformation of these *djinns* into trees is subdued in the
plain, anti-performance style. Mohamed el Anrif just gets her offstage,
so compact and brief is his performance.[27]

His story honors tradition. For one thing, he probably learned it from
someone before him; oral transmission is the defining feature of these
pieces. For another, it is an adaptation of Madagascar's best-known
legend (which he may not directly know). In the legend, Ranoro, a
water-princess from the sea, comes on land and marries a mortal. Her
one condition is that her origin must be kept secret. When her husband
breaks her taboo, she instantly returns under water, but by leaving her
children behind, she becomes the ancestral mother of a clan. Rather
like the figure of Liberty in the United States or Marianne in France,
the female body of Ranoro is a political symbol. She comes from a
family whose members cannot be seen or mentioned. Her watery origin
symbolizes her foreignness. Even the euphemism 'salt', which would
remind a hearer of the sea, cannot be spoken. Because she dies in water,
Ranoro has no tomb, hence no family who might make demands on her
husband.[28] In the legend, losing a wife is the man's tragedy. In Mohamed
el Anrif's adaptation to the folktale genre, the husband accepts the king's
rejection of her. The essential remodeling is to adapt the search for a wife
— the main plot line of so many Indo-European folktales — to Mayotte's
values: to transform it into a warning against marrying outside your
social group. The plain style contrasts with the reverent attitude of the
legend, yet the taboo has the same force as before, because marriage is
the heart of all the social politics.

Ranoro (taking her as an 'original') undergoes many transformations
in Southwest Indian Ocean folklore. It's less easy to determine the
attitude in a piece told by Mansour Kamardine, of the village of Sada.
A man catches an octopus thinking to dry it, but secretly it cooks and
cleans for him. Hiding under the bed, he discovers the secret and insists
on marrying this woman. But one day in an argument, he mentions

her octopus nature, and instantly she leaves for the water in a huff.[29] Obviously a husband isn't allowed to cast aspersions on his in-laws, but the difference of species already has tipped off the audience. Is the octopus a parody of that revered ancestor from long ago? 'Parody [says Herbert Lindenberger, about European operas, of all things] stresses the continuity of a tradition at the same time that it deflates earlier works within the tradition'.[30] Both stories deflate Madagascar's nostalgia and reverence for ancestors into Mayotte's favorite concern about the dangers and contradictions in marriage. As one reads more and more tales collected by Claude Allibert, parody and kindred remodelings are seen to constitute tradition in this society.

Parody is obviously mocking when El Hadad Mohamed reworks the Indian fable of The Ungrateful Snake Returned to Captivity. An ugly, hairy giant is released by a poor fisherman from a copper pot he has accidentally landed. The witty giant shouts to his captor, 'CHOOSE HOW YOU'RE GOING TO DIE', and explains his threat: 'IN MY FIRST YEAR OF PRISON, I PROMISED BAGS OF DIAMONDS TO WHOEVER WOULD LET ME OUT. SECOND YEAR, I PROMISED SEVEN HOUSES WITH SERVANTS, BUT NOBODY LET ME OUT. SO THIS YEAR I PROMISED THAT WHOEVER OPENED THE POT WOULD DIE. UNLUCKY YOU'. In ancient versions of the fable, another character advises the man to put the creature back into captivity, but in Mayotte the fisherman does it alone: 'I ACCEPT, BUT I HAVE TO SAY, I DON'T BELIEVE YOU WERE IN THAT POT, BECAUSE HOW COULD YOU, SO BIG AND FAT, HAVE DONE THAT? NOT EVEN YOUR FOOT COULD HAVE GOT IN THERE'. The giant falls for the trick and goes back into the pot. The softhearted fisherman lets him out only when he pleads. Since that day, he is the richest man in the world — an inexplicable ending, but a cute one. He must have got those diamonds.[31]

At first an outsider won't grasp a local person's attitude towards the authority figures in Sharifuddin Emile Nizari's tale of a father and his two sons, but the mockery of Islamic education makes for a well-told story with a rapid-fire ending and justifies translating it in full.

MAGANDJA TOOK HIS TWO SONS TO ENROLL THEM IN THE QUR'AN SCHOOL. THE FATHER ENTRUSTED THEM TO THE FUNDI, BECAUSE THE BOYS COULDN'T GO THERE EVERY DAY AND RETURN NEXT DAY. THE ELDER STUDIED BRAVELY AND WILLINGLY, BUT HIS LITTLE BROTHER REFUSED TO MAKE THE SMALLEST EFFORT. WHEN HE LEFT SCHOOL, THE BIG ONE LEARNED HIS LESSONS WHILE THE LITTLE ONE PLAYED WITH HIS FRIENDS. AFTER THREE OR FOUR MONTHS, THE OLDER ONE SAID TO HIS

FATHER, "IF YOU COME AND GET US, YOU HAVE TO TAKE ME, BECAUSE I KNOW LOTS OF THINGS AND MY BROTHER DOESN'T KNOW ANYTHING!"

AFTER THEY SPENT MANY YEARS IN SCHOOL, THE BOYS WERE AGAIN VISITED BY THEIR FATHER. HE THOUGHT NOW HIS SONS HAD A GOOD EDUCATION. HE SAID TO THE MASTER, "I'VE COME TO GET MY SONS, BUT I'M LEAVING ONE OF THEM WITH YOU". THE *FUNDI* THOUGHT [IT OVER] AND SAID, "TAKE THE LITTLE ONE". BUT THE FATHER WANTED THE BIGGER ONE. AFTER A LONG DISCUSSION THE *FUNDI* AGREED THAT THE FATHER WOULD TAKE THE OLDER ONE. WHEN THE FATHER AND THE OLDER ONE HAD LEFT, THE *FUNDI* SAID, "NOW I'M GOING TO DO EVERYTHING I CAN TO EDUCATE YOU".

THE OLDER ONE, AFTER SPENDING TWO OR THREE WEEKS WITH HIS FATHER, SAID TO HIM, "I WANT TO FIND A WAY TO HAVE MONEY". "WHAT, SON?" "I WANT TO CHANGE INTO A BILLYGOAT, WE'LL GO FROM VILLAGE TO VILLAGE AND YOU'LL SELL ME. BUT YOU HAVE TO BE CAREFUL NOT TO SELL ME IF WE GET NEAR MY *FUNDI*." THE FATHER AGREED AND THEY STARTED OUT.

THEY CAME TO A VILLAGE. AS SOON AS THE FATHER SAID HE WAS SELLING HIS GOAT, A MAN BOUGHT IT FOR A LOT OF MONEY. THE FATHER TOOK THE MONEY AND LEFT. HARDLY HAD HE GONE BEFORE THE GOAT ESCAPED FROM HIS BUYER. JUST AS HE REACHED THE OTHER END OF THE VILLAGE, HE TURNED BACK INTO A MAN AND FOLLOWED HIS FATHER. THEN THEY WERE NEAR A VILLAGE. THE BOY TURNED INTO A GOAT AGAIN. BUT THE FATHER MET HIS SON'S *FUNDI* AT THE ENTRY TO THE VILLAGE. HE BOUGHT THE ANIMAL. HE TOOK IT HOME AND TOLD HIS LITTLE PUPIL TO TAKE THE KNIFE AND KILL THE GOAT. BUT AS THE BOY KNEW THAT GOAT WAS HIS BIG BROTHER, HE HID THE KNIFE. THE *FUNDI* TOLD HIM TO COME AND HOLD THE GOAT, AND HE WENT LOOKING FOR THE KNIFE HIMSELF. AS SOON AS THE *FUNDI* WENT INTO THE HOUSE, HIS PUPIL LET THE ANIMAL GO. WHEN HE WAS FAR OFF, THE BOY SAID TO HIS *FUNDI* THAT THE ANIMAL HAD RUN AWAY.

THE MASTER WENT OUT OF THE HOUSE AND CHASED THE ANIMAL. WHEN HE WAS CLOSE TO CATCHING HIM, THE ANIMAL TRANSFORMED INTO A LITTLE BIRD AND TURNED THE MASTER INTO A SPARROWHAWK. WHEN THE SPARROWHAWK WANTED TO GRAB THE BIRD, IT TURNED INTO A PIECE OF MONEY AND FELL INTO A POCKET OF A MAN THERE. THE SPARROWHAWK TURNED INTO A MAN AND TOLD THE MAN WITH THE COIN IN HIS POCKET TO GIVE IT TO HIM. THE OTHER ONE ANSWERED, "YOU DIDN'T GIVE ME ANYTHING". "LEAN DOWN A LITTLE AND SHAKE YOUR POCKET". AS SOON AS HE LEANED OVER THE COIN FELL OUT. THE *FUNDI* BOWED AND PUT OUT HIS HAND TO TAKE IT. BUT IT TURNED INTO A GRAIN OF RICE, AND THE *FUNDI* INTO A CHICKEN WANTING TO EAT THE RICE. BEFORE IT HAD TIME TO EAT, THE GRAIN TURNED INTO A WILD CAT AND ATE THE CHICKEN.

AFTER THAT DAY, PEOPLE KNEW THE PUPIL CAN BE SMARTER THAN THE MASTER.[32]

No doubt Maître Allibert was listening.

[handwritten margin note: So does that all mean "Parody ← tales" cloths?]

Parody points to the capacity for plural meaning that Mayotte *[handwritten: Hmm.]* inherited from its plural ancestors. From Madagascar's storytelling tradition, it learned how to renegotiate culture through irony. Only a generation after the French conquest (1896), local storytellers in Madagascar ridiculed style and structure in a parody myth about how Europeans were inflicted on the Malagasy for a broken taboo. At the beginning God has already withdrawn from earth, and the Malagasy are praying to him for a deity to live with them. In answer they receive a sealed chest which they must not open; 'OTHERWISE BIG TROUBLE WILL COME TO YOU'. They violate the prohibition and release the first European. Thenceforward they are punished by the presence of Europeans among them — more capable and clever, better educated, and never to leave.[33] Making satiric use of mythic motifs — the taboo on looking into a box, and the release of troubles when a forbidden casket is opened — the piece is an image of the style of myth. It honors and twits tradition at the same time; through parody it invents a new genre, the pseudo-myth.

Fairy Tale in Parody

Serious, satiric, and playful imitation are all present when our friend Mohamed El Anrif narrates a Hansel-and-Gretel-like tale, a version of the ubiquitous cycle The Children and the Ogre (no. 15 in Grimm). He says, it's the story of a brother and his sister, seemingly orphaned, she pregnant. They go out to gather some of the delicious legume *ambatry* and come upon a trove of eggs under a tree. Like all pregnant women, the sister had a keen interest in those eggs. Although she wants them all, at first they take just one, wondering, 'WHOSE ARE THESE?' She puts a batch of them into her basket and covers them with *ambatry* (secrecy rules). As the two flee away, they meet the owner of the eggs, a frightening *djinn*, who interrogates them: 'WHERE ARE YOU COMING FROM, YOU HUMANS?' They already have the object of their search, but the boy also has a magic drum, which forces the *djinn* to dance while the boy sings his answer and the girl trembles. They get out of there and run home, where the girl eats all the eggs raw. The narrator excuses her *faux pas*: that's an action she isn't responsible for, a pregnant woman's act is involuntary. She confesses when her brother comes home. They repeat the theft and the gourmandizing the next day, but on the third day, she goes alone (unaccompanied by scary movie music), her brother following behind. When the angry *djinn* threatens them, the brother comes out and vanquishes the *djinn* by beating the drum. They escape and resume their domesticity.[34]

The plot — children undergoing dangers, helped by a magic object — is adapted to conflicting values. Is it a touch of Islam, or mere folktale convention, or both, that to survive, human beings require more than their own strength? We are to identify with a thieving boy and girl who escape, not through commendable behavior, but only by way of the magic drum the boy has been carrying all along. Well, where did he get that drum? (A tale in the next chapter gives the answer.) Is Mohamed el Anrif's wisecrack about a pregnant woman's desires bringing trouble a clue to the attitude of his piece, or just a wink at his audience? Different values are juxtaposed.

Theoretical, formal patterns like the making and breaking of friendship reside half-recalled in the memory of tellers and audiences. Folklorists use them to handle the huge numbers of texts they have assembled. One such, early in the Stalin era, was the Russian formalist Vladimir Yakovlevich Propp. Wanting nothing to do with live storytellers or any obscure African island, concentrating on his texts of Russian tales, Propp discovered an interesting three-part sequence. Firstly, the hero is tested. Secondly, he reacts appropriately, and thirdly, he is provided with a magical agent, like that drum. Though it's missing from Mohamed el Anrif's brother-and-sister tale, the 'donor sequence' is essential in many tales. Take a story collected by Noël Gueunier. Two young wives seeking a cure for barrenness (which can lose them a husband) seek help at the house of an ancient woman, the donor. Her door will open only if she speaks a magic formula: 'IF YOU ARE HUMAN CHILDREN, MAY THE DOOR OPEN! IF YOU ARE SPIRIT (*LOLO*) CHILDREN, MAY IT STAY TIGHT SHUT!' That is their first test; the door does open. They then light her fire (common courtesy getting them past another test), and she rewards them by providing magic rice in a magic pot, with magic meat. Later both get pregnant.[35] It's possible to read an entire piece as being organized around Propp's donor sequence.

The Maiden in Mayotte

An example is a tale widely told tale in Europe and North Africa, The Maiden Who Seeks Her Brothers.[36] Typically, the young heroine is isolated, separated from her seven or twelve brothers; she must find them after they have been transformed into ravens or animals. Through most of the plot, her test is to keep silent, which doesn't prevent her getting a royal husband. What gets her through the test is submissiveness to wrongful accusation, exile, and almost death. At the end the family is reunited. In real-life Mayotte, keeping a family together is challenged by the potential conflict between a mother's ownership of her house and a father's authority outside the home. The image of a woman respected for keeping silent ought also to be popular, but only one version has been collected, from Bwanali Sanda (not to be confused with Bwanali Said).

At the outset, he says, the girl is orphaned. The audience will understand that she therefore requires a husband, and any marriage arrangement would have to be made by her brothers. So they set out.

ONCE THERE LIVED A FAMILY MADE OF THE FATHER, THE MOTHER, AND SEVEN CHILDREN, THE LAST A GIRL. ONE DAY AFTER THEIR PARENTS' DEATH, THEY DECIDED TO GO VISIT SOME VILLAGES.

The maiden is offstage. They meet a man (not found in European versions of the tale) who lays on the boys the kind of interdiction they ought to have got from their dead father.

ON THE WAY THEY MET A MAN WHO ASKED THEM WHERE THEY WERE GOING. THEN HE ADDED, "BOYS, YOU WILL FIND A RIVER NEXT TO THE FOREST, AND THE WATER FROM THAT RIVER IS SACRED. THAT MEANS NO ONE HAS THE RIGHT TO DRINK IT." THE CHILDREN KEPT GOING. WHEN THEY GOT TO THE RIVER, ONE OF THEM STAYED DEAF TO THE OLD MAN'S ADVICE AND DRANK. HE WAS INSTANTLY TRANSFORMED INTO A SHEEP. THEY CONTINUED ON THEIR WAY, AND WHEN THEY GOT TO A VILLAGE, THEY SAW AN OLD LADY RELIEVING HERSELF. THE OTHER FIVE BOYS BROKE OUT LAUGHING AND WERE IMMEDIATELY TRANSFORMED TO STONES.

They were being tested; they have failed; they are punished. But the sheep, as the remaining male, retains responsibility for her.

THE ONLY ONES LEFT WERE THE GIRL AND THE SHEEP. THEY WENT INTO AN OLD WOMAN'S HOUSE; SHE WENT TO THE KING'S PLACE TO REPORT THEIR PRESENCE.

This character, who profits by carrying news to the king, is the first of many old-lady messengers, or tale-bearers, we meet in Mahorais tales. Her speaking is crucial. The girl is silent — not forbidden to speak but enhancing her mystery by keeping her transformed brother's secret.

> THE KING CAME TO GET THE GIRL AND TOOK HIM BACK TO HIS PLACE, WITH THE SHEEP. THE GIRL SAID NOT A WORD. THE SOVEREIGN MARRIED HER BUT SHE STAYED MUTE. THE SHEEP ATE EVERYTHING THE GIRL ATE.
>
> A FEW YEARS LATER, THE KING AND THE GIRL HAD A BABY. [THE NARRATOR REMINDS HIS HEARER,] EVERYBODY IN THE VILLAGE SAID THAT THE KING'S WIFE WAS MUTE. THEIR SON GREW UP.

Now the story has a self-declared hero.

> HE DECIDED TO DO SOMETHING TO MAKE HIS MOTHER SPEAK. HE TIED HIMSELF UP BY THE NECK, CLIMBED A TREE, AND LET HIMSELF HANG AT THE END OF THE ROPE.

That does it. The threat of losing the last member of her family makes his mother speak at last.

Only now does the maiden, a wife at last, break her silence; she speaks from her maternal role to save her son and maintain family.

> "I HAD SIX BROTHERS, FIVE GOT TRANSFORMED INTO STONES AND THE SIXTH IS A SHEEP. IF YOU DIED THAT WOULD BE AWFUL FOR ME!" SAID THE BABY'S MOTHER.

But keeping the hero in the foreground, Bwanali Said goes into another donor sequence. The old-lady-magician-donor tests the boy; by imitating his mother's silence, he is provided with a magic object, which will enable him to get his reward, and her secret, which gives him power over her.

> THE BOY DECIDED TO GO FIND THE OLD WOMAN'S PLACE, WHERE HIS UNCLES HAD BEEN TURNED TO STONE. THE WOMAN DID ALL HER WONDERS, BUT THE BOY DIDN'T LAUGH. THE OLD WOMAN TOLD HIM TO LIVE WITH HER. SHE TAUGHT HIM WHAT HAD TO BE DONE TO TRANSFORM PEOPLE TO STONE AND TO HUMAN BEINGS. THEN SHE SHOWED HIM A CALABASH WHERE HER SOUL WAS. "IF THAT GETS BROKEN, I WILL DIE", SHE SAID.
>
> A FEW DAYS LATER THE OLD WOMAN WENT OUT INTO THE COUNTRYSIDE. THE BOY BROKE THE CALABASH AND THE OLD WOMAN DIED. THEN HE TRANSFORMED ALL THE STONES INTO HUMAN BEINGS. THE LITTLE PRINCE WENT BACK TO THE HOUSE WITH ALL HIS UNCLES.

THE MEN COULD BE RECOGNIZED BY THE MARKS THEY HAD ON THEIR THUMBS
BEFORE DYING. THE KING'S WIFE WAS OVERJOYED. SHE CRIED, WALKED UP AND
DOWN, SAID TO THE VILLAGERS TO COME CONGRATULATE HER BECAUSE HER
BROTHERS WERE RESUSCITATED AND WERE HUMAN BEINGS AGAIN. "OH! SUCH
JOY IN THE VILLAGE THAT DAY!"[37]

Yes, the male hero has taken over, but for him to be saved, the woman had
to break silence. Here, as in the 'women's tales' in chapter 3, a woman's
speaking, even if delayed, is a crucial assertion of the importance of her
sex and models the act of a female storyteller.

How did Bwanali Sanda learn The Maiden's tale? Often, especially
in Madagascar, storytellers say they are closely following or copying a
performance they heard, but we can't ask him to identify his teachers.
His version conforms to the tale type; he didn't make it up. Folktales
in Mayotte generally come from Bantu African, Arab, Malagasy, or
European traditions, which don't seem to know the maiden.[38] We are
lucky to have his name attached to this unique text; many of this region's
storytellers have been kept invisible and anonymous.

The Swallowing Cock

The plain style of Allibert's translations reveals plain style in his
narrators, which seems to reflect being interviewed. The trilingual,
never loquacious Mohamed el Anrif uses a plain Shimaore to narrate a
swallowing-monster tale. Does his one-sentence, one-image style seem
plain because he's translating from another of his languages?

A KING HAD A YARD WITH MANY HENS. THERE WAS ONE OF THEM HE LOVED
A LOT. SHE HAD CHICKS BEHIND HER, FUTURE COCKS AND HENS. A YOUNG
COCK, WHEN HE SAW THOSE CHICKS, HE ATE THE HE ATE ALL THE CHICKS IN
THE VILLAGE. THE VILLAGERS CAME TO COMPLAIN TO THE KING. THE KING TOLD
THEM, "EVERYTHING IS MINE, YOU'RE MINE, YOUR HENS ARE MINE, THE COCK IS
MINE. YOU HAVE NOTHING TO SAY!"

THE COCK GREW UP AND BEGAN EATING THE HENS OF THE VILLAGE. PEOPLE
COMPLAINED, TOLD THE KING EVERYTHING WAS HIS, BUT HE HAD TO THINK
THINGS OVER. THE KING ANSWERED, "IT'S ALL MINE!"

THE COCK GOT TO BE AS BIG AS AN OX. HE ATE THE GOATS. HE GREW SOME
MORE AND ATE THE OXEN. THE KING ALWAYS ANSWERED THE SAME THING. THE
COCK BECAME A MONSTER, WENT INTO ONE HOUSE AND DEVOURED A LITTLE BOY,
LEFT THAT HOUSE AND ATE THE NEIGHBOR'S BABY. THE PARENTS DISCOVERED

THEIR BABY WAS GONE AND WENT TO THE KING. THEY SUSPECTED THE MONSTER
WAS NEXT GOING TO EAT PEOPLE. THE KING GAVE THE SAME ANSWER.

 THE MONSTER ATTACKED THE MEN. IT ATE ALL THE MEN. ONLY THE KING
WAS LEFT, AND THE MONSTER ATE HIM. NOTHING WAS LEFT IN THE VILLAGE. THE
MONSTER COULD EAT FORTY OR FIFTY PEOPLE.

The swallowing monster is well known, always a male though seldom
a literal cock. Many people know about a culture hero who rescues
numerous victims from the monster's belly.[39] Historians love this
monster so much that they want him to be real. François Martin, who
spent 1665 to 1668 in Madagascar, reported that some French colonists
had seen a four-headed snake. People of the 1830s said that in early
times, a monstrous snake encircled large villages, some containing as
many as three hundred families, and bit them with its seven-forked
tongue. The good prince Dérafif was said to have killed it with a huge
weapon and scattered pieces of its body all over the country. A hundred
years ago, the monster's cave and swimming pool could still be seen at
Tanifotsy. That proved these events really happened.[40]

 A few years later, Malagasy people asserted that the seven-headed
snake came out of the intestines of dead chiefs. When it had grown
to adulthood, they said, it was large enough to encircle a village and
eat all the contents. Then it would plant its tail in the ground, stand
straight up, and disappear, either into the sky or into a deep lake such as
Tritriva. The variant forms of this popular legend attest to the monster's
tremendous vitality; contending interests can all make symbolic use
of him.[41] For some, the legendary hero Darafify (same name, another
form) personifies the Arab immigrants to Madagascar. Famous for his
gift of prophecy, after landing at Vohémar in the northeast, he leaves
traces of his travels all along the coast. At Sakaleona he leaves dishes
and utensils on a little hill. In an early effort at marketing Malagasy
folk art, the colonist Alfred Voyard shipped one of his relics to France.[42]
Having heard or read all this, I once felt obliged to visit the restaurant
named Darafify, near Toamasina on the east coast. No monster showed
up; dinner was delicious; but dining as a *vazaha* (foreigner), I suppose
that despite my insignificant stature, I became a swallowing monster.
As for the tales, one critic calls them 'a transparent criticism of the abuse
of power', and so indeed they must appear when one man releases the
victims from the swallower's belly and makes them his, well, servants,

thus founding a two-class system all too familiar in Madagascar's history.(43)

Back to Mohamed el Anrif's story:

> WHILE IT WAS EATING THE PEOPLE, IT DIDN'T SEE ONE OLD WOMAN WITH HER
> SON, TWENTY OR TWENTY-FIVE YEARS OLD. THEY LEFT THE VILLAGE TO HIDE.
> THE BOY WENT TO THE SMITH TO GET A SWORD MADE. THE OLD WOMAN
> ADVISED HER SON NOT TO GO FIGHT THE MONSTER. THE BOY DID GO. HE ASKED
> HIS MOTHER FOR A CAKE, AND LEFT. A FEW DAYS LATER, HE WENT TO FIND THE
> SEVEN-HEADED MONSTER.

The necessary scene of struggle between hero and villain turns the monster adversary into a donor.

> THE MONSTER WAS ASLEEP AT THE FOOT OF A HUGE TREE. THE BOY CLIMBED
> A BRANCH AND TICKLED THE MONSTER FROM ABOVE WITH HIS SWORD, UNDER
> ITS EAR. HE CUT OFF ONE HEAD. HE CAME DOWN AND GOT OUT OF THE WAY.
> THE MONSTER WANTED TO GET REVENGE AND HAD ANOTHER HEAD CUT OFF. THE
> MONSTER CAME UP AGAIN AND HAD HIS THIRD, FOURTH, FIFTH, AND SIXTH HEADS
> CUT OFF. THE MONSTER WAS WORN OUT AND FAINTED. HE SAID, "KILL ME!" AND
> THE BOY REFUSED TO CUT THE SEVENTH HEAD. THE BOY WOULD AGREE IF THE
> MONSTER REVEALED HIS SECRET. THE MONSTER TOLD HIM TO CUT OFF HIS LITTLE
> FINGER, HANG IT FROM A TREE, HEAT IT UP AND IT WOULD TURN BLACK. HE TOLD
> HIM, "YOU MAKE A BIG *COUSCOUS*, YOU SET A CERTAIN DAY, AND YOU CUT THE
> FINGER TO MAKE THE PEOPLE COME OUT." THE BOY CUT THE FINGER; EVERYBODY
> CAME OUT AND RUSHED TO THE *COUSCOUS* POT AND ATE.

Now a donor sequence will test the suitor, to ready him for high position. Mohamed el Anrif brings in another fowl, who can't keep a secret but speeds the tale to its end.

> THE KING TOLD THE PEOPLE OF THE VILLAGE THAT WHOEVER KILLED THE MONSTER
> WOULD MARRY HIS DAUGHTER. THE BOY WAS WITH HIS MOTHER. ALL THE VILLAGE
> BOYS SAID IT WAS THEM. THE KING SAID WHOEVER WOULD SIT ON THE HARPOON
> WITHOUT GETTING PRICKED WOULD HAVE KILLED THE MONSTER. NO ONE WAS
> UP TO IT. THE BOY WENT INTO THE VILLAGE AND FOUND AN OLD WOMAN, AND
> TOLD HER NOT TO SAY HE WAS THE ONE WHO KILLED THE MONSTER. HE COVERED
> HIMSELF WITH CHARCOAL AND HID IN THAT WOMAN'S HOUSE. BUT THAT WOMAN
> HAD A COCK WHO HAD HEARD IT ALL. THE KING MADE AN INQUEST. ONE DAY,
> THE COCK SANG, "COCOHICO! THE BOY IS IN THE OLD WOMAN'S HOUSE!" THEY
> SEIZED THE BOY, TOOK HIM TO THE KING AND HE GOT MARRIED TO THE DAUGHTER.[44]

Probably the narrator learned his plain, unselfconscious style from a predecessor. His text suggests he was no schoolboy. No Hemingway could write more plainly than he speaks.

Sparrow as Doctor Know-All

Another experienced-sounding narrator, Maulida Isufa, tells a fine version of Doctor Know-All. This is the tale of a self-mocking charmer (no. 98 in Grimm), whose ingenious victory over authority has had special appeal to African, Caribbean, and African American hearers. It is suitable to matrilocal Mayotte for another reason: it declares that a woman. even symbolized as an insect like the *valala* of Madagascar, is not to be separated from her house.

> SPARROW WAS A POOR MAN, SMART, WITH A WIFE CALLED *VALALA*, LOCUST. ONE DAY AS THEY HAD NOTHING TO EAT, THEY MOVED TO A DIFFERENT PLACE. WHEN THEY GOT TO A NEW TOWN, THEY WENT UP TO THE ROYAL PALACE. JUST THEN THE KING AND HIS WIFE WERE OUT WALKING ON THE ROAD. SUDDENLY THE KING'S RING FELL TO THE GROUND AND A COCK GOING BY SWALLOWED IT. WELL, SPARROW SAW THE COCK SWALLOW THE RING. THE NEXT DAY, THE KING CALLED EVERYBODY TOGETHER TO ASK IF ANYONE HAD SEEN THE RING. OBVIOUSLY NOBODY KNEW EXCEPT SPARROW. IT WAS UP TO SPARROW TO GO BEFORE THE KING. HE TOLD THE KING TO GATHER ALL THE PEOPLE AND ANIMALS TOGETHER AND TO GIVE HIM A STICK AND A CHAIR TO SIT IN. IN FIVE MINUTES THE SQUARE WAS FULL OF ANIMALS AND PEOPLE. EVERY TIME SOMEONE PASSED CLOSE TO SPARROW, HE TOUCHED HIM WITH HIS STICK AND SAID, "IT WAS YOU, WASN'T IT?" WHEN IT WAS THE ANIMALS' TURN, HE TOUCHED THE COCK AND TOLD THE MEN TO KILL IT. THEY FOUND THE RING INSIDE THE COCK. THE KING TOOK SPARROW TO BE A MAGICIAN AND GAVE HIM THIRTY BAGS OF RICE. WHEN HE GOT HOME WITH THE BAGS, SPARROW TOLD HIS WIFE TO GET READY TO LEAVE, BUT LOCUST REFUSED.

Maulida Isufa remembers the rule with trickster stories: tell them in strings.

> ANOTHER DAY, A MAN STOLE THE KING'S TREASURE; THE KING QUICKLY CALLED SPARROW. THE RASCAL BEGGED THE CHIEF TO GIVE HIM A DAY TO THINK. AS THE THIEF WAS AFRAID THAT SPARROW-THE-MAGICIAN FOUND HIM OUT, HE WENT TO SPARROW THAT EVENING AND SAID, "DON'T GO TELLING THE KING I WAS THE ONE WHO STOLE THE TREASURE, AND I'LL GIVE IT BACK WITHOUT A PENNY MISSING."AS SPARROW WAS CLEVER, HE TOLD HIM, "I ALREADY KNEW IT WAS YOU, AND IF YOU HADN'T COME TO SEE ME, I'D HAVE DENOUNCED YOU TO THE KING." SPARROW GOT UP EARLY AND WENT TO TAKE THE TREASURE TO THE KING.

THE KING HAD HIM OFFERED A LOT OF FOOD. BACK HOME, SPARROW TOLD HIS WIFE TO LEAVE THAT TOWN, BECAUSE HE WAS AFRAID HE COULDN'T ANSWER THE QUESTION THE THIRD TIME. HE WAS AFRAID THE KING WOULD HAVE HIS HEAD CUT OFF. BUT LOCUST REFUSED.

From being a clever peasant, Sparrow turns into Ali Baba.

FOLLOWING DAY, SOME MEN STOLE ALL THE KING'S TREASURE AND GOODS. THE KING CALLED SPARROW AND ASKED HIM WHO STOLE IT. SPARROW, VERY WORRIED, ASKED FOR A DELAY OF FORTY DAYS TO ANSWER. HE BOUGHT FORTY CHICKENS AND GAVE THEM TO HIS WIFE. WELL, THERE WERE FORTY OF THE ROBBERS.

THE FIRST DAY, LOCUST COOKED A CHICKEN. THE HEAD ROBBER SENT ONE OF HIS ACCOMPLICES TO LISTEN TO WHAT SPARROW WAS SAYING. THE ACCOMPLICE, ARRIVING IN FRONT OF THE DOOR, HEARD SPARROW, EATING HIS FIRST CHICKEN, SAY THESE WORDS: "THAT'S THE FIRST ONE OUT OF THE FORTY!" THE THIEF, VERY WORRIED, THOUGHT SPARROW WAS TALKING ABOUT HIM, AND RUSHED BACK TO HIS CHIEF TO TELL HIM WHAT HE'D HEARD. THE SECOND DAY, THE CHIEF SENT ANOTHER MAN TO SPARROW, TO LISTEN IF HE WAS TALKING ABOUT THEM. THAT NIGHT HE ARRIVED IN FRONT OF THE DOOR AND HE HEARD SPARROW SAY, WHILE EATING HIS SECOND CHICKEN, "THAT'S THE SECOND ONE OF THE FORTY!" THE THIEF HURRIED TO GO TELL THE CHIEF WHAT HE'D HEARD. AND EVERY NIGHT THE CHIEF SENT ANOTHER THIEF. THE NIGHT OF THE FORTIETH DAY, THE CHIEF WENT HIMSELF AND HID BEHIND THE DOOR AND HEARD SPARROW SAY THIS AS HE WAS EATING: "THERE'S THE LAST, THE HEAD OF THE FORTY!" THEN THE CHIEF WAS CONVINCED SPARROW WAS TALKING ABOUT THEM. AT NIGHT THEY WENT TO APOLOGIZE IN FRONT OF SPARROW, SAYING THEY WERE GOING TO GIVE BACK THE TREASURE. THE NEXT DAY THE KING GOT BACK ALL HIS GOODS.

To escape the king's questions, Sparrow disguises himself in rags, like a poor farmer, and starts throwing stones at birds. Maulida Isufa adds punning (untranslatable) to his other skills.

ONE DAY THE KING AND HIS MINISTERS GOT TOGETHER TO FIND A WAY OF KILLING SPARROW. JUST THEN A SPARROW AND A LOCUST CAME INTO THE ROOM. THE KING CAUGHT THEM AND PUT THEM UNDER A PLATE. HE CALLED SPARROW AND SAID, "IF YOU MANAGE TO GUESS WHAT'S UNDER THAT PLATE, I'LL GIVE YOU ALL MY FORTUNE, BUT IF YOU DON'T, I'LL HAVE YOUR HEAD CUT OFF!" SPARROW, NOT KNOWING WHAT TO ANSWER, SAID, "IF IT WASN'T FOR LOCUST, SPARROW WOULD NOT BE CAUGHT TODAY!" THEN EVERYBODY APPLAUDED THAT GOOD ANSWER. HE EXPLAINED THEN THAT HIS WIFE WAS THE CAUSE OF WHAT HAD HAPPENED. AS HE WAS POOR, THE KING GAVE HIM HIS PLACE. SPARROW THEN SAID TO LOCUST, "LET'S LEAVE TOWN!", BUT LOCUST REFUSED.[45]

If not for Locust, who identifies herself with her house, Sparrow would have flown away. That stubborn wife cannot be moved, as if she were a human Bwé Foro. A wife is almost identical with her house.[46]

Being a narrator means making your own choices about what to offer and how closely to imitate your source. Bwanali Said knows very well how to string trickster episodes together. Mahamudu Abiamri makes an attempt to join two tales, but the result is unsatisfying.[47] Musbahu Abderhamani and Abdourahmane Hamada have absorbed some of the Arabian Nights, whether from reading or hearing.[48] Every one of their sixty-seven performances, however we evaluate it, is a response to its particular interpersonal situation, using plots and characters from the past to allude to the present.

Remodeling the Dilemma

In Africa, the dilemma tale is an interactive genre that encourages the audience to guess out loud its response to the story. The narrator takes the plot to an unresolvable point; then the hearers must chime in to determine how it will end. (It took Internet sages a while to invent the interactive.) They are expected to attribute thoughts and desires to the characters, and to discuss and evaluate their behavior. The genre is not much known in Europe, where audiences remained better behaved until the arrival of rock and roll, but in Africa it heightens the close relation between narrator and audience. The genre did travel to the Indian Ocean but didn't sink deep. In one Malagasy example, three men meet at a crossroads and vow to learn shooting, woodworking, and thievery. They go off to acquire their skills, and when they meet again, they see a *drongo* bird laying eggs. One shoots a single egg, the second steals the rest but breaks one, and the third repairs the egg. Hearers are to decide which man is the cleverest.[49]

Maanli Fayadhinddine told M. Allibert one unresolved tale that looks like an adaptation to Mayotte's marriage customs. Four brothers are suitors of the same girl but don't know it. Her father does know it, and profits from the knowledge by playing trickster.

ONE MONDAY MORNING, THE ELDEST WENT TO THE GIRL'S PARENTS TO ASK FOR HER IN MARRIAGE. THAT WAS SUMBUI. THE PARENTS TOLD HIM TO GET READY FIRST AND COME BACK ON THE FIFTH DAY. BUNKU WENT NEXT. THE PARENTS TOLD

HIM TO COME BACK ON THE FOURTH DAY. MLADJÉ GOT THERE; HE WAS TOLD TO
COME BACK ON THE THIRD DAY (THAT IS, IN THREE DAYS). AS FOR LAUL, HE HAD
TO COME BACK THE SECOND DAY, THE NEXT DAY.

Now the narrator, or his source, stages a farcical scene. The four travel
separately and come in together. Each one sat down on a chair and
lowered his head, so as not to see the others' faces. The father offers his
daughter to the one who can come back from a long trip with 'SOMETHING
INTERESTING AND NECESSARY'. Departing separately, they return with good
stuff: a resuscitating perfume, a flying carpet, a mirror showing what's
happening far away, and a magic protective ring. Each one keeps his
hand under his shirt, BECAUSE THEY DIDN'T WANT TO SHOW THE OTHERS WHAT
THEY'D GOT. THEN THE ONE WITH THE MIRROR SAID, 'COME AND LOOK! THE
MIRROR SHOWS THE GIRL IS DEAD!' Time to cooperate: they use the carpet to
transport them, the ring to protect them from a band of enemies, and the
perfume to bring her back to life. The narrator catches not his audience,
but the girl's father in the dilemma. THE FATHER COULD NOT CHOOSE
AMONG THEM, and the girl remained with no fiancé. The four brothers
end as separate as they began.[50] Who is the trickster here, the father
for breaking contract? The narrator, for that skillful twist? The person
he learned the story from? Is none of the suitors of proper descent?
Creolization loves to blend genres. *Ha!*

Amazing quote

'Tradition is the creation of the future out of the past'

Henry Glassie's epigram points to Claude Allibert's motive for collecting
folktales.[51] What would they tell him about Mayotte's early days? The
African tricksters and the swallower, the Indian seven-headed monster,
the creature (woman, *djinn*) whose name must be concealed, the
messenger bird who transforms itself, the cow as a mother symbol,
the self-created hero — all are relics and survivors of the corpus of
narratives (collected and uncollected) he calls mythology. Convincingly
he argues that the various swallowers in Mahorais narratives are a blend
of the African swallowing monster, the seven-headed snake from India,
and the dragons people saw on Chinese porcelain. 'The seven-headed
snake becomes a seven-headed cock, and the Bantu trickster Sungura is
baptized Bwanawasi... under the Perso-Swahili influence of the Shirazi
Uba-Nawas'.[52] A crucial moment for storytelling, and for the island's

social structure, came when Persian-style patriliny and patrilocality was introduced to the matriliny and matrilocality practiced by the Bantu-Malay population. Whether the immigrants in the thirteenth century were greeted with celebrations or fear, whether Islam was forcibly imposed or welcomed, the confrontation of dissimilar languages and traditions caused languages and narratives to mix and hybridize. Cultural mixing became normal practice of the contributing cultures: Bantu African, Swahili, 'Indo-Aryan', the supposedly Persian Shirazi, and whatever elusive settlers had come before them. M. Allibert's deep searches into Mayotte's past lead to the mildest possible conclusion about cultural mixing: 'It seems that diverse influences have piled up to form the mythology of the islands and archipelago of the western Indian Ocean'.[53]

Diverse influences show Mayotte to be a mixed society from the beginning. Its history is an example of creolization, the process whereby people in situations of unequal power renegotiate their cultures and thereby create new folklore. In the Southwest Indian Ocean islands as in the Caribbean, songs, stories, and displays were created from 'violent, fragmented, and disjunct pasts'.[54] Since new stories and songs continue to be created, it's ironic that our three collections are such excellent documents of the mixing in Mayotte's village life. The nostalgic picture of such a past is drawn by a writer from Grande Comore.

> As soon as a child is able to understand the language, his/her grandmother teaches him/her folktales, taboos, and riddles. Generally tales and riddles are said on nights of the full moon. She recites tales and poses riddles, and the children come around her to listen. They are very attentive to the tales.[55]

The picture is a favorite memory, whether accurate or not, of western-educated African diplomats. What Claude Allibert's fifty-three narrators do not do is to tell him accounts of spirit possession, which is a frequent and important experience for people in Mayotte.[56] Obviously they and he agreed on what sort of story he was looking for. Usually imitating or recalling someone else's performance, they show deep attachment to the land and its history; they offer him old trickster stories, interpretable as social criticism; sometimes they offer serious, playful, or satiric pieces without discoverable sources — Mayotte originals. Often they are alluding to the subordinated status of their island.[57] To me their

Are the tales ill told? (handwritten)

narratives seem to say more about 1970s Mayotte than about its history. Analogously in Mauritius, Patrick Eisenlohr finds the life stories of Hindus to be bringing the past to their present, 'building relationships of experienced closeness and distance between remembered events and places and the narrator's self'.[58] In Madagascar, anthropologist Philippe Beaujard finds Tanala narrators continually sounding the theme of conflict between those who claim to have sprung from the soil (*tompontany*) and nobles who assert power over them and claim their land. Narrative performances are ideological thrusts.[59] Paul Ottino traces this technique far back into the Malayo-Polynesian secret languages of Madagascar's remote past, and the well-recognized habit, in Malagasy oral literature, of alluding to the unspoken.[60] So often, M. Allibert's informants — the students anyway — seem to be performing for their interviewer, alluding to their relationship to him. As he listens, the thrusts are gentler, but a similar conflict is behind their stories. Stories in the following chapters ask to be read as alluding to other, untold stories.

Endnotes

1   Claude Allibert, *Contes mahorais* (Paris: Académie des Sciences d'Outre-Mer, 1977), p. 113. 'Origin of place-name' is catalogued as Motif A1617 in Stith Thompson, *Motif-Index of Folk-Literature. a Classification of Narrative Elements in Folktales, Ballads, Myths, Fables, Mediaeval Romances, Exempla, Fabliaux, Jest-Books, and Local Legends* (Bloomington: Indiana University Press, 1955–58). Subsequent notes throughout this book refer to Thompson's index.

2   Lee Haring, 'Performing for the Interviewer: A Study of the Structure of Context'. *Southern Folklore Quarterly* 36.4 (1972): 383–98.

3   M. Allibert collected a good many other place legends, which treat the ownership issue indirectly: about the origin of a tree name (p. 42), or of natural features (pp. 110–11, 112, 117–18), the fatal power of a cemetery (p. 122), and the fear of foreigners (pp. 78–79).

4   *Contes mahorais*, p. 127. Motifs: F703, Lands with extraordinary names; J2287, Belief that island may be towed by ships to new location; D1812.3.3, Future revealed in dream.

5   *Contes mahorais*, p. 34. Motif Q552.3.3, Drought as punishment.

6   *Contes mahorais*, pp. 104–05.

7   *Contes mahorais*, p. 109. *Démon* may be translating the Kibushi word *kaka*, or it may designate some other hostile being. Motifs: W125, Gluttony; Q325, Disobedience punished.

8   Sophie Blanchy, 'Proverbes Mahorais', *ASEMI* 12, 3–4 (1981), 109–32 (p. 113).

9   *Contes mahorais*, p. 14. Motifs: T100, Marriage; C520, Tabu: touching ground; C984.3, Flood because of broken tabu; reversal of D452.3.1, Transformation: sand to rice; A1617, Origin of place name; C430, Name tabu.

10   *Contes mahorais*, p. x.

11   Ibid., pp. 69–70.

12   Ibid., p. 6.

13   Noël Gueunier and Madjidhoubi Saïd, *Contes comoriens en dialecte malgache de l'île de Mayotte. La Quête de la sagesse* (Paris: Éditions Karthala, 2011), p. 106, n. 1. Richard F. Burton, trans. *The Book of the Thousand Nights and a Night, a Plain and Literal Translation of the Arabian Nights Entertainments* (N. p., n. d.), 4:261–65. Hasan El-Shamy, *Folktales of Egypt* (Chicago: University of Chicago Press, 1980), pp. 219–20. Inea Bushnaq, trans. *Arab Folktales* (New York: Pantheon, 1986), p. 273. Abdallah Daoud and Amina Kassim Bashrahii, *Zamani. Hale za shikomori. Hadisi za kikomori* (Moroni: CNDRS, 1983), p. 109.

14   It is found in Émile Birkeli, 'Folklore sakalava recueilli dans la région de Morondava', *Bulletin de l'Académie Malgache*, 6 (1922–1923), 185–417 (pp. 240–45, 258–61); L[ars] Dahle and John Sims, *Anganon'ny Ntaolo'* (Tananarive: Trano Printy Loterana,1971), pp. 52–53; Charles Renel, *Contes de Madagascar* (Paris: Ernest Leroux, 1910), 1: 77–81 and 2: 265–67. Mayotte is part of Madagascar's large culture area.

15   *Contes mahorais*, pp. 25–27. Motifs: K139, Other worthless animals sold; K1827, Disguise as holy man; K525.1, Substituted object left in bed while victim escapes; K1410, Dupe's goods destroyed; F981.3, Animals killed by trickster's breaking wind; Q583, Fitting bodily injury as punishment; K842, Dupe persuaded to take prisoner's place in sack; killed; K843, Dupes persuaded to be drowned in order to get riches. In several Malagasy stories as in this one, the drowning trick is placed at the end and leads to motif

L161, Lowly hero marries princess. That last trick, persuading a dupe to be put into a sack and thrown into the sea, is told in eastern and western Europe, India, Indonesia (did it migrate from there, with the earliest settlers to Madagascar?) and all over Africa. It is also told by both Native Americans and Black people in the United States. M. Allibert heard it as an independent story from Hamada Sufu (pp. 115–16). Like Bwanali Said, Hamada Sufu credits Bwanawasi with playing off the imaginary king of the sea against the real king of the village. The heart of their method is to use traditional material as a critical perspective on the power relations in which they live. Motif K842 forms part of types ATU1525A, ATU1535, and ATU1737 in Hans-Jörg Uther, *The Types of International Folktales: A Classification and Bibliography*, FF Communications no. 285 (Helsinki: Suomalainen Tiedeakatemia, 2004). This work, the standard reference for the folktale, is referred to in subsequent notes throughout this book.

16 Denise Paulme, *La Statue du commandeur: essais d'ethnologie* (Paris: Le Sycomore, 1984), pp. 13–54.

17 The classic American version is Joel Chandler Harris, *Nights with Uncle Remus: Myths and Legends of the Old Plantation* (Boston: Houghton Mifflin, 1883), pp. 23–25. Type ATU175, The Tarbaby and the Rabbit.

18 *Contes mahorais*, pp. 31–33. This is a cognate of a tale I collected in Mauritius (*Stars and Keys: Folktales and Creolization in the Indian Ocean* (Bloomington: Indiana University Press, 2007), pp. 85–90). Trickster's refusal to help dig a well was told to me in Kenya. The capture by tarbaby is part of tales 2.3.103 (Sakalava) and 3.2.175 in my *Malagasy Tale Index*. Motifs: D1840, Capture by deception; K741, Capture by tarbaby (= ATU175, The Tarbaby and the Rabbit). The unusually lively dialogue between tortoise and king in this version marks the teller's skill.

19 Paulme, *Statue*, p. 97. Dell Hymes expounds the dialectic idea in 'Folklore's Nature and the Sun's Myth', *Journal of American Folklore*, 88, 350 (1975), 346–69.

20 *Contes mahorais*, pp. 1–2. This is a version of ATU2034C, Lending and Repaying: Progressively Better Bargain. The progressively lucky bargains (motif N421.1) dominate several Malagasy tales with different characters, without the trickster frame (*Malagasy Tale Index*, pp. 155–56).

21 *Contes mahorais*, pp. 35–36. The animal translated as Hedgehog is the Malagasy tenrec (*trandraka*), an animal almost as big as hare. Motifs: K359.2, Thief beguiles guardian of goods by assuming equivocal name; K475, Cheating through equivocation. The symmetrical counteractions of this pair appear to be modeled on Malagasy stories about the inseparable

tricksters Ikotofetsy and Imahaka (*Stars and Keys*, pp. 117–33). When Hare and Hedgehog make and break friendship, they are acting out a durable narrative template that shapes many African tales. A trickster and dupe, whom any audience will recognize as real-life enemies, make a contract with each other for their common benefit. Predictably, trickster betrays his partner's trust and the friendship falls apart. I recorded one case of it in Kenya, then recognized it in an African-derived story, collected by one of my students from a church friend of Jamaican background (Alan Dundes, 'The Making and Breaking of Friendship as a Structural Frame in African Folk Tales', in *Structural Analysis of Oral Tradition*, ed. Pierre Maranda and Elli Köngäs Maranda (Philadelphia: University of Pennsylvania Press, 1971), pp. 171–85; Lee Haring, 'A Characteristic African Folktale Pattern', in *African Folklore*, ed. Richard M. Dorson (Garden City, NY: Doubleday, 1972), pp. 165–79). The pattern is not aesthetically neutral: it carries a poignant message about the precariousness of interdependence. As T. W. Adorno observed, the truth content in art 'speaks primarily through the form rather than through themes or opinions'. Peter Uwe Hohendahl, *Prismatic Thought: Theodor W. Adorno* (Lincoln: University of Nebraska Press, 1995), pp. 84–85.

22   Maurice Fontoynont, and Raomandahy, 'La grande Comore', *Mémoires de l'Académie Malgache* (1937), pp. 76–77. Motifs: K890, Dupe tricked into killing himself; G523, Ogre deceived into stabbing himself.

23   Storytellers don't rigorously distinguish a *djinn* from a *lolo* or a *dyab*. A *djinn* from the Islamic point of view is 'an alternative species of being'. All three are regarded as more or less fictional, in contrast to the real spirits that often arise in people. Michael Lambek, *Island in the Stream: An Ethnographic History of Mayotte* (Toronto: University of Toronto Press, 2018), p. 152.

24   A less cynical tale featuring the advice to 'Consider the end' was collected a century ago among Sakalava, in northwest Madagascar: André Dandouau, *Contes populaires des sakalava et des tsimihety de la région d'Analalava*, Publications de la Faculté des Lettres d'Alger (Algiers, 1922), pp. 347–56. Many Mahorais and their tales have Sakalava ancestors.

25   *Contes mahorais*, pp. 49–50. Motifs: F271.5, Fairies clear land; J21.1, 'Consider the end.'

26   *Contes mahorais*, pp. 8–9. Motifs: D1030.1, Food supplied by magic; D431.3, Transformation, leaf to person; C31.2, Tabu: mentioning origin of supernatural wife; C952, Immediate return to other world because of broken tabu.

27 He probably chose his style in response to the interview situation. In the very different setting of western Oregon (U. S. A.), the anthropologist Melville Jacobs discovered the same style when he recorded and translated over a hundred narratives from Mrs. Victoria Howard, one of the last surviving speakers of the Clackamas Chinook language. 'She translated her dictations adeptly into English', he explains: 'Story dictations in a native language, and renderings in English by bilingual informants, display... compactness and brevity'. Melville Jacobs, *The Content and Style of an Oral Literature: Clakacamas Chinook Myths and Tales* (Chicago: University of Chicago Press, 1959), p. 266.

28 R. P. Callet, *Tantaran'ny andriana*, trans. G.-S. Chapus and E. Ratsimba (Antananarivo: Librairie de Madagascar, 1958), 1:573.

29 *Contes mahorais*, p. 134. A similar parody is in Noël J. Gueunier, *L'oiseau chagrin: contes comoriens en dialecte malgache de l'île de Mayotte*, compilers Noël J. Gueunier, and Madjidhoubi Said, trans. Noël J. Gueunier, illustrator Razafintsalama, Asie et monde insulindien (Paris: Peeters, 1994), pp. 66–77. Motif: C932, Loss of wife for breaking tabu. Mansour Kamardine, who appears in the documentary film 'Mayotte, le département abandonné de la France', by Sebastien Daguerressar, has served as Mayotte's representative in the French National Assembly..

30 Herbert Lindenberger, *Opera, the Extravagant Art* (Ithaca: Cornell University Press, 1984), p. 102. I am grateful to Rachel M. Brownstein for this reference. I discuss the topic in 'Parody and Imitation in Western Indian Ocean Oral Literature', *Journal of Folklore Research*, 29, 3 (1992), 199–224.

31 *Contes mahorais*, pp. 47–48. ATU155, The Ungrateful Snake Returned to Captivity.

32 *Contes mahorais*, pp. 96–97.

33 Dandouau, pp. 358–59. Motifs: C321, Tabu: looking into box; C915.1, Troubles escape when forbidden casket is opened.

34 *Contes mahorais*, pp. 4–5. Type ATU327, The Children and the Ogre, comprises this and dozens more tale types; it is a 'supertype'. Motifs: H1212.4, Quest assigned because of longings of pregnant woman; F359.1, Eggs stolen from fairies, an Indian motif; K772, Victim enticed into dancing, captured; D1415.2, Magic musical instrument causes person to dance; T571, Unreasonable demands of pregnant women.

35 Gueunier, *L'Oiseau*, pp. 2–19.

36 ATU451. Nos. 9 and 49 in Grimm.

37   *Contes mahorais*, pp. 120–21. Type ATU451, The Maiden Who Seeks Her
      Brothers. The ATU catalogue (pp. 267–68) shows how seldom this tale has
      been told in Africa or Madagascar. Motifs: C273, Tabu: drinking water;
      C960 and D510, Transformation by breaking tabu; D135, Transformation:
      man to sheep; C460, Laughing tabu; N711, King accidentally finds maiden
      and marries her; D758, Disenchantment by maintaining silence; H1194.0.1,
      Task: causing silent person to speak; H1194, Task: making person laugh;
      E711.2.1, Soul in gourd; H64, Recognition of disenchanted person by
      physical attributes.

38   Could tale type ATU451 have been brought from France? Only if Bwanali
      Sanda's version looked anything like, say, the thirty-six French versions
      carefully catalogued by Paul Delarue. It does not. Paul Delarue and Marie-
      Louise Tenèze, *Le conte populaire français: catalogue raisonné des versions de
      France* (Paris: G. P. Maisonneuve et Larose, 1976–2002), 2: 129–40. The
      maiden's passivity can be seen in three related Grimm tales: The Twelve
      Brothers, The Seven Ravens, and The Six Swans.

39   Fictional versions come from Swahili traditions: George W. Bateman,
      Zanzibar Tales Told by Natives of the East Coast of Africa (Chicago: A. C.
      McClurg, 1901), pp. 155–79; Jan Knappert, *Myths and Legends of the Swahili*
      (Nairobi: Heinemann Educational Books, 1970), pp. 187–89.

40   Dandouau, pp. 380–85.

41   *Malagasy Tale Index*, pp. 131–35.

42   Dandouau, pp. 382–85.

43   Paul Ottino deftly uses the swallowing monster to explain the dynamic
      of creolization in Madagascar and the Comoros: 'Between the African
      coast, the Comoran archipelago and Madagascar, these Islamised people
      of Arab, Persian, even Indian origin, accompanied by Zanj Africans
      (themselves coming from the ensemble of the old coast of Azania from
      southern Somalia as far as the Mozambique of today), were to constitute,
      by the very extension of their religious, economic, and familial networks, a
      true bridge that facilitated the circulation of men, goods, and ideas, among
      them themes like that of the swallowing monster [so] widespread in
      Madagascar'. 'Le thème du monstre dévorant dans les domaines malgache
      et bantou', *ASEMI*, 8, 3–4 (1977), 219–51 (p. 247). A classic version: Renel
      3: 59–62.

44   More or less ATU300, The Dragon-Slayer. Mohamed el Anrif stays close
      to a Betsimisaraka dragon-slayer tale recorded a century earlier, Renel 3:
      140–42. Motifs: F911.6, All-swallowing monster; W151, Greed; B11.2.3.1,

Seven-headed dragon; B11.11, Fight with dragon; F913, Victims rescued from swallower's belly; C422.1, Tabu: revealing dragon-fighter's identity; H83, Rescue tokens; H1531, Spine test; L161, Lowly hero marries princess.

45   *Contes mahorais*, pp. 39–41. ATU1641, Doctor Know-All, is well known in mainland Africa. A sample is Robert Cancel, *Allegorical Speculation in an Oral Society: The Tabwa Narrative Tradition* (Berkeley: University of California Press, 1989), pp. 184–90. Motifs: K1956, Sham wise man; N611.1, Criminal accidentally detected: 'that is the first' — sham wise man; N688, What is in the dish: Poor Crab.

46   Sophie Blanchy, *Maisons des femmes, cités des hommes. Filiation, âge et pouvoir à Ngazidja (Comores)* (Nanterre: Société d'Ethnologie, 2010), pp. 239–69.

47   *Contes mahorais*, pp. 82–85.

48   *Contes mahorais*, pp. 51–54, 57–61, 82–85.

49   Renel 3: 118–19. William R. Bascom, *African Dilemma Tales* (The Hague: Mouton, 1975), p. 52. The dilemma tale, as known in Madagascar and Mayotte, comes closest to one tale type, The Four Skillful Brothers (ATU653), but the Indo-Eurocentric type classification fails to capture the genre because it leaves out the audience. Dilemma tales demonstrate that non-western people engage in discussions of moral problems that are as deep as anything dreamt of in your philosophy.

50   *Contes mahorais*, pp. 86–87.

51   Henry Glassie, 'Tradition', in Burt Feintuch, ed., *Eight Words for the Study of Expressive Culture* (Urbana: University of Illinois Press, 2003), p. 176.

52   *Contes mahorais*, pp. x-xi.

53   Claude Allibert, *Mayotte: plaque tournante et microcosme de l'océan indien occidental* (Paris: Éditions Anthropos, 1984), p. 207.

54   Sidney W. Mintz and Richard Price, *An Anthropological Approach to the Afro-American Past: A Caribbean Perspective* (Philadelphia: University of Pennsylvania Press, 1976), p. 302.

55   Djoumoi Ali M'madi, 'Transmission traditionnelle des savoirs et des savoir-faire à Ndzaoudze, M'Vouni', master's thesis (M'vouni, Grande Comore), 1989).

56   Michael Lambek, in *Human Spirits: A Cultural Account of Trance in Mayotte* (Cambridge: Cambridge University Press, 1981), makes it clear that Mahorais people classify their narratives and separate their genres.

57   I paraphrase Fredric Jameson: these fictional themes or characters 'are themselves simply so many allusions to a more basic ideological "sign" which would have been grasped instinctively by any contemporary reader but from which we are culturally and historically somewhat distanced' Fredric Jameson, *The Political Unconscious: Narrative as a Socially Symbolic Act* (Ithaca: Cornell University Press, 1981), p. 200. Bridging that distance are the notes by our three collectors, which translate the symbolic language of verbal art into a language their readers will understand.

58   Patrick Eisenlohr, *Little India: Diaspora, Time, and Ethnolinguistic Belonging in Hindu Mauritius* (University of California Press, 2006), p. 142.

59   Philippe Beaujard, *Mythe et société à Madagascar (Tanala de l'Ikongo): le chasseur d'oiseaux et la princesse du ciel* (Paris: L'Harmattan, 1991), p. 421.

60   Paul Ottino, 'Un procédé littéraire malayo-polynésien: de l'ambigüité à la plurisignification', *L'Homme* 6, 4 (October-December 1966), 5–34. The British Protestant missionaries in the nineteenth century did the best they could to eliminate ambiguity and irony, with notable success (Lee Haring, 'Interpreters of Indian Ocean Tales', *Fabula* 44 (2003), 98–116). Translation changes everything.

So many questions from this chapter!

2. Varieties of Performing

That Difficult Girl

Noël Gueunier's collecting visits to Mayotte began in 1975, when he was teaching in Madagascar, and continued until 1983. Knowing the language kinship of the two, he could expect that the folktales he would find would be related to tales already collected. He engaged Madjidhoubi Said as a student to teach him Kibushi, the island dialect of Malagasy. Presently the positions were reversed, and as his collaborator, Said interviewed, recorded, transcribed, and helped to annotate Gueunier's translations of their 136 tales. Their information about local references and code-switching helps the reader imagine the diversity of performances by the sixty-five narrators. We see storytellers tossing in a word to help their hearers, listening for their reactions, and keeping ever close to their audience. We also see them telling the same tale over and over. At first we think, this is what I was afraid of, this is why 'folklore' is boring, endless repetition of some not very interesting story.

Admittedly the first twenty-three of Gueunier's texts are versions of the same plot. Then on examination it turns out to be the most interesting story of them all. A heroine refuses eligible men (thus disobeying custom: a woman is expected to marry, period). She marries a man she chooses, who turns out to be an animal or *djinn*, and must be rescued. Admittedly again, it is not a favorite plot in Europe, but it is a favorite of audiences in Africa, Madagascar, and the Indian Ocean islands. I heard it in in Mauritius.[1] Gueunier and Said heard it from seventeen different narrators in six villages of Mayotte: nine old women, three not-so-old women, three young men, a little girl, and one old man.[2] Why is it so popular there?

    https://doi.org/10.11647/OBP.0315.02

First, because it features the interaction of a woman with a *djinn*. Second, because it treats the most important of all social topics — marriage, which secures the position of a woman as child bearer and assures the continuation of family and village. Third, because its insistence on making a correct marriage evokes the pattern Mahorais have inherited from their earliest settlers, the Bantu-Swahili from east Africa. The pattern of tracing kinship through your mother is what anthropologists call *matriliny*. (There is no word for assigning storytelling to women; 'it's traditional'.) After Islam was brought to the Comoros by the Shirazi arriving from Persia, matriliny survived, through conversion through the centuries of plantation slavery and colonial neglect. In the controversies over independence in the 1970–80s, matriliny was still doing its best to survive. The tales collected by Noël Gueunier, Claude Allibert, and Sophie Blanchy rely on a complex based on matriliny: marriage, mother, home, identity, and indigenousness. The oft-told tale has been studied by a team of French folklorists, who call it the *fille difficile*, the difficult girl.[3] They side with her parents.

One version comes from an old lady, one of many accomplished storytellers in the Kibushi-speaking village of Kany Kely. Gueunier conceals the names of all his storytellers:

> I have deliberately avoided giving their names, and most often I have concealed the names of the real persons whom the taletellers like to introduce more or less maliciously into their narrations. Naturally folktales are not, as a rule, matters of moment for Comorans; they are lies. But these lies are sometimes the occasion to get off criticism, even satire..., and I would not have wanted to risk seeing the written texts come back on their authors.[4]

Village storytelling in Mayotte happens among people who know one another well. As the old lady narrates to her neighbors, one occasionally interrupts her Kibushi with whispered French words. She organizes her version around the girl's rescuer, her young brother, who is *Betombokoantŝôro*, Covered-With-Ulcers. After a classic opening formula, she describes the members of the family.

I insert captions in italics for the segments of her story.

Kings were living   Rich ones were living

Viziers [ministers] were living   Poor ones were living

There was a man with children, girls, boys

THE LAST-BORN WAS A BOY
THERE WAS THE FIRST-BORN, THE MIDDLE ONE, THE NEXT, THE LAST-BORN.

The family's equilibrium is about to be menaced.

Her Excessive Marriage Demand: AND THIS GIRL, THE ELDEST, WHOEVER CAME TO ASK FOR HER IN MARRIAGE, SHE DIDN'T WANT HIM. ALL THE ONES COMING TO ASK FOR HER IN MARRIAGE, SHE DIDN'T WANT ANY. HER FATHER SAID, "WHO DO YOU LIKE?"
SHE SAID, "IF SOMEBODY COMES THAT I LIKE, I'LL TELL YOU".
"OH?"
"YES".

A *kaka* (cannibal ogre) arrives from a village he has devoured, disguising himself in ceremonial Arab dress. A *kaka* is not sharply distinguished in Kibushi language from a *lolo*, and Shimaore speakers tend to call all these dangerous creatures *gini, djinn*s. They are to be distinguished from the spirits that sometimes possess people.[5]

His Disguise: HE PUT ON HIS *DJOHO*, PUT ON HIS SHIRT, PUT ON HIS BIG TUNIC, PUT ON ALL HIS JEWELRY, YOU WOULD HAVE SAID A HANDSOME YOUNG MAN.

Acceptance of the Suitor: AS SOON AS HE CAME IN, SHE SAID TO HER PARENTS, "THAT'S THE ONE! HE'S THE ONE I LIKE".
"HE'S THE ONE YOU LIKE?"
"YES".
"HE'S THE ONE YOU LIKE?"
"YES".
"FOR SURE?"
"YES".

The repeated dialogue emphasizes this young woman's stubbornness. That's why the Africanist scholars call her a *fille difficile*.

The Marriage: THEY RECEIVED HIM, THEY CELEBRATED THE MARRIAGE.

The cannibal, having only one motivation, takes her to his place, imprisoning her, her sisters, and her ulcerous little brother. In real life, men move in with their wives, because it's women who own the houses. Listeners would have spotted this counterfactual as identifying the *kaka*. But in case they didn't, the narrator reminds them, all the people, he'd eaten them.

Revelation of His Original Nature: The *kaka* goes out every day, returning at midnight and bringing with him storm, darkness, rain — it was terrible. He means to devour his victims, expecting them to be asleep, but their brother wasn't asleep. A listener says, 'THE SICK ONE WASN'T ASLEEP?' 'NO, HE WASN'T ASLEEP. HE SAID TO HIMSELF, "IF I KEEP QUIET, MAYBE HE WON'T EAT ME".' The *kaka* inspects the sleeping sisters: 'WHO'S THIS?' He has to ask three times before the boy figures out, 'IF I DON'T ANSWER, ISN'T HE GOING TO EAT ME?' and sings,

> "THAT'S FIRST-BORN
> FIRST-BORN GETTING HER PAY.
> SHE'S SLEEPING, *KAKA*, SHE'S RESTING".

Both sing in a dialect of Kibushi slightly different from the narrated parts. 'Getting her pay', Gueunier notes, means that being eaten by the *kaka* is what she deserves for disdaining other men and disobeying her parents, but the boy smears himself in the same words.

> "SO WHO ARE YOU?"
> "I AM BETOMBOKOANTŜÔRO,
> BETOMBOKOANTŜÔRO GETTING HIS PAY,
> HE'S SLEEPING, *KAKA*, HE'S RESTING".

That happens three times. Evidently, he thinks his sores are divine justice.

Next day, the boy said to his sisters, 'YOU KNOW THIS HUSBAND YOU HAVE HERE IS A *KAKA*?' The sisters refuse to believe him until the *kaka* returns the next night and they repeat the sung dialogue until the *kaka* swallows the boy. BUT JUST WHEN HE SWALLOWED HIM, THE [BOY] HAD HIS KNIFE WITH HIM, AND HE CUT HIM FROM HERE [NARRATOR GESTURES TO HER THROAT] TO HIS GUT. THE *KAKA* BEGAN SPINNING AROUND, HE RAISED A STORM *OOO-OOO*, HE TRIED TO CATCH THE SISTERS BUT DIDN'T... 'AY-EE! YOU'VE GOT PEPPER, HUH? YOU'VE GOT PEPPER! AY-EE, AY-EE, AY-EE!' As the *kaka* bangs around, the boy cuts his way out, gets swallowed again, and keeps cutting till he has slain the *kaka*. It is the narrator's distinct touch that the boy, like the heroes of certain Indian tales, does not forget to cut off its fingernails and toenails.[6] Now her hero has taken center stage.

Breaking of the Marriage: THEN HE WENT TO HIS SISTERS, STILL IN THE HOUSE. 'SO, WHAT ABOUT YOU GETTING TURNED DOWN? WHAT IF I HADN'T COME? YOU'D BE DEAD RIGHT NOW.' NO REPLY FROM THEM, EXCEPT 'WELL, COME ON, LET'S GO BACK NOW'.

'GO BACK HOW? HE'S NOT ALONE, THERE ARE OTHERS LIKE HIM. SO FIRST WE'LL DO DIVINATION. WAIT TILL I LOOK AT THE STARS FOR THE DAY, THE HOUR, THE MINUTE WE CAN LEAVE'.

Destiny of the Characters: Finally, on a day he deems auspicious, he leads them back to their mother, where at last his sisters praise him, with another word for his ailment. 'IF NOT FOR LETEKINGA, WE WERE DEAD!' They tell their adventures. SO THEY PERFORMED THE *SHIDJABU* CEREMONY [AGAINST MISFORTUNE] FOR THEM. THEY GOT A SCHOLAR, PUT THEM IN THE MIDDLE OF A CIRCLE TO RECITE THE *SHIDJABU*, AND THEN BROKE UP. I LEFT THEM THERE, I DON'T KNOW HOW IT ENDED.[7]

When Noël Gueunier recorded it, the *fille difficile* was not yet known to be the most popular of all folktales in Africa. Researchers asking for stories in Cameroun have been offered this one first, as I was in Kenya.[8] It is the most oft-told story, much better known than Uncle Remus's tarbaby. How the *fille* got to Mayotte is not obscure: most Comorans are of African descent. But, you say, what happened to that unruly young woman, who was supposed to be the heroine? Well, Mayotte is not the only island where males are allowed to dominate. Indeed in most versions, the rescuer is female — a sister, a sister surrogate, or the wife's little daughter, but in this variant the rescuing hero is named for his scars, which look as if he's been hit with a spade. They cause him to be scorned by his family, but why wouldn't an audience love him? A deformed or defective hero triumphs in the end of so many tales. So this version of the *fille* tale, featuring him, is not irregular; probably it was the one the narrator's audience already knew. That doesn't mean it is 'the' Kany Kely version: Gueunier recorded dozens of storytellers in that village. It means that even within a relatively small community, a recognizable tale is told in variant forms.

He's a *djinn*, or a *kaka*, or a *lolo*

The remembered parts of Gueunier's twenty-one versions are traditional; so are the differences. All the narrators show the girl refusing all suitors. Sometimes he is disguised as an Arab, sometimes she just picks him out (an instant crush). Always he takes her to his place, which is often the forest, Africa's locale for wildness. The discovery of his *kaka*, *lolo*, or *djinn* nature varies according to the teller.[9] One will have him refusing human food: a *kaka* prefers a rotten diet, which listeners will recoil from. Others have him detected by the girl's brother for killing geese and ducks. Another has a talebearing shepherd tip off the king about him. The marriage is broken when the wife escapes in various ways, with whoever has accompanied her. Three narrators give them a lift home on the back of a *Kirombo* bird, singing and pursued by the *kaka*, who will soon meet his destiny in a burning house. One young man in Hakoa allows him to escape to the neighboring island, Anjouan.

For several narrators, marrying the cannibal husband is their chance to sing a dialogue. It is a moment in the narrative when they blend the sister's discovery of the *kaka*'s true nature with her moment of initiation into the true nature of males.

> Now that man was a KAKA. When he worked, he had horns sticking out, a tail sticking out, eyes sticking out. So when she called "Hey, brother-in-law," he snapped back "Chiria chair nyonga, chiria nihonga mshia, chiria mashie!" [Back in, horns, back in, tail, back in, back in].

'Comoran ogres [Gueunier explains] resemble a monstrous bird: they have feathers (*volovolo*) and wings like a bird, but also a tail (*mokla*) and horns (*ampôndo*) like an animal', which they can retract if discovered.[10]

> She got there with the plate she was carrying to him. But he started asking — he held his head like this:
>
> > "What's this, sister-in-law?
> > What's this, sister-in-law?"
> > > "That's my head for carrying
> > > my head for carrying, brother-in-law
> > > my head for carrying."
> > "What's this, sister-in-law?
> > What's this, sister-in-law?"
> > (It was the KAKA asking.)
> > > "That's hair for weaving baskets
> > > hair for weaving baskets, brother-in-law
> > > hair for weaving baskets."
> > "What's this, sister-in-law?
> > What's this, sister-in-law?"
> > (He's asking her about her face.)
> > > "That's my face, to make up
> > > my face, to make up, brother-in-law
> > > my face to make up."
> > "What's this, sister-in-law?
> > What's this, sister-in-law?
> > What's this, sister-in-law?"

"THAT'S EARS TO HEAR WITH
EARS TO HEAR WITH, BROTHER-IN-LAW
EARS TO HEAR WITH."
"WHAT'S THIS, SISTER-IN-LAW?
WHAT'S THIS, SISTER-IN-LAW?"
"THAT'S EYES TO SEE WITH
EYES TO SEE WITH, BROTHER-IN-LAW
EYES TO SEE WITH."
"WHAT'S THIS, SISTER-IN-LAW?
WHAT'S THIS, SISTER-IN-LAW?"
(HE'S ASKING HER ALL THE PARTS OF HER BODY, HE'S ASKING WHAT IT IS.)

The two continue their dialogue down her body till they get to the part she calls THE WORK OF THE WORLD (*mambo ya dunia*). Her skill with euphemism wins the debate. 'WELL, MY SISTER-IN-LAW, YOU KNOW HOW TO TALK. GOODBYE, SISTER-IN-LAW, GOODBYE. EWA!'[11]

Many tales show that all a woman needs to assert herself is to be able to talk back to a man, but this one's command of language also asserts human power over the *kaka*. The main attraction is doubtless the verbal striptease, which is featured by six of Gueunier's narrators.

The plot of the *fille*'s tale is always recognizable; the differences and localizations lodge it in memory. It has no 'original', no hallowed or canonized form. Its only existence is in the performances of storytellers, which differ from one another as performers and audiences do. Folktales have no 'original'. Performers learn by listening to other performers. Their performance of the *fille* comes into existence by their absorbing and transforming of other performances. In Mayotte, the Middle East, and nearly every other place in the world, 'stories may be offered as entertainment, but they are selected for reasons particular to the audience at hand, and often interpretable as interpersonal comment, critique, or admonition'.[12] Gueunier's many texts, indeed all verbatim folktale texts, reveal folktale style to be a mosaic of quotations. Phrases, images, and rhythms recur. Formulaic openings and closings are repeated in fixed phrasings. The cannibal husband is always disguised; the *fille* always escapes. What the academy calls plagiarism is the heart and soul of the storyteller's practice. Little knowing he was describing oral folklore, the playwright Jean Giraudoux said, 'Plagiarism is the basis for all literature, with the exception of the very first, which is unknown anyway'.[13]

What about language? Western people always want to know what language is spoken in an island like Mayotte. The answer is plural. As you travel across Mayotte, Gueunier remarks, you go from one village speaking Shimaore, supposedly the old Comoran, to another speaking Kibushi, their dialect of Malagasy, and then back again.[14] Both nowadays have to cope with Ndzuwani, which is spoken by immigrants from Anjouan looking for work, immediately spotted by their accent, trying to avoid deportation because they are illegal. Kibushi, coexisting with Shimaore, blends Malagasy with Makhuwa, a language from Mozambique. What an embarrassment of riches. So, it is no surprise that Gueunier notes plenty of code-switching; his narrators use it as a strategy for characterization. A *kaka* switches into some unintelligible language of his own, or a woman character gains recognition through singing in a different language from what the narrator has used up to then. Mayotte's cultural mix is honored by the switching.

He Demands What Anthropologists Call Uxorilocality

In the tale, the girl's desire and the cannibal's devouring appetite both are forces. To achieve a proper marriage, to fit into society, she must temper her desires and learn obedience. A man's animal nature can't be erased by a disguise of Arab costume and gold teeth.[15] The depth of social obligation is signaled when the *kaka* says he will take his newlywed to his place. Custom expects a wife to reside with or near her parents. Anthropologists call this custom 'uxorilocality'. Sophie Blanchy points out its advantages.

> Since in the Comoros every marriage must end someday, is not uxorilocality at first sight a guarantee for the woman, who will certainly be repudiated or abandoned, but not thrown out into the street? It also means that parents are always there, close by, always taking care of their daughter, sister, her children. Husbands come and go, the family remains.[16]

The *fille*'s story takes her back to her parents. In a few versions she dies, but commonly that fate is reserved for the *kaka*. Uxorilocality (you have to love that word, that's why I repeat it) is the antithesis of the matriliny of early history days, the identification of a mother with her house, and the identification of a daughter with her mother. With metaphor, irony, ambiguity, and figurative language, the narratives preserved actors and incidents from old stories whose coded language of resistance conveyed messages about the present. So, when they narrate the fille, Gueunier's twenty-one storytellers say less about sexuality than about the need to recognize a person's identity. Hence, they all emphasize the image of the suitor's disguise. Putting it more broadly, the meanings of Mahorais tales are not undecidable; they are variable, because from Africa and Indonesia, the storytellers inherited a virtuosity with secret languages.[17]

One young narrator makes that point by pushing the girl's defiance into absurdity. He departs from convention by making the girl's father the initiator of the marriage. To the man in the robe and fez this poor fellow imposes one condition on the marriage: 'MAHARY NY ZANAKO TY [WHAT SHE BRINGS TO THE MARRIAGE; HER DOWRY] IS TSY MANGERY AÑATY NY HERIN*ANDRA ANEKY, NO SHITTING FOR A WEEK.' The husband-to-be agrees, forgetting he is part human and urged on by his *kaka* appetite. They have the wedding that same day. For five days he holds out; then, under the feeble, human-sounding lie that his mother is ill, he goes to the forest, fills a crab hole with his shit, and immediately goes back to Hakoa, where the tale was being performed.[18] By making the *kaka* ridiculous, the narrator exaggerates the contrast between a 'real' marriage and what is conceivable with this foreigner. The fille tale, with its comments on marriage and the sex-gender system, is popular because it points to life's unresolvable ideological contradictions. If its popularity would be incomprehensible outside some social context, listeners in Mayotte might see that *djinn* husband as an agent of the colonizing power.[19]

The *fille* tale is astonishingly adaptable, ever popular when told straight. Part of it can be attached to another tale; parody is always an option for the clever artist commenting on power differentials.

The Crustacean Campaigner

The skeleton of a story, says a great folktale scholar, 'sometimes as a whole, sometimes only as rudiments, appears as the most stable, oldest and most tenacious element in the tale tradition'.[20] In an oft-told tale like the *fille*, the skeleton is always visible even if most of the body is missing. Several of Gueunier's storytellers use the head — the girl's refusal of suitors — to begin other, wildly unrelated tales. That young man telling the 'no shitting' story in September 1976 was using the familiar opening to comment on the Comoran independence movement. The girl's refusal is not central to his piece; probably he knew the folktale collector would recognize it. His most important character is neither that nubile girl nor her rescuer, but a talking animal. A singing crab will campaign for his party. It's into the crab's hole that the *kaka* deposits his shit. Already the girl is offstage. The crab will proclaim the *kaka*'s real nature — like the little sister in more standard versions, but more loudly.

Coming out of the hole, the crab picks up the turd, dries it in the sun, and parades it through all the villages from Kombani to Mrowali (a trip well known to the audience). He sings in Shimaore about finding it. *Bengava* is the husband; if *pingiri* means anything, it is the crab's name.[21]

> PINGIRI, PINGIRI, PINGIRI,
> BENGAVA SHIT IN FRONT OF MY DOOR,
> MINE! PINGIRI.

The offended villagers tell him to go away, but having now taken the stage, the crab will sing the information again and again. Like any campaigner in the wrong place, he is despised and rejected. At Mrowali, he is still carrying the turd and still singing. The chief, a true colonial administrator, sends him on to the next village, Mtsangamuji. There, the self-important chief Hoseny Be (Big Husain) throws him out, more angrily than the other one. Is this any more than local satire?

Fig. 5 'Mayotte is Comoran and will always remain so'. Photo by David Stanley, CC BY 2.0, Wikimedia Commons, https://upload.wikimedia.org/wikipedia/commons/6/64/Mayotte_is_Comorian_%2810896486873%29.jpg

In fact, it is, because of the political position the narrator is taking. The crab speaks for him and his audience of September 1976. They agree that Mayotte should remain attached to France. The independence movement they reject was not new. Two years earlier, independence for the four Comoros had been proclaimed by the first president, Ahmed Abdallah, but soon it was torpedoed when the mercenary Bob Denard ousted him. Then in 1975 Mayotte seceded from the Comoros. A few months later, a referendum confirmed that Mayotte would be a 'territorial collectivity' of France, but conflicts continued raging, right there in Hakoa. Anyone, even a crab, speaking for the *Serelame* party, which favored Comoran independence, was bound to get thrown out of every village, because the dignitaries were afraid of making trouble with the French authorities. In the tale they keep ejecting the crab and trying to hush him up, because they hear his song as insulting the king's son-in-law. What with the political partisanship and the continual singing — the audience gets to hear the crab's song eleven times — the young narrator's political position will have made a hit with the men listening, who were ready to march against the *Serelame* party.[22] His comment on local events even sounds the ownership theme, of the place legends in the previous chapter, when the crab assails the alien who shit on Mayotte's land. Ultimately, the *soroda* party won: it did fasten Mayotte more closely to the metropole. The narrator, attaching a piece of the *fille* story to the current conflict, enacts a dialectic between the past of inherited tradition and the present of 1976 politics. His tale is a miniature of the blending beloved of creole storytellers. *Hmm.*

A Magic Drum

Another use for the *fille*'s first move is to attach it to the classic fairytale plot of a young man going in quest of a wife. Offhand that trajectory would not seem to match up well with the story's fierce lesson about cannibal husbands, but in a tale from Kany Kely (yes, another from Kany Kely), the young woman refuses all suitors except the one who can fetch the *ngoma la mshindro wa saba*, the seven-beat drum. 'BUT THAT DRUM', says the young narrator, 'YOU COULDN'T GRAB IT SO EASILY. THAT DRUM WAS KEPT BY *LOLOS* [SPIRITS]. THE SPIRITS KEPT IT IN A HOUSE, THEY GUARDED THE HOUSE, TO GET THERE YOU HAD TO GO THROUGH ONE ROOM, THEN ANOTHER, A THIRD, AND LIKE THAT TO THE SEVENTH ROOM, BEFORE YOU

REACHED THAT DRUM, AND IN EVERY ROOM, THERE WERE SPIRITS STAYING THERE, SLEEPING THERE, GUARDING IT'. Several men try and fail. Young Mady (pronounced MAHdee) vows to capture it and marry the girl. It seems even a rebellious woman requires a man to fulfill her destiny. From then on, every move Mady makes is traditional folktale stuff, which the narrator adapts.

Life tokens, for instance, signal the welfare of a departed hero. Mady leaves his two mysteriously named dogs with his mother as a life token. If she hears them scratching and howling, or if the grass withers, she is to unleash them. As a mother should, she gives him cakes (*makary*) and water for his journey. Another favorite device is the charm he is to speak when he reaches a rock. It opens only when he recites the charm (remember 'Open, Sesame!'). The donor he finds happens to be an old woman covered in feces. Graciously he bathes her (thus passing a hero's test). Her advice, and the charm she gives him, will enable him to get the magic object. He is to travel alone to the *lolos*' house and listen for them; some, she says, will be talking strange phrases in their sleep, while others lie awake watching for thieves. Only on a second visit does he hear their surrealist talk: 'HEY MADY, I SAW YOU! I SAW YOU! GIVE ME THAT DRUM, GIVE ME THAT BED, EH, THE RAT, THE CHICKEN, THE BANANA-TREE!' Reciting the charm, he gets past the sleepers, dons a cap of invisibility, quietly picks up the drum and escapes back to the old woman.

The magic of that drum is that it will beat itself if touched.[23] Sure enough, a leaf falls on it and it beats, awakening the *lolos*. As these unusually potent characters pursue him, they clear their path by felling coconut trees with their testicles (this is a young man narrating, remember). He is rescued by his dogs, but his return home is a false ending. The narrator, or his source, delays the real ending with a few more flourishes an audience will recognize. The mother, thinking her son already dead and mistaking him for a deceptive intruder, faints and must be revived with water. Next day an old woman, coming for fire, thinks she recognizes Mady; she runs to tell the king the news. At last the complete hero, with his task accomplished, Mady marries the king's daughter. 'So MADY BECAME KING, HE TOOK THE KING'S PLACE, THE GREAT KING OF THAT VILLAGE'. Thenceforward the drum survives, to announce everything that happens in the village. 'I LEFT THEM THERE,' says the narrator. It's better to follow his example and not attach some mythical meaning to the drum. He has followed the fairytale sequence: the hero's struggle with *lolo*s, his victory over them, his pursuit and rescue, his unrecognized arrival, his final ascent to the throne.[24] Whoever devised this blend — either the young narrator or those he learned it from — has created a new structure by joining the *fille*'s refusals to the fairytale skeleton. Creole style loves such convergences of traditions and unpredictable novelty.

Back to Madagascar for a digression, actually a radical adaptation and shift of genre: the first move of the *fille difficile* story shows up in a pseudo-historical myth-legend. Three young men build a canoe, paddle for three months, and reach an island, where they find an Indian, an Arab and a Somali merchant. 'Back in their own country, they are rejected by the princess whose hand they sought. She prefers a fourth man who has brought her an unknown plant', namely *manioc* (cassava), which becomes a staple for that region of Madagascar.[25] The *fille* is recognizable in that princess; the origin myth about the local diet conforms well enough to expectations; but the whole plot is modeled on the widespread tale of The Four Skillful Brothers, who compete unsuccessfully to win a princess's hand by finding her something very rare. Because they fail the competition, she remains unaffianced, and no one lives happily ever after.[26] The piece yokes together seemingly unrelated traditions in a creole blend.

Recognition Is Vital

Back to Kany Kely and the fundamental issue of the *fille*, how to make a proper marriage. Narrators generally create suspense around discovering the suitor's real nature. Knowing their audiences will recognize the handsome suitor as both human and *kaka*, they make a point of his disguise: a ceremonial robe, a beautiful fez, Arab costume, gold teeth. Recognition is the very point of playing up the half-gluttonous, half-incestuous relation between the cannibal *kaka* and the sister-in-law who will rescue the wife. The naming-of-parts dialogue between them turns on the same theme.

For a narrator in Wangani, the *fille*'s story was not enough. 'Sometimes it happens', Denise Paulme writes of Africa, 'that a first theme, complete in itself, is not enough for the narrator. He passes immediately to a second part, which is in fact another story conforming to a different formal type from the first'.[27] Having begun with the six familiar moves and having shown the sister-in-law's verbal skills, the Wangani lady (probably remembering her source) changes the wife from victim into a folktale heroine, who immediately takes control in a larger plot ('Do as I say'). The sisters will set forth and have adventures.

Departing from home, they find a 'good ogress' mother surrogate, who summons the legendary *Firikombe*, a magic bird 'as big as an airplane', to provide their transport. He first demands and instantly devours ten kilos of rice (cannibal *kaka*s are not the only gluttons). Then he flies them to the *djinn* husband's house, where they spit and defecate. How many women in the audience identify with that gesture? But in the story it's magic. They load onto the bird everything of the *lolo*'s that they need. Securely in folktale country now, they mount the bird and are taken home. *Firikombe*'s magic allows a realistic touch: when the two women land on the roof of the house, it almost collapses. Once they are deposited on the ground, they reassure their mother and turn into *bourgeoises* in a postcolonial country: taking all the *lolo*'s goods, they open a shop.

> Anyway that's what the old liars say.
> (Audience member: — Like you!)
> Naaah! Audience laughter.

On his return, the *lolo* has not changed character. Knowing his gang is coming to eat, he digs a hole to hide in. Only his giant teeth are visible. A baby *lolo* from his gang spots them as a toy, but the adult *lolo*s dig the villain out and start some water boiling, while he pleads with them in vain.

> No, no "sorry", we came from home to eat here, you want us to go back hungry?
> He can't escape; they throw him into the boiling water, and each *lolo* starts cutting off a piece.
> (Audience member: They didn't even cook him?)
> Oh, you think they need their meat cooked?
> So, then they said, "What a fool, trying to trick us, we get married, we invite everybody to eat our wives and he lets them run away!" They

FINISHED HIM OFF. THEY ATE THE *LOLO*, AND I CAME HERE, THEY DIDN'T GIVE ME [ANY].[28]

The energy and narrative skill of this lady from Wangani, evident in print, were encouraged by her audience's reactions to her blending familiar plots. They were never slow to interrupt her.

She may also have been the narrator of a different sort of blend, a tale dictated in Wangani a year earlier, which retells a very well-known literary source, under the name of Avonà. The Beauty with Golden Hair (*La belle aux cheveux d'or*) is one of the *contes des fées* written by Countess Marie-Catherine d'Aulnoy in France at the end of the seventeenth century. She was the initiator of the French fashion for fairy tales, indeed was the inventor of that term. Evidently the woman of Wangani learned it orally while living among a French-speaking family.[29] Knowing the source, Gueunier discerns what makes Avonà a distinctly Mahorais tale. In Mme d'Aulnoy's story, three suitor tasks are required of the hero, whereas for the Wangani narrator, he need only conform to a more popular pattern and slay a dragon on the path. On the way, the narrator was about to list the places Avonà would traverse but wasn't sure Gueunier would know them. Avonà, being a blend of Europe and Mayotte, must have not only a donkey, a sword, and two sacks, but also those two necessaries of a Mahorais hero, water and *mokary* (bread). The dragon, though pleased to see three meals coming (I FORGOT THE DOG; HE HAD A DOG TOO, the narrator interjects), is slain, and the marriage is celebrated — on condition of satisfying one trace of the *fille difficile*. This new queen now sets Avonà two more tasks. He fulfills them, but one proves fatal: the king breaks the bottle containing the 'water of death' and dies from touching the liquid. Should we have foreseen her reaction? 'NO ONE CAN MARRY ME BUT YOU, AVONÀ'.[30] The blend succeeds, the tale is told. This movement from a French literary source to a creole retelling, so nicely documented, is characteristic of a colonized society, where oral and literary narration have fed each other throughout history.[31] Produced within a situation of social subordination, the Wangani narrative blends traits from markedly dissimilar cultures.

Enough of the *fille* tale for the moment. Mayotte's outstanding version will be presented, with its teller, in chapter 3. We turn back to Bwanawasi.

Fig. 6 A *pirog*. Photo by Perrine Pépin, CC BY-SA 4.0, Wikimedia Commons, https://commons.wikimedia.org/wiki/File:Pirogue_1_Mayotte.jpg

Bwanawasi Wants to Take the King's Throne

Code-switching, so easy in Mayotte, seems especially appropriate for a tale about a trickster. Judging from newspaper accounts in Mauritius and street talk in Seychelles, bringing codes together is the Indian Ocean rule; judging from Gueunier and Said's fieldwork, storytellers easily and casually display their multilingualism. Isn't code-switching the real native language of Mayotte? One narrator mixes 'lexicons of Arabic origin (*ezy*, power, *serikaly*, state, policy, *ubati*, people, nation) and French origin (*prezidā*, president, *pour*, *contre*), without counting [Shimaore] words (*mrumwa*, slave, *shiri*, seat, throne) and authentic [Kibushi] ones (*ampanjaka*, king, *hasa*, work, forced labor)'.[32] His story is worth digressing into, though it repeats incidents we've already seen. Early in the performance, Madjidhoubi Said asked the narrator, in Kibushi, 'This Bwanawasi, what kind of person was he?', and the narrator replied in Shimaore, HE WAS THE SMARTEST ONE OF [THE KING'S] MRUMWA [SLAVES, IN KIBUSHI]. Later, again switching codes, he says, 'YOU

KNOW, IN *SERIKALY* [POLITICS, ARABIC] *TOUJOURS* [ALWAYS, FRENCH] THERE ALWAYS HAVE TO BE SOME PEOPLE WITH THE PRESIDENT, SOME PEOPLE TO BE *CONTRE* [AGAINST, FRENCH] THE PRESIDENT. *TOUJOURS* LIKE THAT IN *SERIKALY*. OKAY! So he begins with a king, his only daughter, and Bwanawasi as one of his workers.'

> HE HAD A GOOD TIME PLAYING, DID BWANAWASI. EVERY TIME THE KING ORDERED A JOB, HE SAID TO HIS RELATIVES, "LET'S NOT DO IT! HE THINKS HE'S SOMETHING."... WELL, *YAANI* ["THAT IS" IN KIBUSHI], WHAT HE WANTED WAS TO GET HOLD OF THE KING'S THRONE. HE DIDN'T LIKE THAT THAT FELLOW OCCUPIED IT. THAT'S WHAT HE WANTED...
>
> THERE WAS ONE GUY WHO WAS *POUR* THE PRESIDENT, *YAANI*, AGREED WITH HIM. HE WENT TO TELL [THE KING] EVERYTHING BWANAWASI SAID, WHATEVER BWANAWASI SAID WHEN HE PUT OUT AN ORDER.

The king decides to have Bwanawasi stuffed into a sack and thrown into the sea, but his slaves leave him on the shore because they've forgotten their paddle. Papa Saidy comes by with some cattle, and the audience laughs at what will come next. WELL, THE GUY IN THE SACK, BWANAWASI IN THE SACK, HEARD PAPA SAIDY COMING. He tries to convince Papa Saidy to let him out.

> PAPA SAIDY SAID, "WHAT DID YOU DO TO — ?" *NON, NON, NON!* HE DIDN'T SAY THAT. I FORGOT.
>
> INTERVIEWER: THINK, IT'LL COME BACK.
>
> NARRATOR TO AUDIENCE MEMBER: "COME, COME CLOSER IF YOU WANT TO TALK. WE'LL BOTH TALK IT OVER...." (THEY CONFER, HE RESUMES) "COME AND LET ME LOOSE AND YOU GO IN. BECAUSE THE REASON THEY PUT ME IN THE SACK, THEY TOLD ME TO MARRY THE KING'S DAUGHTER, AND I DIDN'T WANT TO. SO, THEY PUT ME IN THIS SACK." THERE.
>
> INTERVIEWER: OKAY, KEEP GOING.

Papa Saidy falls for the trick and is drowned, while Bwanawasi makes away with his cattle. When he is discovered alive, he runs his next trick of changing places and gets the king drowned.

> HE WENT BACK WITH THE *PIROG*, CAME BACK HERE, MARRIED... WHO? THE KING'S DAUGHTER. THE KING WAS DEAD! HE STAYED THERE HE WAS THE ONE WHO RULED, AND HE USED THE MONEY HE'D GOT FROM SELLING THE CATTLE AND GAVE ORDERS.
>
> INTERVIEWER: HE TOOK THE PLACE OF...
>
> NARRATOR: HE WAS THE ONE WHO TOOK THE PLACE OF THE KING. POSITIVELY! YOU SEE HE WAS A *PÔLITIKY* [CUNNING ONE, IN SHIMAORE]. HE SUCCEEDED IN TAKING THE KING'S PLACE, AND HE STAYED *MAKINI* [WELL-BEHAVED, SHIMAORE],

STAYED WITH THE KING'S DAUGHTER. THEY WERE BOTH THERE, AND HE WAS THE
ONE WHO COMMANDED THE *UMATI* [PEOPLE, ARABIC AND SHIMAORE].[33]

A more engaging, witty, or politic performance of this classic power
reversal would be hard to find. It is totally deliberate, says Gueunier.
'Political power of kingly times is assimilated to that of the French
colonial administration. For the narrator (and doubtless generally in
Comoran ideas) the two powers have the same character: arbitrary
forced labor, and especially acting as informer — presented here as
the regular way of keeping power in place.'[34] The narrator has no fear
of being recorded. Claude Allibert's schoolboys were subtler, or more
cautious.

Varieties of Switching

There's not much difference or effort for these storytellers between
switching languages and switching channels. A few minutes on
YouTube will remind you that moving between speaking and singing
is essential to African and African American performance style. In
Madagascar and the Comoros, channel-switching conveys meaning.
'In all Malagasy folktales and myths', writes the ethnographer Philippe
Beaujard, 'song... represents the "normal" mode of communication in
the beyond, whether that means Heaven or the world of the dead, or
between the beyond and the world of the living'.[35] In Gueunier's texts
there is little communication with the dead, but plenty of singing.
Even if a Mahorais narrator launches into her story without an opening
formula, or summarizes it instead of giving it full performance, she will
give the songs in full, as many times as needed. As inseparable as the
many languages is song from spoken narration.

For an old lady of Mtsangamuji, song dominates speaking. A cannibal
kaka typically eats all the villagers but for a mother and child he didn't
notice. Seeing no more to eat, he and his gang leave. The boy identifies
himself as a hero by asking his mother for cakes (*mokary*) and telling
her to plant a *hintsa* (basil) as a life token; then he sets out to kill the
monster. Most of the rest of the piece is sung dialogue between mother
and son, mixing Shimaore and Kibushi. He drags back a monster.

HERE IT IS,
HERE IT IS, MAMA,
HERE'S THE NYOKA [SNAKE],
HERE IT IS, MAMA,
HERE'S THE NYOKA,
HERE IT IS.

Exclaiming 'There's my son', the mother repeats his song, examines the snake, and rejects it.

THAT'S NOT THE NYOKA,
THAT'S NOT IT, MY SON,
THAT'S NOT THE NYOKA,
THAT'S NOT IT, MY SON,
THAT'S NOT THE MAN-EATING NYOKA.

He throws away that monster, sets out again, and comes back with another monster; they sing the same dialogue. On his third try he succeeds, and the narrator's performance ends as the hero and his mother again exchange verses, her accepting his victory: 'AH, THAT'S THE MAN-EATING NYOKA.'[36] More impressive than the old lady's linguistic skill is her channel-switching.

Indian Ocean storytellers often seem to think song is the essence of their story. They feature song to convey important information. In Seychelles (where few songs were recorded before the age of music videos), song has ever been the privileged channel for revealing truth in tales. The word Nelzir Ventre in Mauritius used for his narratives was *séga*, which otherwise means a kind of song, sometimes with dancing. In Mayotte, even a seemingly incomplete narration will not omit a needed song, sung in toto. If the defiant girl sings her refusal of suitors, her narrator can rely on her audience's memory of the story, but she gives the songs in full. A woman returning to the sea sings goodbye to her mortal husband. Birds sing the identity of a persecuted heroine, or she herself gets recognized by her song, sometimes after being transformed to a bird. A *kaka* sings such enticing songs, in an obscure language, that his gang members dance to the seaside and drown. A gentler *kaka* teaches a child a song he can use to protect himself from other *kaka*s. A song can require the performer to include onomatopoetic imitation of the beating of a bird's wings.[37] Sometimes a song is so obscure that the narrator will explain it to the collector, but sometimes it is untranslatable.

Codes, Channels, Contact

All these devices exist to establish and maintain closeness between narrators and audiences. Opening and closing formulas function like quotation marks in print. When a storyteller says, NIPETRAKA AMPAÑARIVO, NIPETRAKA HOLO BE NY TALOHA, NITARIMY, TEO REO, TEO REO, TEO REO, [THERE LIVED THE RICH, THERE LIVED THE GREAT ONES OF OLD TIMES, THEY BROUGHT UP CHILDREN, THEY WERE THERE, WERE THERE, WERE THERE], he or she is reminding his audience that a certain kind of discourse is coming. The familiar tale will end with a familiar formula: RANGO ZAVAN'IO MOARO NDREKY VOALAVO TSY FANDEY TANDRIKY ÑANY, [AFTER THAT, RAT AND CAT DID NOT GET ALONG, UP TO TODAY].[38] A favored closing formula in Madagascar marks the line between fiction and fact: 'NOT I THE LIAR, BUT THE ANCIENTS WHO INVENTED THIS TALE.' With this nod at how easy it is to break taboo, the storyteller excuses himself or herself; the same formula sometimes opens a tale. In other islands a formula begins a dialogue. A Mauritian storyteller says, 'SIRANDANN!' His audience must answer 'SANPEK!' In Réunion, Gérose Barivoitse would say, 'KRIKÉ!'; to continue recording him, Christian Barat had to answer, 'KRAKÉ MESYÉ! KRAKÉ, SIR!' When Daniel Fontaine, also in Réunion, brought in birds to help his hero, he would ask his audience, 'WHAT DID HE SAY TO THE BIRDS?' and answer his own question. Relying on audience awareness reinforces the connection. Also, a parody relies on memory of its source.

Formulas themselves can be tailored to a particular audience. Here is a woman in Mbuini, tossing a bit of genre criticism to the investigator:

> THERE WERE KINGS, THERE WERE RICH PEOPLE, THERE WERE POOR PEOPLE, THERE WERE OAZIRY [VIZIERS, MINISTERS], THERE WERE THE BIG ONES OF OLD TIMES. THEY WERE LIVING, THEY WERE LIVING THERE — THINGS IN STORIES HAPPEN FAST — THERE WAS A KING IN A VILLAGE, AND A RICH MAN AND A POOR MAN.[39]

A more tradition-minded old lady in Poroani makes the same remark, but adds an older dialogic formula.

> KINGS WERE LIVING, RICH PEOPLE WERE LIVING, VIZIERS WERE LIVING, THEY WERE THERE, THEY WERE THERE. IT'S AN ANGANO, DOESN'T TAKE LONG.
>
> — WHO SHRANK YOUR WAIST, WASP?

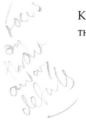

— Wearing a belt to go to the ceremony.
— Who made your bottom red, Spider?
— Sitting on the red ground.[40]

The switch of verbal registers is a signal or courtesy to the audience, to help them frame the fiction. An opening formula invites them into the world of metaphor; a closing formula will bring them back to their everyday world. One supremely accomplished narrator is especially free with her opening formula.

Hale halele [tale from old times]

The audience responds with the untranslatable '*Gombe!*'

There was a man among men.
Waka [Yes]!
There was a man and a woman. Yes. And a child, like my little Maridja here.[41]

This is Anfiati Sufu, of Mtsapere village, drawing her home life into her story and blending its realm with the 'real' world.

Even when being recorded, narrators remind their audiences of familiar names and places they share. The most skillful narrators set their stories in the most recognizable territory. One young woman narrator does it firmly: 'There was a great king [*ampanjaka*], he lived in a village like, let's say, this place named Poroani. Now there was another king in a place like, let's say, Bandrele. And the Bandrele one had two daughters...'[42] Another narrator leads her characters along the southwest coast of the island so as to name every village and charm her listeners by imitating all the local accents.[43] A third gives to one of those old donor women, who live in caves to escape the *kaka*, the name of a celebrated local healer — the person you would go to for talismans — so that the woman who consults her acquires magic resources, which assure her security and food.[44] Gueunier himself, as editor, can't resist stepping into the story realm: 'The parents settled their infirm daughter in the forest near Mavingoni, very far (on Mayotte scale: about 6 km) from Poroani [where the story was being told]. When she marries, she will settle in the properties of her princely husband in Dembeni, not far (2 km) from Mavingoni.'[45] All this place-dropping is not 'local color'; it draws the audience in.

Listen to another of those old ladies from Kany Kely telling her *fille* tale: when the wife's brother has convinced her of her husband's true nature;

> AS SOON AS HE LEFT FOR THE BUSH, THEY QUICKLY STARTED PACKING THEIR THINGS, *KUTSHU KATSU KUTSHU*. LIKE WHEN ZAKIA WAS AT MALAMANI WITH MADY HELY AND SHE WENT TO FOLLOW HER HUSBAND TO SOHOA, THAT DAY SHE RAN AWAY AND CAME BACK TO KANY. (GOOD STORY, YES? TRUE OR NOT?)

Gueunier explains: the narrator 'is recalling an incident... known to her listeners: it happened to [Zakia], as to the heroine of the story, to follow a husband to another village, and finding herself miserable there, to flee and return home to Kany'.[46] The common memory brings her closer to her audience and crosses the boundary between narrative levels, as she does again in the closing formula ending her story. It's finished. Earlier we noticed a narrator commenting on a particularly fanciful moment, 'THAT'S WHAT THE OLD LIARS SAID,' only to be interrupted by somebody alluding to the formula, 'LIKE YOU!' She snaps back, 'NO!' In Mayotte as in West Africa, the dialogue gives the narrator 'some assurance that he [or she] is being heard, that his [or her] word is getting through, and that it can be given back... Even when [formulas] are no longer understood, they are never forgotten'.[47] Some narrators know perfectly well how conventional a fixed phrase can be: '*ZAHO TSY HIVOLANA "OLO BE NY TALOHA,"*' [I WON'T SAY 'THE GREAT MEN OF OLD TIMES'].[48] Mahorais audiences feel comfortable interrupting and helping the narrator; they often know both the story and the devices of narrators, so that performance is collaborative.

In literary theory, crossing between fiction and fact has been regarded as transgressive and elegantly christened *metalepsis*.[49] Not so in oral narration, where it is a convention of style available to any storyteller and is welcomed by audiences. In creole culture it fits well with people's delight in incorporating heterogeneous materials into a single performance.

Two Heroes, One Self

The narrator of the first tale Gueunier collected in Mayotte puts much effort into staying close to his audience. His conception of performing ignores the boundary between fact and fiction. By stating the title of his tale — not a frequent practice of Mahorais, African, or Malagasy performers — he announces himself as a storyteller. He mixes languages as so many others do, but he also declares himself and his friend to be the real-life counterparts of the story's main characters and inserts topical references into traditional story features. He starts his story with himself as he is and ends it by awarding his other-self hero a successful, conventional folktale marriage. Perhaps that is his fantasy for his future: an individual whose inheritance is his tool for living in a new dispensation without forgetting the old. He blends traditional incidents with projections of his own identity.

To begin with, he calls his heroes by familiar Islamic names. Hasan and Husain ibn Ali were the two grandsons of the Prophet; after Hasan's death, Husain became a martyr, killed in the battle of Kerbala in 680 C. E.[50] Their names are often given now to male children, as guarantees that they will enter Paradise. For a pair of heroes who are almost clones of the storyteller, the names are aspirational.

> THERE'S A STORY CALLED HASAN AND HUSAIN. THEY ARE TWO FRIENDS, SAY
> LIKE ME AND ZAKARIA. WE'RE VERY GOOD FRIENDS. IF I'M AWAY FROM HIM FOR
> A MINUTE, I GET SAD. IF SOMEBODY GIVES ME A LITTLE SOMETHING, ANYTHING, I
> WON'T EAT IT ALONE, HE GETS SOME OF IT. SO — TWO BROTHERS, FROM THE SAME
> FATHER AND MOTHER, DON'T LOVE EACH OTHER LIKE THAT.

Not brothers, then, but like sworn brethren or blood brothers: best friends, at first indistinguishable and inseparable. They contrast with the twin tricksters in Madagascar tales, who are barely distinguishable, whose disputes or separations are always ephemeral, and who always end up together. Hasan and Husain are young men like the narrator and Zakaria, inseparable up to a point when Husain outgrows Hasan and becomes a folktale hero. Husain's father was a big *moalimo*, a man with power in the invisible world.

> WELL, IN THAT VILLAGE, PEOPLE DIDN'T PLAY THE DRUMS, THEY DIDN'T PARTY.
> SO, ONE DAY THEY WENT TO LOOK FOR SOMEBODY WHO COULD MAKE DRUMS, LIKE
> MADY MARY IN MRONABEJA [A REAL CRAFTSPERSON].

Inseparable rebels, the ones who build themselves the small, fantastically decorated mud houses called *bangas*, where Mayotte's boys hole up during adolescence and reinforce their rebelliousness. They order three drums to be made and vow to play them, defying the king. Nothing bizarre or fanciful here. The village, and its drum-maker using trees from the forest, are quite realistic.

> LIKE IF ME AND ZAKARIA WENT — AND THEY SAID, "WE WANT YOU TO MAKE
> US SOME DRUMS, BUT SECRETLY". SO, WHEN THEY CAME, HE SAID, "DRUMS?
> THE KING DOESN'T ALLOW US TO DO THAT STUFF." WE SAID, "WE WANT THEM
> ANYWAY". THE DRUM-MAKER SAID, "*JUSTEMENT* IT'S FRIDAY, *JUSTEMENT* TODAY
> IS FRIDAY. YOU COME BACK TOMORROW, COME EARLY TOMORROW. I'LL LEAVE MY
> TOOLS OUTSIDE, YOU GO BY THE FOREST, AND LEAVE WITHOUT GOING THROUGH
> THE VILLAGE". SO, THEY SAID, "OK". NEXT MORNING THEY WENT STRAIGHT
> THERE. THEY DIDN'T GO TO HIS HOUSE; ONE OF THEM WENT THROUGH THE
> FOREST, ON A WINDING ROAD COMING OUT FARTHER OFF.

Conventionally folktales remove their hero from a family background. That happens to Hasan and Husain only after they have (formally) left home and taken the father character with them. Then they polarize.[51] The making and breaking of their friendship is a solidly African pattern; their deceptive agreement to kill fathers is definitely Malagasy; the *moalimo* father may be simply another local person. Blending is the rule.

Ten days later, 'THERE THEY WERE, POUNDING THE DRUMS, *TRITRIM*, *TRITRIM*, *TRITRIM*, AND THE PEOPLE IN THE MOSQUE CAME OUT AND STARTED DANCING, SOME OF THEM STARTED BOXING'. An evocation of former times, when boxing (*morengy*) went together with drum-beating.[52] Listeners might recall that magic folktale instrument that causes monsters or ogres to dance. Soon, as the worshippers emerge, their embroidered go-to-mosque clothes will show the dust from the boxing matches. A few days later, the boys resume playing, against the king's order; they even lie (as any villager might do) to protect their drum-maker. The king's intervention is realistic enough; so is their only punishment, the destruction of their instruments.

Now the narrator moves his boys from the ordinary world into the folktale world, blending together two well-known trickster motifs. To declare their independence, Hasan and Husain go off on their own in the roles of trickster and dupe. Firstly, they agree to farm a piece of land together; when only Hasan's rice fails to grow, the audience will recognize the fragility of a contract like this.[53] Then, leaving behind the making-and-breaking pattern, the teller goes into a deceptive agreement to kill their fathers. Husain's *moalimo* father has probably

heard deceptive-agreement stories himself; anyway, his narrator knows
them well enough to get him out of danger and blend in a deception by
substitution.[54] The *moalimo* saves the friendship by supplying a remedy
to make Hasan's rice grow, and the teller prepares to separate the two
pals, who will leave home after harvest. But not without this excellent
father. Stowed away in a trunk on board, he retains divine power, and
'EVERY DAY AT MIDDAY GOD PUT HASAN TO SLEEP (HE WAS A *MOALIMO*), GOD
PUT HIM TO SLEEP. THEN HUSAIN WENT AND WAKED UP HIS FATHER, OPENED
[THE TRUNK], GAVE HIM FOOD. LIKE THAT, MIDDAY AND EVENING'. Guided by
the father's foreknowledge, they sail on to a point where Hasan is left
ashore, with his father's blessing and ample food.[55]

Firmly in the land of fiction, and needing the old man to provide also
for his son, the narrator remembers the roc in the Arabian Nights, the
giant bird who carries off men in its claws.

> THEN HE SAID, "HUSAIN, I'M GOING TO DIE (IT'S HIS FATHER SPEAKING), I'M
> GOING TO THE OTHER WORLD NOW. AFTER I DIE, YOU WASH ME, YOU TAKE ME AND
> PUT ME IN THAT TRUNK AND LEAVE ME UNDER A ROCK. AFTER THAT A MONSTER
> WILL COME [*HAVY*, LITERALLY SOMETHING SINISTER FROM THE LEFT], CARRYING A
> BIG OX — IT WILL COME HERE WITH THE OX, AND WHEN IT GETS HERE, YOU HIDE
> UNDER A ROCK WHILE IT EATS THE OX, AND WHEN IT'S DONE (IT IS A *LOLO*) GET
> UP ON ITS WINGS AND YOU'LL GO." AND THEN HE SAID, "YOU HAVE RECEIVED MY
> BLESSING IN THIS WORLD AND THE NEXT." JUST THEN HE DIED. IT WAS ALL OVER.

He could be remembering the roc without ever having read the *Nights*:
recollections of it often recur in all Islamic countries. As predicted, along
comes a flying *raha*, monster, with a big bull it will eat. Husain jumps on
the monster's back, it gives him needed transport to his next place, and
as it spies its next meal, Husain escapes.

Quickly he encounters a donor woman, who cries;

> "YOU'RE DEAD! THAT'S IT! YOU ARE THE ONE STEALING MY CATTLE!"
> HE SAID, "GRANDMOTHER, I DIDN'T STEAL YOUR CATTLE." AND HE HAD A
> LITTLE BOOK WITH HIM, FROM HIS FATHER. SO, HE SAID, "I DIDN'T STEAL YOUR
> CATTLE. BUT ME, THIS AND THAT IS WHAT'S HAPPENED TO ME", AND HE TOLD HER
> EVERYTHING. IF I TOLD IT, IT WOULD BE TOO LONG.

At this point, if Husain went back to the top of his story and told it
again, a Comoran audience would probably welcome the repetition.
Recapitulating is conventional; anyone who attended a Qur'an school

knows how to do rote memorization. But this narrator lacked patience for the reprise, which would retard the plot and lengthen the performance. Telling his story, Husain passes the donor's test and gains recognition as a *moalimo*'s son.

> HE TOLD HER HIS WHOLE STORY, WHAT HAPPENED TO HIM. THEN HE SAID, "IF YOU DON'T BELIEVE ME, SIT HERE AND YOU'LL SEE IT COME BACK AND GRAB AN OX. LET'S HIDE HERE."
>
> AS SOON AS HE SAID THAT, THE THING CAME. IT LOOKED, LOOKED, TILL IT FOUND ONE, PICKED IT UP AND LEFT. NOW THE GRANDMOTHER BELIEVED HIM. WELL. HE KNEW DIVINATION, HE KNEW BOOKS.
>
> THEY MOVED THE CATTLE AND WENT BACK TO THE HOUSE. AT THE HOUSE THE GRANDMOTHER MADE MOKARY [CAKES], MADE TEA.

At this point, a folktale hero should search for a king's daughter we (and maybe Husain) didn't know he should set out to find. The narrator combines the classic folktale plot with the forbidden chamber (which conceivably he could have heard from Bluebeard[56]). The *dady* (grandmother) takes him in to a house belonging (like everything else) to the king, where there are sheep he can eat. The grandmother trusted him. She gave him all the keys to the house, but said, 'See this key, the key to that room? Don't open it!' That was the room the king's daughters stayed in. She said, 'Don't open that one!' He said yes.

Tempted though he is to violate the interdiction (thus following folktale tradition), he resumes a realistic self. He takes up the bachelor life *à la manière française*, living alone, eating mutton chops from the sheep outside, and studying. Graciously he suggests the *dady* move her cattle away, lest she lose them,[57] but knowing life is more interesting if he plays fairytale hero in real life, he violates the interdiction.

> SO, ONE DAY HE SAID, "TS! WHAT'S THE STORY HERE? WHY DID THE *DADY* TELL ME NOT TO OPEN THAT ROOM?" HE WAS A MAN, SEE, HE WAS LUCKY. HE SAID, "WHY DID THE *DADY* WANT TO STOP ME FROM OPENING THAT ROOM? I'M GOING TO OPEN IT AND SEE WHAT'S INSIDE". HE TOOK THE KEY, OPENED IT. WHEN IT WAS OPENED, HE FELL OVER. BEAUTIFUL GIRLS, OOOH! THE GIRLS WERE JUST BATHING, HE LOOKED AT THEM, WONDERING WHICH ONE TO GO FOR. HE LOOKED HARD AT THEM, TOOK ONE BY THE HAND, LED HER. HE LOCKED THE DOOR AND HAD HER CLIMB UP TO HIS PLACE UP ABOVE. WHEN THEY GOT UP THERE, HE FIRST WENT TO GET A POT [FOR HER] TO COOK WITH.

No, they're not going to have sex; setting up housekeeping in a trial marriage marks him as an adult.

> THEN ONE DAY THE *DADY*, THE DAY AFTER, THE *DADY* SAID, "HUSAIN, YOU DON'T COME DOWN TO EAT ANY MORE? WHAT'S GOING ON?"
> HE SAID, "OH, I JUST GET A SHEEP AND ROAST IT, SO I'M NOT HUNGRY".
> "REALLY?"
> "YEAH".
> IT WENT ON LIKE THAT, UNTIL "BUT HUSAIN, SHEEP EVERY DAY, HOW IS THAT? WHEN YOU CAME HERE YOU DIDN'T ROAST SHEEP EVERY DAY".
> HE SAID, "I GOT INTO THE HABIT, I GOT THE HABIT. I GET ONE THAT DOESN'T LOOK GOOD, I ROAST IT. I'M TIRED OF EATING RICE EVERY NOONTIME, TIRED OF ALWAYS EATING LIKE THAT".
> "REALLY?"
> "YEAH".

Such realistic dialogue between grandmother and grandchild registers changing times in the 1970s. Rice every day was the old Malagasy diet; meat every day is seen as French. Only a few years after the story was recorded, an elder said, 'Rice, we don't do it anymore, nobody raises it, no woman would crush it'.[58] The *dady* has to play a nurturing, maternal role on discovering he has hidden away the king's daughter. At her remonstrance he takes her back to the king, making her again the object of his search. Still talking like a modern lad, he is bold enough to seize the magic object he will need next.

> BUT AFTER FIVE DAYS, HUSAIN SAID, "*DADY*, MAKE ME SOME *MOKARY*, I'M GOING TO GO, GOING TO GO GET MY WIFE".
> "TO GET YOUR WIFE?"
> "YES".
> "BUT YOU KNOW THAT PASSAGE IS FORBIDDEN TO GO INTO. THERE ARE GUARDS EVERYWHERE. IF YOU GO THERE FROM HERE, YOU'LL RUN INTO THE GUARDS."
> "JUST MAKE THE *MOKARY*, I'M GOING". SHE MADE THE *MOKARY*. HE HAD HIS FATHER'S BLESSING, SO... SHE MADE THE *MOKARY*, SHE GAVE HIM THE *MOKARY* AND HE LEFT.[59]
> HE WENT TILL HE MET TWO MEN. HE ASKED, "HOW ARE YOU?"
> THEY SAID, "FINE".
> "FINE?"
> THEY SAID, "YES". WELL, HE WENT AWAY FROM THEM, DISTANCE *CINQ MÈTRES* [FIVE METERS], AND BEGAN LOOKING AT THEM THE WAY SOMEONE DOES WHO KNOWS MAGIC. HE LOOKED AT THEM, STOPPED THEM, SAYING, "STOP A MINUTE". HE CAME UP TO THEM AND ASKED, "TELL ME, THOSE STICKS YOU CARRY, WHAT

DO THEY MEAN?" THEY SAID, "WHAT THEY MEAN, WHOEVER CARRIES THIS STICK,
LIKE IF YOU'RE BEING ARRESTED BY THE *ẐANDARMO* [GENDARMES], YOU JUST HIT
THE GROUND WITH IT AND THEY'RE ALL TIED UP!"

"AH?" THEY SAID YES. "WHY DON'T YOU GIVE ME ONE, SINCE YOU'RE
ALREADY HERE?" THEY TALKED IT OVER, FINALLY AGREED. HE BOUGHT IT AND
WENT OFF. AS HE WENT, HE DIDN'T BOTHER TO ASK THE WAY.

With the magic stick he ties up the king's guard (who look very much
like *gendarmes*), then the king himself, and demands his wife. The king
knows to stay in character: he poses a suitor test.

BUT HE PUT ALL THE GIRLS IN A LINE. THEY'D LINED THEM UP, AND HE INSPECTED
THEM, AND — HE INSPECTED THEM, BUT HE SAID, 'AHA, MY WIFE ISN'T HERE!
HAVE HER COME OUT!'

THEY SAID, "THERE AREN'T ANY MORE WOMEN, THEY'RE ALL HERE".

HE SAID, "UH-HUH, A WOMAN I SLEPT WITH, I WOULDN'T RECOGNIZE HER?"
HE KEPT SAYING, "SHE'S NOT HERE!" THEN THEY GOT HER, HAD HER COME OUT,
SAYING, "OKAY, COME OUT!" SHE CAME OUT, BUT THEY SEIZED HER AND PUT HER
IN THE MIDDLE OF THE REST. BUT HE, AS SOON AS SHE CAME OUT, HE WENT AND
TOOK HER BY THE HAND. HE SAW HER, TOOK HER, AND LED HER AWAY. HE SAID,
"THIS IS MY WIFE".

SO, THEY DID THE WEDDING RIGHT AWAY.

I LEFT THEM THERE AND CAME TO STAY HERE.[60]

The quest for a wife ends the story rather hastily, contrasting with the
detail the teller provided about acquiring the drums or voyaging by sea.
The teller makes little of the oft-told test of identifying one woman from
others. For him to project himself and Zakaria into such a fantasy, to
make metalepsis the organizing principle of his narrative, demonstrates
the creole aesthetic, which appropriates whatever real-life elements are
at hand into the fairytale model. This method of performance enacts
the mental habit the anthropologist Claude Lévi-Strauss calls *bricolage*;
it animates the creativity in creolization.[61] The young man of Kany Kely
— the village that gave Gueunier forty-five other pieces — performed a
new narrative, created in Mayotte and unclassifiable in an existing tale
type. Yes, he is an author.

Fig. 7 Market in Mayotte. Photo by Msire, CC BY-SA 4.0, Wikimedia Commons,
https://commons.wikimedia.org/wiki/File:March%C3%A9_Mayotte.jpg

Quest, Displacement, Recognition

The grandest of Gueunier's translated narratives was recorded from
a fast-talking young man in the village of Mronabeja, in a relaxed,
expansive manner. His theme is recognition, or identity. His piece
has three big chapters: a hero's quest for a wife, her displacement by
a false bride and rescue, and the persecution of her daughter, who
finally vanishes into a continuity with her mother. The narrator keeps
his audience with him through a long performance; for instance he
gives a walk-on role to a well-known musician whom the audience
will recognize. His characters use strange words; an essential song is
almost omitted until a hearer prompts the narrator; but his panoply
of traditional motifs holds their attention. Knowing with regret that
the main character's name is awkward for a foreign reader, and that a
verbatim translation would be too much for your patience, I summarize
his story, with direct translations in small capitals.

His first chapter closely follows the model of a Sakalava story; the rest looks more improvised and original. The hero-of-a-difficult-name is a *jeune homme difficile*, who refuses girl after girl summoned by his kingly father. 'IT WAS THE SAME THING LIKE THAT TILL THEY'D MADE THE TOUR OF THE WHOLE ISLAND OF MAYOTTE'. Hearing of his desire, a champion harpoon-thrower goes to the king and says, 'THERE'S A GIRL IN MAJUNGA [MAHAJANGA, THE CLOSEST MALAGASY TOWN], AS SOON AS YOUR SON SEES HER, HE'LL BE ATTRACTED TO HER'. Such news-bearers always get quick action. The king finds his son four extraordinary companions: Harpoon-Thrower the messenger, Squints-to-Aim the marksman, Arm-Stretcher of the long arm, and Far-Seer, who sees great distances.[62] Since these wonderworkers don't, in the end, help find the lad a wife, they are only a flourish of the narrator — the first of many.

The wearisome trip to Majunga is entertained by the Harpoon-Thrower's singing, which pleases the audience and speeds up the boat. Only now does the narrator give his hero his difficult name, Ndramohamiñy, something like 'Jack Armstrong'. On their arrival, things still move fast. When Ndramohamiñy explains their intentions to the local king, he promptly sends for his daughter upstairs, and she promptly faints as soon as she sees the hero.[63] Ndramohamiñy sprinkles water on her face, revives her with a magic charm, and now it's his turn to faint and be revived. The scene demonstrates that she is his equal in rank and hence a suitable wife. The first chapter ends as the marriage is agreed on and celebrated.

The second chapter, often told as an independent tale, is a false bride story: the newlywed wife is displaced and mistreated by her treacherous slave.[64] The king agrees to let Ndramohamiñy take his daughter back to Mayotte, and asks her which slave she wants to take along. 'THE SLAVE I WANT IS THIS ONE, TANGARIRA'. Audiences can recognize the name Tangarira from other tales: she is a *kaka* in disguise. When they arrive at a sandbar and Tangarira suggests they go for a dive, she also audaciously proposes a false-friendship wager, as if they were equals: 'AFTER WE DIVE, THE ONE WHO COMES OUT FIRST WILL TAKE HALF HER FATHER'S LANDS AND GIVE THEM TO THE ONE COMING OUT LAST'. 'OH, YES?' 'YES.' SHE AGREED. The narrator's skillful use of dialogue underlines the absurd presumption of this would-be slave and the innocent submissiveness of the newlywed. Tangarira comes fast out of the water, dons the wife's fine clothes, and commands, 'LET'S GO, LET'S GO, LET'S GO!' The pathetic abandoned wife wonders why her new husband didn't at least take her back to Mayotte and set her on a higher rock, which would be the place of exile for a cast-out heroine.

Instead of leaving his heroine in danger, the narrator gives her a sequence of suspenseful scenes. She resigns herself to God's will. The tide rises, bringing sharks. 'AT FIRST IT WAS LOW TIDE, SHE WAS DRY, THEN THE TIDE CAME UP TO HER ANKLE, THEN HER LEG, THEN HER THIGH, THEN WHEN IT CAME UP TO HER WAIST SHE PULLED HERSELF UP LIKE THIS, AND SHE SAW A THING LIKE AN ALMOND LEAF FLOATING DOWN, IT FELL AT HER FEET'. Keep your eye on that almond leaf.

Fig. 8 Almond leaf. Photo by Renjusplace, CC BY-SA 4.0, Wikimedia Commons. https://commons.wikimedia.org/wiki/File:Terminalia_catappa,_country-almond,_Indian-almond,_Malabar-almond,_sea-almond,_%E0%B4%A4%E0%B4%B2%E0%B5%8D%E0%B4%B2%E0%B4%BF%E0%B4%A4%E0%B5%8D%E0%B4%A4%E0%B5%87%E0%B4%99%E0%B5%8D%E0%B4%99._Leaf_.jpg

Instantly she knows this magic object will give her powers. She picks up the almond leaf, pronounces a charm over it, strikes it, puts it under each armpit in turn, and transforms into a bird. Thus, she is able to follow her husband's boat and perch atop its sail. From there she sings to him, but is recognized by Tangarira, who orders a stick thrown at her. It misses. Their contest has begun, made suspenseful by the wife's transformations.

Now, transformed into the almond leaf, she follows her husband back to Mayotte and transforms herself into a pineapple. Tangarira, ever the hungry *kaka*, sends a man to pick the fruit four times, but always it transforms back to the almond leaf. Spitefully Tangarira must give up that round. Next the wife re-transforms into a bird, follows them, perches aloft, and again sings her identifying song; she avoids a stone they throw at her, and transforms herself into ripe bananas. Again, when they try to pick the fruit, she transforms back into the almond leaf. Tangarira gives up the chase, and the party returns to their village.

The next scene, another gesture to the audience, will reveal the *kaka*'s true nature. The king sends for a musician named Langa, 'the surname of a musician, celebrated all over Mayotte and even in the other Comoros, who is a specialist in this kind of music'.[65] Ordinarily the word denotes a musical genre rather than a performer. People are suspicious of Tangarira: 'LOOK AT THAT FACE, THAT FACE, IT'S LIKE A DONKEY'S FACE.' Not her unusual diet of locusts, but the huge amount of them she demands, now draws the attention of an unexpected new character, a boy who calls the hero *zama*, Uncle.[66] As she devours her locust feast, he discovers her *kaka* horns, tails, feathers, and big eyes, but she catches him. Then in a tale-within-a-tale scene, the boy goes to his grandmother (*dady*) and recounts his exploit in detail. The narrator uses this convention of embedding to pause and let his audience review the events up to this point.

Two or three months go by, with no fear of losing the audience. We learn the heroine's name, Cow's Daughter (which links her with other heroines we shall meet).

> THAT FARANANOMBY, FIRST SHE STAYED IN THE FOREST, THEN SHE WENT INTO IN A TREE NEAR THE RIVER, SHE STAYED THERE, SHE HAD BECOME AS BEAUTIFUL AS THE FOURTEENTH-DAY [FULL] MOON. SO, WHILE SHE WAS THERE, THE GIRLS DIPPING THEIR GOURDS SAW HER SHINING FACE REFLECTED IN THE WATER AND [THINKING IT'S THEIR OWN AND REMEMBERING TANGARIRA'S] SAID, "OH NO! I'M NOT DRAWING WATER FOR THAT UGLY THING. THAT FACE LIKE A DONKEY'S. SSS! HUH!"

The young man knows how well this scene, recounted in many a tale, evokes women's enviousness, but it's his innovation that girl after girl mistakes Farananomby's aristocratic face for her own slave visage. Breaking their gourds, the slave girls refuse to work for Tangarira. They return to the village and hide without telling what they saw. Every time one comes for water, another gourd gets broken; at last, an old woman comes, knows that face is not her own, and becomes the agent of the reconciliation. Farananomby asks her to speak to Ndramohamiñy and bring back all her things so she can go home, 'BECAUSE WHAT HE DID TO ME, IT'S WORSE THAN ANYTHING HE COULD DO TO ME, AND YET I'M STILL ALIVE, I'M STILL IN THIS WORLD'. The old woman breaks her gourd, takes her stick and goes running and falling, running and falling, running and falling, back to the village; she finds Ndramohamiñy and beats him with a stick, *pan, pan, pan!* because he mistreated that beautiful girl (another innovation). Wanting the marriage to be celebrated, people go to Farananomby and beg her, and she refuses. Finally, Ndramohamiñy agrees to set Tangarira on the threshold of their house, where Farananomby can tread on her as she goes in. Langa plays his music, an ox is slaughtered, at last the marriage is done.

That punishment, plus the restoration of wife to husband, feels like an ending. Is the story over?

No, this young narrator is in no hurry. He will repeat the punishment when he finishes, but now he knows Farananomby's trials have to continue. In his third episode, which again resembles other tales told separately, her baby daughter will be kidnapped and then rescued. At the point where his Sakalava forerunner said, 'TWO YEARS LATER, FARANANOMBY GOT PREGNANT', the Mahorais storyteller wants to hold his audience: 'THEY WENT ALONG, WENT ALONG, WENT ALONG, SHE GOT THROUGH THE FIRST MONTH, THE SECOND, THE THIRD, THE FOURTH MONTH, THE FIFTH, THE SIXTH, THE SEVENTH MONTH, THE EIGHTH, AND THE NINTH, AND AFTER NINE MONTHS AND NINE DAYS, SHE GAVE BIRTH — SHE GAVE BIRTH TO A FINE LITTLE GIRL'. That kind of flourish takes confidence. But Farananomby is not yet safe. Inexplicably, a pseudo-donor lady puts a strand of palm in Fara's hair, and while she is briefly absent, the old lady grabs the baby, removes one of its eyes, and absconds with it. Farananomby, as before, weeps at her misfortune, resigns herself, transforms into a bird, and goes into the forest, from which she repeats her earlier attempt to be recognized in song. Just then, the narrator has to be reminded by one of his audience members which song to sing.[67]

Marriage and secrecy are inseparable throughout. The transformed wife hears of her husband's return, falls to earth, retransforms to a woman, dies, and is buried. The baby in the forest, being her mother's daughter, is clairvoyant: she knows the secret of who her real parents and grandparents are. Still with one eye, she is sent to Qur'an school, but when she gets home, the old lady covers her with fat and won't let her bathe, without explanation of the disguise. Then, from some other tale, arrives a magic object that looks like candy, named by a word no one knows: 'THAT THING WAS CALLED A *VAKOROMANGA*.' Trying it, the little girl divines that it is a gift from her dead mother, so she visits her mother's grave and buries pieces of *vakoromanga* (whatever that is) at the head and foot. Gold-bearing trees grow there, another secret, discovered by a honey-gatherer. When the king tries to pick the golden fruit, it turns into an almond leaf every time, echoing the earlier segment. (You wonder where to get these almond leaves.) He announces a suitor test — to pick the fruit — for which the little girl at last is summoned. Only she succeeds.

Foreshadowing the end of the tale and acting as her mother, she sings an identifying song and orders a new golden throne. The power of her song causes the tomb to start trembling; people start to run away in fear, but they are stopped by the king. The tomb opens and out comes Farananomby. 'THERE SHE SAT [ON THE THRONE], AND NO ONE COULD TELL WHICH WAS THE DAUGHTER AND WHICH WAS THE MOTHER. AND THE GIRL'S EYE, THE MISSING ONE, IT CAME BACK LIKE BEFORE, GOD GAVE IT BACK TO HER.' With this variation on the identical-women motif, beloved of Malagasy storytellers, the Mronabeja narrator brings his tale around to mother-daughter identity. A stinging fly provides the answer by lighting on the girl. Instantly, ironically, Farananomby says, 'DAUGHTER, I AM DEAD', and kills the fly. The assembled people accept a bit of divination never seen before; mother and daughter are recognized, restored, and merged. The king's daughter, who was to be the prize in the suitor test, must remain unmarried, not that anyone remembers.

Yet the narrator is not done, for he gives Farananomby's husband the last word:

'AND THAT OLD WOMAN, THAT TANGARIRA CAME, AND I TOLD HER, "LOOK AFTER MY DAUGHTER," SHE TOOK MY DAUGHTER WHEN I WENT TO THE TOILET, AND WHEN I CAME BACK, I DIDN'T SEE MY DAUGHTER. I WAS SO SAD, I DIED FROM

IT, AND TODAY GOD AND THE PROPHET, WITH MY LITTLE GIRL, HAVE COME TO
BRING ME BACK TO LIFE. I WANT TO GO RIGHT NOW INTO THAT TOMB, OR ELSE I'LL
GO BACK TO MY MOTHER'S IN MAJUNGA'. She agrees to stay only on condition
Tangarira is again tied hand and foot and placed where she will tread
on her. 'AFTER THAT HER THROAT IS TO BE CUT. WHEN I'VE SEEN YOU CUT HER
THROAT, THEN I'LL STAY, BUT OTHERWISE I'M NOT STAYING, I'M GOING HOME'.

Perhaps hearers recognize her threat to play the legendary woman who
returns under water because her husband broke her taboo. Anyway, she
is now in charge. Once her order is carried out, there is another banquet
and more dancing, 'AND I LEFT THEM THERE AND CAME HERE'. Finale.[68]

Seldom indeed does an oral storyteller dictate to an investigator
a story so packed with precise, fascinating, sometimes mysterious
details. The dimensions and elaboration of his story bring him to the
fore among Gueunier's narrators. From one point of view, the whole
text 'is organized in such a way that at its strongest points, the meaning
remains *undecidable*; from then on the signifier no longer lets itself be
traversed, it remains, resists, exists and draws attention to itself.'[69] To an
audience in Mayotte, however, the meaning is decidable in many ways.
They may even debate it. Multiple possible interpretations constitute
one excellence of the performance; the other is the narrator's creativity.
His combination of innovating with repeating what he has learned
defines his creativity.

My Tail

Spotting Tangarira as an impostor in that story is easy, since we feel
automatic sympathy for the young bride. A surprising amount of a
storyteller's tone, humor, irony, and allusion — most of what makes
an oral performance entertaining — can be felt from print. But there
are puzzling moments. It's clear that the cannibalism of *kaka*s or *lolo*s
subsumes their libido, but one of Gueunier's narrators gives us a
puzzling *lolo*. The master storyteller this time is Dady ny Saidy, of Kany
Kely (uniquely identified; *dady* means grandmother, remember).[70] She
tells a Hansel-and-Gretel-type story: the children fall into the ogre's
power, the ogre is deceived, and they escape. Hunger and destitution
are realistic details, but her main character is outlandishly contradictory.
How can a *lolo* be both a threat and a help? Which is the oddity, the *lolo*
or the narrator?

Her tale begins conventionally: a boy and girl are abandoned by their destitute parents. Abandoned children are so common in folktales that you wonder whether they are only fantasy, and how many times they have been abandoned in this island, where families are so cherished. The boy makes his way to the house of a *lolo*, an old spirit-lady in the donor role. Gueunier comments, 'This ogress acts like a good Mahorais housekeeper', making her food in advance and heating it for the table. When she blandly goes out to pick flowers, he reacts as any prisoner should and sneaks some of the food out to his starving sister. When the *lolo* comes back, ominously bringing wind and rain (Dady's sound effect 'Ooooн!'), she spreads her flowers nicely on the bed, and goes to wash and change her clothes. Preparing to eat, she opens the rice pot — nothing there. She opens the sauce pot — nothing there. She knows whom to blame: not the boy. 'Aн! [ɪᴛ ᴡᴀѕ] ᴍʏ ᴛᴀɪʟ!', as if her tail could voluntarily emerge from hiding and steal her food. When she becomes angry and excoriates herself, the narrator switches from Shimaore into Kibushi: 'Tᴀʙᴜ! Tᴀʙᴜ ɢᴏᴇѕ ᴛᴏ ᴘɪᴄᴋ ꜰʟᴏᴡᴇʀѕ ᴀɴᴅ ᴍʏ ᴛᴀɪʟ ᴄᴏᴍᴇѕ ꜰʀᴏᴍ ʙᴇʜɪɴᴅ ᴀɴᴅ ᴇᴀᴛѕ ᴍʏ ʀɪᴄᴇ!'

What does that name say about her character? Being both jailer and helper is certainly ambiguous. It would be hard to find another case of a folktale character so conflicted internally, a cannibal who 'gathers flowers in the woods to perfume her house before eating the refined meals she has cooked by the book', a *lolo* who 'continually shifts between flattery and ridiculous cajolery and the most violent threats'.[71] Her name translates as *tourment* — agony or torture. Usually a *lolo* is punished by a victim's family, but Tabu (once the boy has gone off with her food) builds a sizable fire. Taking revenge on her tail, she burns herself to death. She is not the first stupid ogre one has met, only the clumsiest. Once out of danger, the boy recounts his adventures to his sister — these characters do like to give accounts of themselves — and moves them both into the empty house to enjoy the plentiful stocks of food Tabu left behind.

Why isn't the story over, as it was when told in Madagascar?[72] Dady ny Saidy's priorities are those she shares with Mayotte's other storytelling women: get the sister married off and include an episode in praise of her own craft. So, to move the story forward, a slave of the king reports the girl's beauty to him; seeing her, the king faints (that keeps happening), then marries her. Wedding guests arrive from four named villages. Among them (surprise) are those destitute parents who first cast out the brother and sister. All along, the children's identities could have been known, but what finally gets these two to recognize their children is a storytelling event: the boy wordily narrates all the adventures up to that point. Dady ny Saidy, ever the performer, makes the telling of a story her climactic moment. Such embedding, says a great critic, 'is an articulation of the most essential property of all narrative. For the embedding narrative is the *narrative of a narrative*.'[73] The parents ask forgiveness, the son says it was all God's will, they all set up house together, and the family founds a large village.

Dady ny Saidy ends her story by personalizing the conventional formula 'I left them there' with acknowledgment of being recorded.

I LEFT THEM THERE. I STAYED WITH THEM A WHILE. I TOLD THEM, "I'M GOING BACK [HOME], MY GRANDCHILDREN ARE WAITING FOR ME". I WENT BACK AND COME HERE. "SEE", I TOLD THEM, "I'M GOING TO SEE MY GRANDCHILDREN." I HAVE A GRANDSON, SEE, WHO JUST CAME FROM MADAGASCAR. MY GRANDCHILDREN IN THE VILLAGE ARE UPSET: "WHAT HAPPENED, GRANDMA? WHAT HAPPENED, GRANDMA?" SO, I'M GOING, I'LL TALK WITH MY LITTLE HUSBAND.[74]

It is a classic old woman's joke. Both the grandson and the little husband are Noël Gueunier, who had just arrived from Madagascar. Old ladies, not only here but in Africa, like to play at pretending a young man will be a husband or lover.[75]

Dady misses no opportunity to blend past convention with present circumstance. Her story is a new creation on the stupid ogre model. Whom could she be satirizing, in that portrait of a mother figure both nurturing and stupid? Could she be doing what African Americans call signifying, i. e. telling a story as criticism of someone present to hear it? Signifying, says Roger D. Abrahams, 'can mean any of a number of things:... the propensity to talk around a subject... making fun of a person or situation... to stir up a fight between neighbors by telling stories...'.[76] What connects African American signifying to the verbal art of the Indian Ocean is that speakers in both cultures habitually use indirection, metaphor, and irony. Her story is a new creation, like The Dog's Daughters in the next chapter.[77]

Some Versions of Parody

Many folktale performances (for instance the ones Claude Allibert translates) are serious, modest attempts to hand on to the interviewer a narrative the informant has heard. Parodies are likely to be playful. They rather complicate the old image of African folklore as simple and monochromatic. Some storytellers in 1970s Mayotte liked to parody old styles as a means of commenting satirically on present realities. One of them starts her story conventionally, contrasting a king's daughter with her friend, a poor girl, at the seaside. The poor girl loses her doll, which she calls *zanako*, 'my child', into the water. Ignoring her friend's mockery, she goes in after it; under water she meets kind, generous foster parents. 'THEY GAVE HER HER CHILD, THEY GAVE HER CLOTHES, THEY GAVE HER LOTS OF THINGS, PUT THEM IN A CHEST AND GAVE THEM TO HER'. An old lady donor (still under water) gives her a test, which she passes, and magically arranges her flight home with all her presents. Then her rich, jealous girlfriend tries for the same rewards without success. The narrator is relying on well-known models: a young woman is helped by a generous surrogate mother; her unkind sister fails at imitating her good fortune; rich and poor have contrasting fates. Still, the rich girl's defeat is a Mayotte touch: she is devoured by cannibals, not named as *lolo* but with the same diet. Once she is eaten, they toss a thigh bone to that kind lady. Then the narrator gives us 'a veritable parody of the classic story motif wherein a bird of good omen [the roller-bird *Leptosomus discolor*] comes to restore the lost daughter to her parents'.[78] First a series of birds refuse to carry the word of her fate to the girl's father as he prepares her *grand mariage*. Then the bat, ironical in the role of bird of truth, reaches the village, sings an identifying song five times, and drops the bone. The king recognizes it, and the *mariage* turns into a funeral ceremony ('Indeed, my lord, it followed hard upon,' as Horatio remarks at a similar double bill). The tale ends in tears. 'These abrupt conclusions [says Gueunier] are much appreciated by the juvenile audience; young narrators seem to prefer them to any other'.[79] A taste for parody bonds the younger generation the whole world around.

Similarly abrupt, inclusive, and parodic is a legend about the village of Mtsamangamuji. The younger of two orphaned girls catches and raises a fish, which in time grows to full size and invites her to visit him under the sea. Though she is fearful, the fish reassures her and plays foster father; indeed he protects her from being devoured down there. The main feature of the performance is his boastful song, which we hear five times before the narrator gives us her sudden, unexpected conclusion. The fish finds her a young man to marry, but the two don't stay under water. NITERAKA, NITERAKA ATÀ NDREKY TANÀNA NAVY BE, IZY KAMO MTSANGAMUJI-TSIKA TY [THEY HAD CHILDREN, SO MANY THAT THEY MADE A BIG VILLAGE, AND THAT IS EXACTLY OUR VILLAGE OF MTSAMANGAMUJI].[80] Isn't this a parody of the Ranoro legend of Madagascar, which we saw in the previous chapter? Both tale and legend explain a present population as having been engendered by the lady from the sea. Blending folktale and legend, the piece is a serious, non-mocking parody.

Ranoro plus parody plus satire gives a Kany Kely narrator an allegory. Ordered by the king to cut the leaves from a wild date tree (*morandra*), a man sees a beautiful woman emerge from the tree. She protests this violation of the environment: 'WHO ARE YOU, DESTROYING MY HOUSE?' Yet she agrees to come out of the forest and marry him, on the same condition as Ranoro: he is not to say her name Morandra, which is the tree's name too. When he reveals the name to a friend, consequence is immediate. FA NEHEY TÔPONY ATO, SHE KNEW RIGHT AWAY. Four times she taps the ground with a stick, calls back the children, and takes them back into the tree.[81] Secrecy is precious. Giving away the island's secret destroys its posterity. The satire is clear, but it's not a funny story. Parody is not always playful or mocking.[82]

The general rule these storytellers follow is stated by the anthropologist Pierre Maranda: 'the life of myths [or folktales or jokes] consists in reorganizing traditional components in the face of new circumstances or, correlatively, in reorganizing new, imported components in the light of tradition'.[83] Storytellers in Mayotte have faced new circumstances many times: Islamization, colonization, enslavement, immigration. They have responded by reorganizing traditional plots, characters, and even genres, sometimes seriously, sometimes comically. The creativity in Morandra's story, and many other tales, lies in how successfully the teller (or a predecessor) reorganizes, parodies, or remodels existing components. A novelty like Hasan and Husain feels traditional because the teller inserts his local references among components from the African-Malagasy repertoire (for instance the deceptive agreement to kill fathers). At bottom it is remodeling that makes oral folktales so different from one another, and social-political circumstances that shape them. Parodies are a game of the powerless.[84]

Parody in that vein ridicules contemporaries by disguising them as characters from the past. Kings of old Madagascar, says Gueunier, were no longer of interest in 'a society founded on fidelity to the village community, under the more or less arbitrary sway of a foreign authority'.[85]In his tales, the characters called 'kings' are caricatures of colonial civil servants, district chiefs, or local administrators. One is some kind of treasurer or paymaster. 'The master of that Treasury is still a king, necessary so that the narrative will conform to the conventions of the folktale, but the disguise is rather transparent'.[86] He is far away from the grandiose figures of traditional sovereigns who are encountered in the older Madagascar tales. Social contestation delivers its jab in the form of disillusioned satire, as if to say it's in the nature of power to be corrupt. As the impact of alien language and tradition liberates creativity in American immigrant narrators, so it does for Mahorais narrators under colonization.[87] The storyteller's game is to participate ironically in tradition.

Other parodies of Ranoro affirm people's attachment to the land they own. For instance, a woman of Mbuini (who commented, ZANAKA ANGANO TSÀRE HELA [THINGS GO FAST IN STORIES], made sure to follow tradition: she performed the required song all seven times, while telling of a poor man who catches and dries octopuses. While their captor is out, they open the door of their cage and make their way back to the sea as their leader sings, 'BOSS DOESN'T EAT ME, DOESN'T SEND ME AWAY'. His job was to eat them. To the delight of the audience, they trek all the way through the villages Bweni, Bambu, Mzuazia, Bweyanatsa, Kany Kely, Kani-Be, and Bandrakuni, with local villagers looking on. The narrator's recitation of the village names and her imitation of local accents are simultaneously entertainment and celebrations of the home place.[88]

The parodist likes to mix genres. Take that string of trickster episodes ending so oddly with Bwanawasi marrying the princess and ascending the throne. Doesn't that ending belong to a different model? Surely marrying the princess belongs to the fairytale pattern. Isn't a trickster like him supposed to violate all the social rules and get punished? Evidently not in a poor colony, where new circumstances demand that storytellers reorganize old material and the poor aspire to riches. The anonymous reorganizers who create 'tradition' allow the message that it's now time for the enslaved to take power. As code-switching reflects the linguistic history, so genre-mixing reflects and negotiates the cultural convergence.

Mockery of serious tales could well have come to Mayotte from Sakalava ancestors. They tell of an ambiguous hero, the opposite of the hero in quest of something valuable, who is yet rebelling against a disapproving father. The parody keeps the quest structure of a hero tale but changes the values. He acquires an undesirable necessity of human life, *loza* (trouble, a buzz word in innumerable proverbs). Determined to find trouble, the hero encounters bees, steps on a snake unharmed, and kills a boar, but these petty victories don't satisfy him. Saying to his father, 'I STILL DON'T SEE TROUBLE; I'LL GO SEE WHERE DAY IS BORN,' he takes eight loaves of bread (a heartier lunch than those *mokary* cakes most heroes get) and leaves home. At the end of the day he meets the son of God, a caricature who challenges him, 'WHERE ARE YOU GOING, AND WHAT ARE YOU CARRYING IN THAT BASKET?' He changes the loaves into goat heads and accuses the boy of stealing; the boy disingenuously ransoms himself by promising to go home and fetch a silver vessel. Having turned his moment for heroic struggle into cowardly retreat, he admits to his father, 'THAT TIME WAS REALLY TROUBLE!' But his ending is ironic. As an unintended result of his quest, he does bring his people something desirable — honey. His successful quest has yielded only a product anybody could have fetched out of the forest.[89] That 'son of God' character gives the game away: the parody is targeting Christianity, as well as storytelling style itself. Anyway, Mayotte has its own reasons for satirizing power figures.

How much 'tradition' does a hearer or reader know? The audience may know the storyteller's sources vaguely; perhaps some recall tellers of the last generation; the western reader is uninformed. The complexity of Mayotte's past might discourage us. Anthropologist Paul Ottino refuses to simplify. Malagasy and Comoran symbols reflect 'Indian and Muslim religious, philosophical, and political representations. From the 13th century on, these converged across India on the Malay peninsula and the Insulindian archipelago, at the same time as Islam and the Bantu [African] world were encountering each other on the shores of the east coast of Africa, producing what was to become Swahili civilization and culture'.[90] Complex enough? It's simpler to picture Mayotte as having four coexisting 'presences': Africa (history, physiognomy, customs, ideology), Islam (ever hovering over people's consciousness), Europe (colonization, mixing, convergence), and Madagascar (language, custom).[91] These presences converge in expressive culture. Responding to that multiplicity by imitating and remodeling, storytellers, dancers, and singers of Mayotte build their heterogeneous, hybrid repertoire. Ranoro becomes an octopus. A myth of the creation of the first woman from a tree is reduced to a caricature: an old man carves a woman, to replace a wife the king has stolen from him.[92] Remembering India, they award a king's daughter to a snake born of woman, to be his wife.[93] Now, in whatever oral performances survive French television, the accumulated stories have become 'a chain or network of texts in dialogue with each other'.[94] Formal and stylistic imitation, transformation, remodeling and parody of sources now unknown or irretrievable, as well as allusion to tales audiences will recognize, survive as tools of the powerless.

Bako the Ventriloquist

Remodeling an inherited narrative to comment satirically on a present reality is a potent way to build a close relation to your audience, especially of the young. Style and genre in parody are means of bringing the past to bear on the present. Take the motif of a child sold or promised to an ogre. Many traditions know it — France, India, Indonesia.... Who would think of parodying this motif to portray a mother who 'delivers her child to her lover to get rid of him, as he is proving to be an obstacle to their liaison'?[95] Who but an old grandmother in an African island, surrounded by her grandchildren and their friends under a tree, unembarrassed at the triangle in her modern melodrama? I summarize her piece.

Bako (Little Guy) has never seen his father, who is so uninterested in parenting that he stays out at work all day. One day Bako learns another reason. Accompanying his mother taking lunch to his father, he asks why the dish is so small. His mother doesn't explain to him, but the performer explains it, because her grandchildren are listening. There's a third dish for the mother's secret lover, who soon comes to complain, 'WHY DIDN'T YOU BRING ME MORE TO EAT THE OTHER DAY? I'M DYING OF HUNGER'. She explains Bako's interfering, and he says, 'WHAT ARE WE GOING TO DO WITH THIS BOY?' We don't expect her to say, 'KILL HIM'.

She hides her lover, with his sword, under the bed and calls the nimble but reluctant Bako. As she is about to beat him, he says, 'OH, OH! How

BIG THEY ARE!' Not the coconuts she wants him to bring, but her lover's eyes: 'LOOK UNDER THE BED, THIS MAN, WHAT BIG EYES HE HAS!' The lover flees. With his sword the mother chases Bako into the forest. One of the listeners has to make sure: 'EVEN THOUGH THAT'S HER SON?' The narrator repeats her words in reply. In the forest Bako finds another scandal: his father is mounting the cows, one after another. 'SO, BABA [POP], THIS IS WHAT YOU DO HERE? THIS IS WHY YOU ARE IN THE FIELD SO LONG?' The father chases him back to the mother; they agree, 'TSY MANJARY, HE'S NO GOOD'. Rejected by parent figures, Bako leaves home. Where is the old lady getting her material — from the movies? She is modernizing African or Malagasy tradition.

That melodramatic episode is only the first. Hiding shirtless in a tree, Bako falls in with three thieves and introduces himself to them as *Ampangalatra Bengy*, the Goat Thief. After they share meat and go to sleep, the boy enacts his new name by stealing their food and makes his way to some king's big garden. 'THE KING WAS THERE, IN HIS STONE HOUSE, HIS DAUGHTER WAS THERE TOO'. Bako doesn't yet know what the audience guesses, that he will be a suitor for the king's daughter. The watchman's wife suddenly boasts to her husband by quoting two Qur'anic words: 'FROM WHERE I SIT, I CAN SEE THE THRONE AND THE FOOTREST,' i. e., I know all the mysteries of the universe, and the other world as well.[96] Hearing her quote scripture, perhaps noting its irony in this context, Bako challenges her to find his lost shirt, but instead the couple take him to the sleepy king, a cynical portrait of authority. He would be obliged to listen to the boy's story if he didn't assign him a task. He is to bring back a rather unusual lion, on loan to another king's pasture in nearby Shungi. (Yes, Shungi is a real place nearby. No, the only lions in Mayotte are in these stories.) Of course he succeeds (he's a hero now); with time the lion grows fat. The king sends over one girl, then another and another, trying to get Bako so drunk he will kill the animal. Bako has a much better plan: he deflowers each girl and sends her back. Only the last one resists. He kills the lion, and the rival king tauntingly says, 'I TOLD YOU YOUR HERDER WOULDN'T BE ABLE TO BRING THAT ANIMAL TO PASTURE, AND NOW IT'S DEAD!' Bako has not told his king that news.[97]

Now comes the aged storyteller's tribute to the arts of the word. This is the only ventriloquist dialogue in Mayotte's folktales, but it fits both the theme of disguise and the practice of storytelling, in which a narrator can speak through one of her characters. The boy, to respond to the king's questions, carves a dummy of himself to present to the king, under the Arabic name *'Adjabu-l-fikira*, Mental Marvel. He debates with the dummy what to tell the king; only the truth will draw a laugh.

> "MENTAL MARVEL, WHAT ARE YOU GOING TO TELL THE KING TO EXPLAIN YOU KILLING THAT ANIMAL?"
>
> "HE SENT HIS DAUGHTERS SO I WOULD GET DRUNK AND KILL IT. HE SENT HIS FIRST GIRL, AND WHEN SHE GOT THERE I DEFLOWERED HER, AND HE SENT ANOTHER, I DEFLOWERED HER, AND HE SENT THE OTHERS UP TO THE LAST, WHO DID SUCCEED IN GETTING ME DRUNK. AND IF HE DOESN'T BELIEVE ME, LET HIM EXAMINE HIS GIRLS AND HE'LL SEE, THERE'S ONLY ONE WHO'S STILL A VIRGIN."
> Audience laughter.

The rival king claims the gold and is outraged that the girls have been deflowered.[98]

What ends the performance is the most pointed parody of all. Now that Bako has accomplished his task, he can marry the princess, as expected of a folktale hero, but the rival king insists that the boy take his daughter as well. Bako's last word to his prospective father-in-law takes him out of ancestral polygamy into the world of French law and secular custom.

> I NEVER LIKED YOUR DAUGHTER. IT WAS YOU WHO PUSHED ME INTO KILLING THE LION. YOU DIDN'T WISH ME WELL, YOU WANTED ME DEAD. WELL, IT'S YOUR SIX DAUGHTERS WHO ARE DEAD. YOUR [LAST] DAUGHTER, I NEVER LIKED HER, YOU FORCED ME TO MARRY HER. SO, I'M NOT DOING IT, I'LL STAY HERE WITH MY OTHER WIFE, I DON'T LIKE YOUR DAUGHTER.[99]

If a true trickster is one who overturns all social norms, a truly creole narrator is one who plays with story conventions, mixes folktale with *bande dessinée* (a comic strip), and mocks accepted attitudes. This old lady is playfully acquainting her grandchildren in Kany Kely with irony, infidelity, and violence. Inheriting and inventing metaphor is the best imaginary vengeance of the oppressed.

The final narrator of this chapter brings all these varieties of parody into a single performance.

The Virtuoso: Comedy, Trickery, Melodrama

Each evening is a re-creation: ephemeral or durable, its success depends wholly on the genius of the artist.[100]

> In ethnographic societies, narrative is never assumed by a person but by a mediator, shaman, or reciter, whose 'performance' (i.e., his mastery of the narrative code) can be admired, but never his 'genius'.[101]

Genius or performance? It all depends on the criteria of your society. There's no such thing anymore as a non-ethnographic society. Roland Barthes, himself a performer, would have admired a performer captured by Madjidhoubi Said, one evening in the village of Hakoa (also spelled Acoua), on Mayotte's west coast, in August 1976. Had he heard his innovations and watched his interactions with his audience, Barthes might have tolerated the word genius for his mastery of Mayotte's narrative code. He was surrounded by a religious celebration, which drew quite a crowd from outside the village for the rites and singing of the Sufi religious practices called *daira*.[102] A small group of men were entertaining one another with stories. 'The atmosphere was unusually steamed up [says Gueunier]... They all had time, and no one wanted to cut the [performance] short. In that situation several stories, which otherwise could be independent, got strung together for over an hour and a half.... The narrator stands out first for the verve with which he modernizes the situations'.[103]

Fig. 9 Fallen baobab, Sazilé beach. Photo by VillageHero, CC BY-SA 2.0, Wikimedia Commons, https://upload.wikimedia.org/wikipedia/commons/2/26/Fallen_Baobab_at_Salizey_Beach_%28Mayotte%29_%2830578354034%29.jpg

His Prologue

At first the young narrator is a little hesitant to ask for a turn: 'I'D LIKE TO TELL MY STORY'. Knowing his audience, he has already chosen an indecent parody, but is confused over how to introduce it. He begins with a mistake of attribution, which he then corrects: 'WELL, I LIVED THERE A LONG TIME... IN FACT I WASN'T THERE, IT'S A STORY FROM MY GRANDFATHER'S GRANDFATHER. THERE WAS A MAN CALLED *WAZIRI KANA-MPUNDRA*,' Minister No-Ass. The vizier's quaint practice is to kill every boy born in his village, with his own fashion of abusing power: his farts are fatal. (So that's the kind of story it'll be.) The villagers, for their safety, pen him up at the edge of town, and the storyteller starts again. 'THERE WAS A YOUNG WOMAN IN THAT VILLAGE WHO WAS PREGNANT, SHE DIDN'T KNOW BY WHOM'. She gives birth to a son, who grows supernaturally fast, like many an African hero. Despite being warned against the poisoned farts, the boy decides to fare forth. 'HE WAS A BOY! YOU KNOW, YOU CAN'T TRUST HIM, ANY MORE THAN AN OX, ANYWAY A BOY AND AN OX, IT'S THE SAME THING'. After watching No-Ass fart every three days, he returns home, tells his mother he's setting out like any classic hero, and soon she thinks he must be dead. But he is hiding in the weeds, to encounter his adversary. He was the same size as Mukadasi, says the narrator, pointing to a boy in the village. Instead of the combat we expect, the fart nearly kills the boy, and he yells like a newborn. To save him, the porters intervene: 'IT'S YOUR FART, WAZIRI NO-ASS, THAT MADE THE CHILD'.[104] The baby is adopted and raised as the *waziri*'s son. 'THAT KID'S NAME WAS — ACH, I DON'T KNOW, WAIT, THE NAME WILL COME BACK TO ME'.

Is the storyteller forgetting or faking? He covers for himself: 'YOU KNOW WHAT THEY'RE LIKE, PEOPLE WHO NEVER HAD A CHILD.' He is feeling energized. The farting demagogue promises to kill anyone his son tells him is an enemy, so the boy gets the vizier's wife beheaded and finishes off the vizier himself. The unnamed son takes possession of all his riches, and for a happy ending he installs his mother on the throne, thus proving that a young man who manages deception, fraud, and murder can find a high place in society.[105] That risky lesson would not escape the attention of a colonized audience, but that night, the listeners doubtless enjoyed the cynicism that emerges from drinking a lot of palm wine.

Kôto vs. Rhampsinitos

Evidently some time elapsed before the storyteller of the evening launched his longer performance. Perhaps he took the first piece to warm up, and then, noticing Mr. Said recording him, saw an opportunity for virtuosic display. He seems to admit that the story he told just now is separate from what's coming. His next hero looks like the same generic boy, but he is ready to give this one a name and put him into one comic situation after another, linking recognizable plots together. He blends unexpected material with the familiar, especially in his last piece. And he is the only Indian Ocean narrator who tells a tale from Herodotus.

Anchoring his piece in Mayotte's oldest tradition, he names the clever lad Kôto (Boy, in Kibushi), instead of the Muslim name a boy would normally be given. Kôto lives at his mother's house (a man's real home), with a father who soon will be proud of him. Already he is a composite character. The right word for him is *staârabo*,

> the word that precisely translates into [Shimaore] the idea of a 'civilization,' which etymologically was 'Arabness' (*ustaârabu*), covering all the qualities of good education, urbanity, and refinement that Comorans attribute to their Arab-Muslim heritage. But since colonization, the word has somehow slid from Arabness into Frenchness; it designates those whom colonial typology called assimilated, i. e. those who have been able to stick to the colonizer model.[106]

Kôto is the trickster hero of a satire, which the Hakoa narrator (or his source) bases on an old tale. Known to Europeans as Rhampsinitos, it was written by Herodotus in the fifth century BCE and is probably older.[107] It depicts the contest for power between a clever thief and king Rhampsinitos. First the thief robs the king's treasury; then he escapes detection so well that he finally attains high office and marries the king's daughter. Some time in the last six centuries, this 'charming sociopath', already known since antiquity, was recognized and accepted by African storytellers as one of their tricksters. Major elements of Herodotus's narrative were performed in Hakoa that night: theft, a trap, a decapitation, a weeping test, and the theft of the corpse.

Kôto is ambitious: 'I want to go work for the king [*ampanjaka*]'. This is no Grimm or Andersen king, not even a village chief, but a twentieth-century bureaucrat, who often absents himself from his colonial-style office, leaving a deputy in charge. His treasury (*bureau*) has a security system, which the narrator calls *courant* (electricity). It gets plugged into two old trickery motifs, trapping a victim and a magic object that holds a victim fast. The editor comments,

> The storyteller has only rough ideas about the effects of electric current. His village, Hakoa, never had electricity, and even Mwamoju or Mwomoju, the principal city in Mayotte (French spelling Mamoudzou), got its permanent installation only in 1978, two years after the tale was collected. For him it's a useful trickster trap: if you touch a wire, you get stuck without being able to get loose, but without being harmed otherwise.[108]

The Theft: Having won the king's confidence, he steals bags of money from the treasury, to his father's delight.

> KÔTO'S FATHER STARTED DANCING, DIDN'T NEED *AZOLAHY*, DIDN'T NEED *AMBIO* [INSTRUMENTS], DIDN'T NEED A THING, HE DANCED TO SEE THAT MONEY, AND SAID, "TRULY, I'VE FATHERED A WINNER FOR A SON, A REAL WORKER, I DON'T NEED ANY OTHER CHILD BUT YOU, I DON'T WANT ANY OTHER CHILDREN, ONLY YOU, YOU ARE A BLESSING, IF I HAVE OTHERS IT MIGHT BE BAD FOR ME, IT MIGHT RUIN ME". SO KÔTO'S FATHER COULDN'T CONTAIN HIMSELF, HE'D GOTTEN RICH!

All that wealth makes him crazy enough to disown his other children, who don't appear in the story. He becomes Kôto's henchman, and we begin to notice the narrator's penchant for dialogue as the father insists on accompanying Kôto to execute the theft. 'This very day, take me with you, we'll both go there together, tonight. We'll take ten bags and the same tomorrow, then done. We'll stock up on rice, and if you get fired later, well, our future is assured'.

But (the trap) he gets caught by the *courant*.

> KÔTO'S FATHER GOT TRAPPED. KÔTO CAME BACK, HE WAS GONE TO GET [THE MONEY], HE CAME BACK AND FOUND HIS FATHER STUCK THERE.
>
> "AH, DIDN'T I TELL YOU, PAPA? I TOLD YOU NOT TO FOLLOW ME, IT'S A DANGEROUS PLACE, AND NOW WHAT I TOLD YOU HAS HAPPENED. SO, WHAT ARE WE GOING TO DO NOW?"
>
> "GO ON WITH WHAT YOU'RE DOING, THEN COME BACK AND CUT OFF MY HEAD".
>
> "BUT YOU'LL DIE!"
>
> HE SAID, "OH, IT'S NOTHING. 'CAUSE THERE'S NO OTHER *MOYEN* [THING TO DO]".

That decapitation motif has been part of the story since antiquity. Kôto cuts off his father's head and removes it, so he won't be recognized when they drag him through the village. Kôto's mother duly weeps. The narrator advances his tale with more and more dialogue.

He told her, "See, what I said to my father is what happened, and this is his head, see?"

She said yes and began crying.

"Quiet, you're making matters worse. I'm telling you, mama, tomorrow around *saa ya vili* [seven o'clock], his body, we'll take it out, and I'll be one of the people doing that. Be careful, they'll go through the whole village looking for the family it belongs to, whoever starts crying, they'll arrest them, so be careful". So, he went in, organized things, got his father's head, took it and buried it, that same night in their yard... Well, Kôto stayed there, and at *saa ya vili* he left, went there, opened the doors, got there, went to work and ran to the king.

The Weeping Test: While his mother weeps in grief, Kôto convinces the soldiers that it's because she has cut her hand with a knife. *The Theft of the Corpse*: He assumes responsibility for watching the body overnight, steals the body, and buries it in that treasured place, his mother's house. Then the narrator shifts genres for Kôto to reveal his true trickster identity.

So Kôto went back and found the guys asleep, when he got there he saw them asleep, Kôto picked up a coconut shell, picked up a coconut shell, took and filled it with shit, that shit, he stirred it so it would be sticky like rice, and he got a tuft of coconut, he took the men's clothes off, he made the tuft all shitty and spread it on the first one's ass, then the next one, right to the last one asleep. He gave them all the same treatment.... When they woke up, they felt their clothes all cold, felt with their hand, and when they smelled it they knew it was shit. "Allahu akbar [Great God], what's all this?" [Audience laughter] "Gee, it smells like shit".

Is it the inspiration of the moment, or his audience's responses, that prompt the narrator to echo scenes where trickster pollutes a house? The soldiers catch on, but Kôto stays in charge. He orders all the houses inspected to search for the body, but ingeniously diverts the inspectors away from his house. In a touch from the business world, he also makes sure he hasn't lost his job with the king. Having proven his worth, Kôto remains the trusted servant. Do the men listening anticipate that he'll marry the king's daughter?

Kôto Tricks the King

Now against his mother's fears, Kôto vows to marry the king's daughter. His riches will take the place of high rank.

"Ke bôko zaho mahampy ampanjaka, I'm as strong as a king, I have lots of money, all the money we have at home, I'm as strong as a king". After he said that, Kôto went and said to the king, "King, I am telling you I want to marry".

The king asked, "How will you arrange to marry? Who do you want to marry? I myself will garanti to get that woman for you".

He said, "Holo hilàkao io, zanakanao iñy, areky helihely iñy, the one I want to marry is your daughter, the youngest one. There is an older one and another after her, but she's the one I want".

The king had no words to answer Kôto, he was embarrassed, he looked at Kôto: "Kôto, a poor man like you wanting to marry my daughter? Hey! Tie up Kôto, come tie him up fast, he has insulted me!"

This is the narrator's ingenious transition to a string of tricks familiar to the audience. Kôto is sewn into a sack and taken to the forest, where with much talk he persuades a passing herdsman to take his place and get thrown into the sea. Then he sells the dupe's cattle. The dupe recounts the adventure to the king, who is unconvinced and sends him into the sea, weighed down with a rock. Does he drown? Need you ask? At length Kôto reappears and persuades the king to follow the herdsman.

The King of the Sea gave me a message to bring you. Here is the letter I'm carrying from the King of the Sea, it's an invitation to a big feast, king. Such splendor, king, such splendor, such splendor at the bottom of the sea! They want you there, you have to make a reply to this letter, I came back just for you. The King of the Sea sent me to you, I have to go back right away!

Once the king has agreed to go, and take all the villagers with him, Kôto gets a stack of old sacks, marks them for royal occupants, puts a stone in each, and distributes them.

Kôto took [the king] and all his relatives, his children and his wife, except only the girl he wanted to marry, she wasn't going to go, because

IF SHE WERE TO GO, HE WOULDN'T WANT TO STAY IN THE VILLAGE, AND WHAT HE
WANTED WAS TO BECOME KING OF THE VILLAGE. THEY ALL DROWN. BACK IN THE
VILLAGE HE WAS THE ONLY MAN. KÔTO WAS THE ONLY MAN IN THE VILLAGE. SO,
HE UNTIED THE KING'S DAUGHTER: "LET'S GO LIVE IN YOUR FATHER'S HOUSE,
BECAUSE FROM NOW ON I'M THE KING OF THIS VILLAGE. YOUR FATHER IS WITH THE
KING OF THE SEA, HE WON'T BE COMING BACK HERE."

Not much of a courtship.

Now that he has the king's money, he wants to marry above his
station. He has become more authoritative: seeing no need to court the
daughter, he merely states his plan of marriage to her. The narrator has
used the drowning-the-dupe motif to replace the king's attempts, in
older versions, to catch the trickster. But instead of a happy fairytale
ending, he needs a transition to his next piece, because a trickster must
always be allowed to escape. 'THEY ATE UP THE KING'S RICHES, THEY ATE
UP THE KING'S RICHES, ATE IT UP TILL NOTHING WAS LEFT. KÔTO RAN OUT [OF
EVERYTHING], KÔTO SAW HE'D RUN OUT, HE LEFT THE VILLAGE'. Blending the
favorite African theme of rebuking a king's absurdity with satire of
colonial civil servants, the Hakoa narrator has transformed an ancient
comic tale.[109] Don't ask where he got it: the history of a tale as ancient as
Rhampsinitos is untraceable.

A Succession of Tricks

'The [African] storyteller [Denise Paulme writes] who judges a one-
movement story to be too short, or who wants to conserve his effects,
will resort to his memory. He will add a second motif to the first, and
— why not? — a third or fourth. The resulting story will be a success to
the extent it remains plausible and two successive sequences hang well
together'.[110] That is what the Hakoa storyteller does: fluently he adds
six scenes in which he can show off with wordy exchanges of dialogue,
surprises, and familiar tricks. The first is the old trick of convincing people
'THE MOSQUE IS GOING TO FALL DOWN, COME, LET'S HOLD IT UP, THE MOSQUE IS
GOING TO FALL DOWN!'[111] That frees him to steal everybody's food and shit
all over their houses. For his second trick he sells a nonexistent bull. He
ties a rope to a tree and leaves the end out, telling people, 'THAT IS ONE
NASTY BULL'. The prospective purchasers discover the trick and yell, 'LA
HAULA LA KUWATI LA BILLAHI! THAT GUY IS A THIEF! WHAT THE HELL! IT WAS

Kôto!' Next (third) he crashes a party in Labatoara (in Pamandzi) and outwits the unwelcoming locals who try to get him drunk. He POURED SOME, DRANK ONE MOUTHFUL, THREW THREE GLASSFULS ON THE GROUND. ONE MOUTHFUL, THREE GLASSFULS ON THE GROUND. He escapes out the back.

For trick no. 4 the narrator gives Kôto magic powers.

> NOW KÔTO, A LONG TIME BACK IN NDZAUDZE, HAD MADE A BOW THAT COULD THROW HIM AS FAR AS MWOMOJU. NOBODY KNEW ABOUT IT. HE GOT AS FAR AS [THE LITTLE ISLAND OF] FUNGUJU BEFORE THE OTHERS SAW HE'D GONE: "KÔTO ISN'T HERE, KÔTO'S GONE!"

Of course they pursue him.

> AND THEY GOT TO FIRASHO, AND HE WAS AT FUNGUJU. HE SAW THEM COMING FROM FAR OFF. HE RAN LIKE CRAZY AND REACHED HIS BOW AND STOPPED AND WATCHED THE ONES COMING AFTER HIM. HE LET THEM GET CLOSE, THEN HE DREW THE BOW AND GOT THROWN ALL THE WAY TO MWOMOJU.[112]

All the tricks are part of the African-Malagasy stock. Mentioning the place names is a surefire device for plausibility. Tsangamôzy is a village not far from Hakoa; Labatoara is the principal village of the island of Pamandzi, which carries on a rivalry with the main island, Grande Terre. Equally familiarizing is the way the trickster Kôto imitates behavior his hearers must know well, like dropping in at parties and dances (trick no. 5). Some revelers give him a demijohn of liquor which he sells, steals, sells again, and steals again, each time drinking a bit and filling the jug with water. Discovering he has stolen their liquor, they think of pursuing him but decide he must be a *lolo*. Kôto goes back to the village to live with the king's daughter. He makes the other women his concubines.

Perhaps Kôto's escape and victory had a special force in 1976, when Mayotte was deciding how to maintain its dependency on France. Or perhaps neither narrator nor audience would care. Any trickster rebels against authority figures.

Fig. 10 Barbara Stanwyck and Fred MacMurray
in Billy Wilder's 'Double Indemnity' (1944).
Public domain, Wikimedia Commons, https://
commons.wikimedia.org/wiki/File:Double_
indemnity_screenshot_8.jpg

Kôto Goes to Hollywood

The pseudo-happy ending launches the narrator's final story. In an unexpected bit of narrative metalepsis, the storyteller reveals the ending he will use: 'Kôto — FINALLY THE KING'S DAUGHTER IS GOING TO KILL HIM, BUT HE DOESN'T KNOW ABOUT THAT'. What? No teller of even the most familiar trickster tale gives away the ending (which is often already known to the audience anyway).[113] To launch his final, 4,000-words-long number, the Hakoa storyteller switches genres into something like screen melodrama. A switch in genre is a typical creolizing move, the kind that loves to form 'fresh cultural forms from the ready-to-hand debris of old ones'.

Folktale and *film noir* are not far apart. Generically, the trickster in oral narratives — ever marginal, ever the social critic, endangered but never destroyed — is the father of Maigret or Philip Marlowe in films. Perhaps some zealous *cinéaste* will uncover a specific source for this part of Kôto's story in the combination of pessimism and romance of the Popular Front films, or the dialogue style of post-World War Two thrillers by Henri-Georges Clouzot or Yves Allégret. We don't know what films he might have seen, or what popular magazines or romances were circulating in 1970s Mayotte, but in the middle of this religious celebration, the young man has mastered dialogue and character relations in the manner of those sources. The first unexpected touch is Kôto's wife coming angrily onstage. 'I'M WARNING YOU, KÔTO, YOU HAVE MISTRESSES, YOU'RE NOT A GOOD HUSBAND. CAN YOU MARRY THE WHOLE VILLAGE? I WANT SOME EXPLANATIONS, KÔTO!' Also unexpectedly, the teller reveals the ending he will use: 'KÔTO — FINALLY THE KING'S DAUGHTER IS GOING TO KILL HIM, BUT HE DOESN'T KNOW ABOUT THAT'. Betraying himself in their dispute, Kôto admits that he exterminated all the village men under pretext of sending them to the King of the Sea. The angry shouting dialogue of the couple, a staple of film and television dramas, is foreign to the speaking style of other Mahorais storytellers or their characters. Equally foreign is the wife's aggressive verbosity, so different from the abstract stylization of most folktale characters. That must have impelled the male listeners to identify with Kôto more than ever. The husband and wife can't stop arguing: 'THEY KEPT ON, THEY KEPT ON, THEY KEPT ON'.

Melodrama's next contribution is an interior monologue, which leads to a slowing of the narrative pace.

> THE WIFE THOUGHT ONLY OF HER PLAN, SHE WANTED TO KILL HIM. SHE THOUGHT ABOUT WHAT MEANS SHE WOULD USE TO KILL HIM. BUT IF SHE KILLED HIM, WHERE WOULD SHE GO? SHE WANTED TO GO GET HER FATHER AND MOTHER BACK. SO, SHE WANTED TO FIND A WAY TO CONVINCE KÔTO TO SHOW HER THE PATH TO GET TO THE KING OF THE SEA'S PLACE... SO, THE KING'S DAUGHTER BEGGED KÔTO, 'TAKE ME THERE, TAKE ME THERE, TAKE ME THERE, OTHERWISE I'M LEAVING!'

Kôto's wife steps out of her folktale role to assert herself. Her reversal of power and gender is nominally prohibited in Muslim law, but real-life Comoran women do manage it, because they own the houses into which men marry. They can oblige their husbands to return to their mothers, but only in shame. In style, the narrator is firmly in control of both old folktale and contemporary melodrama.

Once Kôto confesses all the deaths, his wife turns to the classic folktale grandmother (*dady*) for what she needs. Unlike her folktale predecessors, but like the Hakoa audience, the *dady* is partial to the trickster hero. She plays donor by suggesting several impractical methods of murder.

> FINALLY THE KING'S DAUGHTER REALIZED THAT THE *DADY* WAS TRYING TO PROTECT KÔTO, AND SAID TO HERSELF, "WHAT I HAVE TO DO IS KILL KÔTO WITHOUT

DELAY, BECAUSE OTHERWISE THE OLD WOMAN IS GOING TO CHANGE HER MIND
AND GO WARN HIM, THEN HE'LL KILL ME". SHE ALWAYS HAD HER KNIFE ON HER.

The women's melodramatic dialogue deepens the texture, causes the
wife the kind of severe inner conflict never portrayed in oral narrating,
and retards the movement of the narrative towards the catastrophe.
Kôto and his wife meet again at home; still she is indecisive.

WHEN KÔTO WAS ASLEEP, THE WIFE BEGAN WATCHING HIM SLEEP, WAITED TILL
HE BEGAN SNORING, THEN SHE WENT OUT QUIETLY AND WENT INTO THE OTHER
ROOM TO GET HER KNIFE, ONE OF THOSE VERY LONG KNIVES... SHE WAS THERE
ALL ALONE WONDERING, "AM I GOING TO CUT HIS THROAT? NO, I'LL PLANT IT
IN HIS CHEST. NO, I'LL DO IT LIKE THIS... LIKE THAT..." KÔTO WAS STILL ASLEEP,
NOT SUSPECTING ANYTHING, THE LAMP WAS STILL LIT. SHE CAME VERY CLOSE,
PRETENDING TO STROKE HIM, KISS HIM, MASSAGE HIM TO SLEEP. SHE TOOK THE
CURTAIN AND PULLED IT BACK TO SEE WHERE SHE WOULD HIT. SHE LOWERED THE
KNIFE, PLACED IT, THEN STOPPED, THINKING, "HOW'M I GOING TO GET ALONG IN
THIS VILLAGE WITH NOBODY IN IT?" SHE TOOK BACK THE KNIFE, TOOK IT BACK,
THINKING, THREE TIMES. THE FOURTH TIME, SHE CUT HIS THROAT. SHE PUSHED,
PUSHED SOME MORE, PUSHED AND PUSHED, AND WHEN SHE DREW THE KNIFE OUT,
HIS THROAT WAS CUT. SHE WAS VERY UPSET AT THAT CUT THROAT, SHE STAYED
ALONE.

SHE THOUGHT ABOUT WHAT TO DO, IF SHE TOOK THE KNIFE TO CUT HER OWN
THROAT, SHE WOULDN'T HAVE THE COURAGE. SO, SHE TOOK A ROPE, FASTENED IT
AROUND HER NECK, FASTENED IT TO THE ROOF, TOOK A CHAIR, PLACED IT, GOT
UP ON IT, TIGHTENED IT AROUND HER THROAT, AND THEN SHE KICKED AWAY THE
CHAIR AND WAS HANGED, AND THAT'S HOW SHE DIED.

At this point we recall this narrator is a male, who is allowing his story
to punish the woman and let the trickster escape.

As the performance in Hakoa nears its end, the narrator begins to lose
focus and energy. Instead of dramatizing the burial in a cinematic scene,
he curtails his story to misquote, or rework, a classic closing formula.

THE VILLAGE WOMEN WERE STILL THERE, THE VILLAGE WOMEN WERE STILL THERE...
THEY CAME AND CALLED, NOBODY ANSWERED, CALLED, NOBODY ANSWERED....
WHAT TO DO? THEY WERE ONLY WOMEN. THEY OPENED THE DOOR, WENT IN,
FOUND THE WIFE ALL STIFF, HANGING FROM THE ROPE, AND HIM STRETCHED OUT
ON THE BED WITH THE BED ALL COVERED IN BLOOD AND HIS HEAD CUT OFF. THE
WOMEN WERE STUNNED. "WHAT IS ALL THIS?"... THEY CUT DOWN THE WIFE,
TOOK HER DOWN, LOOKED AT ONE ANOTHER SAYING, "WHAT ARE WE GOING TO
DO? WE ARE ONLY WOMEN! LET'S BURY THEM".

I LEFT THEM THERE, I LEFT THEM THERE, I WENT ALONG. I DON'T KNOW WHAT
HAPPENED TO THAT VILLAGE WITH NO MEN IN IT. SO, I LEFT THEM THERE, WITH NO
MEN, I DON'T KNOW IF OTHER MEN CAME THERE, OR — NOTHING.

Abruptly he ends the tale, we hope with tumultuous acclaim from the
men listening.[114]

All the good Mahorais narrators bend old folktale plots and
characters to the concerns of their time and place. This one is especially
good at blending popular fiction into the trickster tale. Consider the
setting: the crime happens at night in a house of melodramatic despair,
where nothing good can be hoped for. Also notable is the slowing of
the plot: trickster tales like those he had already told, which move
swiftly towards a predictable ending, know nothing of the Hitchcockian
suspense he manages in his last segment. The most prominent *film noir*
touch is making the wife the new central character, a woman too weak
to stand alone except as a Barbara Stanwyck murderess, 'fate's emissary,
a siren leading the man to ruination'.[115] Knowing that her crime will
deprive her of redemption, she seeks only revenge. For her — as for
many women in Mayotte — the world is a dangerous place. Modernizing
gives the listener an exaggerated vision of dangers that don't show up in
most stories about an innocent persecuted woman. Kôto's wife, instead
of being permanently separated from him, joins him in death for the
sake of her family.

Recorded, transcribed, translated, and read, the Hakoa performance
is surprisingly novelistic. Perhaps the young narrator constructed
his performance merely by adding a second piece, then a third, then
a fourth. But in print, his disconnected, picaresque story has a unity,
because through his adventures, Kôto grows. At the beginning he is
ambitious; he begins maturing when he cooperates with his father and
then does away with him. In another Oedipal move, Kôto wins out over
the king by getting him drowned. Having spent all the late king's money,
he makes a rational decision to play tricks on the neighbors. Each time,
his success takes him to a higher position. 'THAT WAY HE FINALLY MADE
ABOUT A MILLION WITH THAT ONE DEMIJOHN'. His final defeat, inevitable
for a folktale trickster, comes in a surprising way; listeners might have
wondered if it could apply to corrupt, deceitful civil servants. Since his
main objective has been to entertain, the narrator avoids the direct topical
commentary we saw in the tale about the crab (incidentally also a Hakoa

product). Finally, both Kôto and his narrator have a great deal to say on all subjects. They and their characters are talkative, communicative, verbose, loquacious, garrulous, longwinded, prolix, fluent, and voluble, if you see what I mean.

Still, the narrator is producing a wholly oral performance. He honors all his sources, putting his memory and skills into practice in response to the social-religious-celebratory mood of the *daira*. His memory, skill with dialogue, and humor stand out there as much as they would at a wake, where again a storyteller would be expected to entertain. The music and dancing around him, what he knows about the men listening to him, the changing status of Mayotte — all are forces motivating him to remodel old features of oral performance. Drawing energy from being among friends, he frees them from any weight the religious ceremony has put on them. They can enjoy an hour and a half of fun. Such improvised assembling of sources has probably been the normal practice in Mayotte.

When men are the narrators, they tell tales about men. When this narrator speaks about Kôto, isn't he often referring to himself? For example, '[Kôto] KNEW A LOT OF THINGS THE PEOPLE IN THAT VILLAGE DIDN'T, HE KNEW THINGS'. People flatter him: 'You ARE AN EXPERT AT PARTIES LIKE THIS, YOU ARE A GOOD DANCER'. Here is a subtler model of self-referentiality than Husain, in the previous chapter. Both Kôto and his narrator are skillful keepers of secrets, practiced at concealing what they know. The trickster hides his intentions or changes his clothes; the storyteller uses words to reveal and conceal at the same time. The female storytellers we shall meet in the next chapter have an equally self-referential subject. Apparently Mayotte is not much different from places we know. After studying the island for many years, the anthropologist Michael Lambek ventures to say, 'relations between the sexes are not without their contradictions and their inequality'.[116] Imagine that.

A Note on Creolization

The tales and storytellers in this chapter have been treated as products of creolization; here is the theory behind that treatment. Linguists, beginning from the assumption that languages change slowly, discovered with surprise that in certain situations, new pidgin and creole languages develop rapidly out of the necessity for one language group to communicate with another. Invasions, conquests, resettlements, and enslavements have forced together peoples carrying different languages and traditions. Members of each group, dominant or subordinate, drew linguistic and cultural forms from the other group. Confronting power differences and conflicts, both groups learned to blend or amalgamate features of language, to negotiate language and culture, and jointly to create something new. What linguists discovered about these modifications of ordinary talk shows up all the more in people's proverbs, riddles, and narratives. Hence *creolization* is the name for the process whereby people in situations of unequal power renegotiate not only language but culture. Through that process they create new art, music, and literature.

Creolization is not just another word for culture change or cultural mixing. It is a consequence of class conflict, if not class struggle. In Mayotte's early history, the ethnic mix we see today resulted from the convergence of peoples — Arabo-Persian Shirazi, Swahili, Malagasy, and Europeans — whose arrivals were seldom peaceful. From the tenth century on, these peoples renegotiated their older models into an Islamic environment. All were sources for social structure, beliefs, cookery, and stories. Indian Ocean Island societies, Noel Gueunier insists, are the result of slavery and maritime trade.[117] Such harsh regimes virtually require renegotiating culture. So does colonization. Centuries of French influence have brought French material and intangible products to Mayotte for selecting and refashioning. Like other dependent cultures, Mayotte has appropriated and remodeled those products in a spirit of ambivalence and sometimes play. The contradictions of the social situation foster ambivalences: matrifocality vs. male-dominated Islam, dependence vs. independence, strict discipline vs. rebellion, sociability vs. concealment. By making ambiguity a feature of style, creole narrative turns silence into speech and makes its figurative language a subversive activity. As we see from that evening in Mayotte, the best storytellers blend diverse imported and new elements to create narratives that are discontinuous and new. The next chapter contains more samples of these new narratives. Neither accidental nor deteriorated assemblages of foreign influences. Kôto's story and others are new creations, which points at the most enduring feature of Mayotte's history: differential identity, differential power — what is sometimes called class struggle.

Endnotes

1   *Stars and Keys*, pp. 147–67.

2   The Index of tellers and locations (below) gives fuller information about the collecting in the 1970s–80s, and lists Aarne-Thompson-Uther tale types for the pieces discussed.

3   Veronika Görög-Karady and Christiane Seydou, ed., *La fille difficile, un conte-type africain* (Paris, CNRS Éditions, 2001).

4   Noël J. Gueunier, *La belle ne se marie point: contes comoriens en dialecte malgache de l'île de Mayotte* (Paris: Peeters, 1990), p. 23.

5   Non-fictional, personal-experience narratives about the spirits that rise up in Mahorais people have been extensively studied by Michael Lambek in *Human Spirits*.

6   Motif H105.5.2, Teeth and fingernails of slain cyclops taken as proof. Stith Thompson and Jonas Balys, *The Oral Tales of India* (Westport, CT: Greenwood Press, 1958), p. 216.

7   *La Belle*, pp. 162–72. Motifs: T118, Girl married to a monster; G82, Cannibal fattens victim; G512.1, Ogre killed with knife.

8   The tale is known in many West and Central African languages, for example Raymond Boyd and Richard Fardon, 'La Fille Difficile Tchamba, Sauvée par un Chanson (Nord-Cameroun)', in Görög-Karady and Seydou, *La fille difficile*, pp. 139–66. In the Democratic Republic of the Congo, Daniel P. and Brunhilde Biebuyck analyzed thirty-six distinct versions, in an article, 'We Test Those Whom We Marry', now difficult to access. East African versions are sampled in Ngumbu Njururi, *Agikuyu Folk Tales* (Nairobi: Oxford University Press, 1966), pp. 4–10; Rose Gecau, *Kikuyu Folktales* (Nairobi: East African Literature Bureau, 1970), pp. 92–99. I discuss Southwest Indian Ocean versions in *Stars and Keys*, pp. 147–67. Three texts from Mauritius, all following the same outline, were published in Charles Baissac, *Folklore de l'île Maurice* (Paris: G. P. Maisonneuve et Larose, 1887), pp. 146–79, and it is a favorite plot in Madagascar (*Malagasy Tale Index*, pp. 271–72, 363–71, 473–74).

9   Horns and tail identify the *lolo*. Cannibalism is the mark of the *kaka*. A *djinn* is often disguised.

10   *La belle*, p. 67 n. 3.

11   Ibid., pp. 68–74. Motifs: G81, Unwitting marriage to cannibal; T118, Girl married to a monster; H509, Tests of cleverness or ability (cf. H509.4, Tests of poetic ability); K1710, Ogre overawed.

12   Margaret A. Mills, *Rhetoric and Politics in Afghan Traditional Storytelling* (Philadelphia: University of Pennsylvania Press, 1991), p. 123.

13   The line is said by a character in Giraudoux's play *Siegfried* and is quoted in Jacques Body, *Jean Giraudoux: The Legend and the Secret* (Rutherford, NJ: Fairleigh Dickinson University Press, 1991), p. 57.

14   *La belle*, p. 11.

15   Detailed studies of the story, with this interpretation, are presented in Görög-Karady and Seydou's *La fille difficile*. From the innumerable versions the authors derive, not an 'original', but a skeleton, or *modèle matriciel*, of the story, containing six narrative essentials. 1. A girl shows herself excessively demanding for marriage. 2. A suitor appears, hiding his real negative nature under a positive appearance, say a fat *lolo* in Arab dress, with gold teeth. 3. She declares her intention to unite with him. The union is concluded. 5. The husband's true nature is revealed. 6. The union is broken. Thus they define a 'tale type', a hypothetical form abstracted from transcribed performances. To confirm the importance of multiplicity, Seydou concludes,'The ensemble of tales produced by a society forms a system in which each constituent yields its total meaning only when compared with others and the play of constants and variables they deploy' (p. 52).

16   Sophie Blanchy and Zakaria Soilihi, 'Le tambour', *L'Espoir* (Réunion), 2 (August 1989), 20–31.

17   Ottino, 'Un procédé littéraire'; Anne Storch, *Secret Manipulations: Language and Context in Africa* (New York: Oxford University Press, 2011).

18   *La belle*, pp. 182–83.

19   Slavery aggravated the fear of being forced to marry outside one's ethnic group (exogamy). Yves Blandenet, 'La diaspora des contes africains dans les mythologies de l'Océan Indien', *Notre Librairie*, 72 (1983), 21–31.

20   Linda Dégh, *Narratives in Society, a Performer-Centered Study of Narration* (Bloomington: Indiana University Press, 1995), p. 37.

21   Noël J. Gueunier and Madjidhoubi Said, *La Belle ne se marie point* (Paris: Peeters, 1990), p. 192, n. 4.

22   'The political struggle between those two parties, much alive in 1975–76, was manifested in actual internal blockades: 'Hakoa people could not set foot on the opposite party's territory, notably Mtsangamuji and Shembenyumba. Sometimes the villages confronted each other in veritable armed expeditions led by prominent men and veterans of the French army'. Gueunier, *La belle*, p. 192, n. 8.

23   A drum plays itself also in an Antankarana tale from Madagascar's east coast. Renel 1:224–27.

24   *Contes comoriens*, pp. 206–19. Motifs: D1601.18.3, Self-beating drum; G512.2, Spirit woman in rock; F455.5.3, Cap of invisibility; B421, Helpful dog; B524.1.2, Dogs rescue fleeing master from tree refuge.

25   Pierre Vérin, *The History of Civilisation in North Madagascar* (Rotterdam: A. A. Balkema, 1986), p. 36.

26   ATU653, The Four Skillful Brothers, known among Sakalava: Dandouau, pp. 373–76.

27   Denise Paulme, 'Morphologie du conte africain', *Cahiers d'Études Africaines* 12, 45 (1972), 131–63 (p. 156). Her description applies even more closely to the Hakoa narrator's string of trickster stories below, provoked by the joviality around him.

28   *La belle*, pp. 138–61. Motifs: G81, Unwitting marriage to cannibal; H509, Tests of cleverness or ability (cf. H509.4, Tests of poetic ability); K1710, Ogre overawed; G551.2, Rescue of sister from ogre by another sister; N825.3, Old woman helper; B450, Helpful bird; B552, Bird carries man; D1101, Magic spittle; D1002, Magic excrements; G510, Ogre killed.

29   Noël J. Gueunier, *Le coq du roi: contes comoriens en dialecte malgache de l'île de Mayotte* (Paris: Peeters, 2001), pp. 146–55. Motifs: B11.6.2, Dragon guards treasure; H335.7, Suitor task: to kill treasure-guarding snake lying around the princess' chamber; H1174.2, Overcoming dragon as task; H105.1, Dragon tongue proof; B375.1, Fish returned to water: grateful.

30   *Contes comoriens*, pp. 22–26, 146–55.

31   Caroline Levine's phrase 'a series of local network clusters' accurately describes an island where one village speaks Kibushi, the next one Shimaore, and both are trying to practice Islamic marriage under French law. The folktales take up 'the daunting challenge of understanding life in a world organized by multiple networks… [They are] sites where multiple forms cross and collide, inviting us to think in new ways about power'. Caroline Levine, *Forms: Whole, Rhythm, Hierarchy, Network* (Princeton:

Princeton University Press, 2015), p. 122. Each network is self-contained yet connected with many other networks. Actors, objects, and incidents of stories, not being independent entities, get their meaning from the relations among them and their networks. Storytellers exercise that competence in mixing and blending them which characterizes all creole societies. Their performances go beyond clarifying people's understanding, to give an answer to the conflicts between networks. Plenty of linguistic energy is prominent in the collectors' transcriptions that are the sources for this book. Even more potent than the networks image, traditional storytelling looks to be the kind of system defined by Gilles Deleuze and Félix Guattari: 'Must it not be admitted that every system is in variation and is defined not by its constants and homogeneity but on the contrary by a variability whose characteristics are immanent, continuous, and regulated in a very specific mode (variable or optional rules)?' Gilles Deleuze and Félix Guattari, *A Thousand Plateaus: Capitalism and Schizophrenia*, trans. Brian Massumi (Minneapolis: University of Minnesota Press, 1987), pp. 93–94).

32   *Contes comoriens*, p. 116, n. 2.

33   *Contes comoriens*, pp. 110–17.

34   *Contes comoriens*, p. 116, n. 2.

35   Beaujard, p. 493.

36   Gueunier, *Le coq*, pp. 42–47. In other Comoran versions the hero gets some reward, but no impostor tries to rob the hero of it, as happens in European dragon-slayer stories. Language is awkward: 'The teller seems to disregard the meaning of *Nyoka* in Shimaore, speaking only of a *kaka* or a '"being", *raha*' (47, note 5). Paul Ottino's brilliant and detailed study of the swallowing monster's versions and variants is titled 'Le Thème du monstre dévorant' (1977).

37   Investigators in Africa have been bound to observe the performers' habit of alternating speech and song, e. g. Bird, Charles, 'The Heroic Songs of the Mande Hunters', in *African Folklore*, ed. Richard M. Dorson (Garden City (NY): Doubleday, 1972), pp. 275–93, 468–77. In situations of convergence or display, the channel draws attention as much as the content of the message. Attention to creolized societies has revealed their delight in multiplying channels of artistic communication: Roger D. Abrahams, *The Man-of-Words in the West Indies* (Baltimore, M.D.: Johns Hopkins University Press, 1983).

38   *Contes comoriens*, pp. 246–48.

39   Gueunier, *L'Oiseau*, pp. 66–67.

40   Because certain possession rituals 'are more or less ostracized by orthodox Islam, the wasp's tiny waist can be interpreted as a punishment', and there is indeed one species of spider with a red bottom. *La belle*, p. 100, n. 1.

41   Blanchy et al., *La maison*, p. 65.

42   *La belle*, pp. 310–11.

43   *L'Oiseau*, p. 130, n. 7.

44   *L'Oiseau*, p. 19, n. 2.

45   *L'Oiseau*, p. 130, n. 7.

46   *La belle*, p. 204, n. 9.

47   Marie-Paule Ferry, 'Telling Folktales — Why?' trans. Lee Haring, *Southwest Folklore* 6, 1 (1986), 1–16. The transgression of narrative levels is analyzed for literary fiction by Gérard Genette in *Narrative Discourse: An Essay in Method*, trans. Jane E. Lewin (Ithaca: Cornell University Press, 1980).

48   *L'Oiseau*, pp. 260–61.

49   A related literary notion is *deixis*, the set of devices whereby literature, or any other act of reference, anchors itself in or refers to a context. Ducrot, Oswald, and Tzvetan Todorov, *Dictionnaire encyclopédique des sciences du langage*, Points (Paris: Éditions du Seuil, 1972), p. 323.

50   Annemarie Schimmel, *Islam: An Introduction* (Albany: State University of New York Press, 1992), p. 21.

51   Polarization like what Hasan and Husain next experience is a 'law' of folktale structure, part of the abstract stylization regulating folktale style. Axel Olrik, *Principles for Oral Narrative Research*, trans. Kirsten Wolf and Jody Jensen (Bloomington: Indiana University Press, 1992), p. 50: Max Lüthi, *The European Folktale: Form and Nature*, trans. John D. Niles (Bloomington: Indiana University Press, 1986), pp. 24–36. If Persian mythology had the influence in Mayotte that Claude Allibert asserts, any duality like this, or the inseparability of the tricksters Ikotofetsy and Imahaka in Madagascar, would be a relic from Zoroastrianism. Allibert, *Mayotte*, pp. 195–226.

52   *Contes comoriens*, p. 365, n. 6.

53   Conventional, but also quite specific to Mayotte: 'It is an occult test: it is known that prosperity comes from parental blessing.... Hasan understands that his rice is not thriving because of the curse weighing on him for killing his father. And he suspects Husain has not killed his [father], since his rice is still flourishing' *Contes comoriens* p. 365, n. 8.

54   The deceptive agreement to kill mothers is traditional among Sakalava or
      Tsimihety: Dandouau, pp. 339–46. Thompson's motif K1840 comprises a
      number of deceptions by substitution; the father's trick here is to substitute
      an animal's blood as proof of the execution, which deserves but does not
      have its own motif number (cf. the Indian motif K512.2, Compassionate
      executioner).

55   'Hasan, pursued by his curse, will sail without ever reaching land, and will
      finally die on his boat' *Contes comoriens*, p. 366, n. 10.

56   A chamber full of human skulls is part of one of M. Gueunier's *fille difficile*
      stories (*La belle*, pp. 82–101). Another shows briefly in Allibert, *Contes
      mahorais*, pp. 57–61.

57   'Thanks to the magic knowledge he has inherited from his father, Husain
      can indicate to the old lady a place where the *djinn* will not come and raid
      her herds' *Contes comoriens*, p. 366, nn. 12–13.

58   Sophie Blanchy, 'Changement social à Mayotte: transformations, tensions,
      ruptures', *Études Océan Indien*, 33–34 (2002), 165–95 (p. 169).

59   'We recognize the formula indicating the hero's departure, even if as in
      this case he will not go far' *Contes comoriens*, p. 366, n. 17.

60   *Contes comoriens*, pp. 348–66. Motifs: P311, sworn brethren, P312, blood
      brothers; Q2, kind and unkind; K1400, Dupe's property destroyed;
      D1415.2, Magic musical instrument causes person to dance; K1840,
      Deception by substitution; D2157.1, Land made magically fertile;
      D1812.0.1, Foreknowledge of hour of death; D1960, Magic sleep; B31.1,
      Roc; H324, suitor test. The line about recognizing a woman he has slept
      with might be the most 'modern' touch of all, updating one of the motifs
      most often used in the repertoire, H161.1, Recognition of person among
      identical companions. Other versions: Renel 1: 65–76 and 3: 19–21;
      Dandouau, pp. 149–53.

61   Claude Lévi-Strauss, *Wild Thought: A New Translation of 'La Pensée Sauvage'*,
      trans. Jeffrey Mehlman and John Leavitt (Chicago: University of Chicago
      Press, 2021), pp. 20–26.

62   ATU513A, Six Go Through the Whole World. Dandouau's text, pp. 255–
      71, though a powerful forerunner, is not 'the source' for M. Gueunier's
      narrator, nor is it unique: a version from Madagascar's east coast is in
      Renel 1: 254–60. A Malagasy prototype for a hero who, rejecting local
      girls, travels over water to fetch a wife is the legend of Rasoanor, which
      is summarized in Étienne de Flacourt's 1661 history book: Paul Ottino,
      L'étrangère intime: essai d'anthropologie de la civilisation de l'ancien Madagascar
      (Paris: Éditions des Archives Contemporains, 1986), pp. 51–52.

63   This favorite moment in Malagasy tales (T24.2.3, Fainting from seeing an extraordinary beauty, evidently of Indian origin) is prominent in a Sakalava tale, The Two Brothers (ATU303: *Stars and Keys* pp. 206–20). I discuss charms in 'Verbal Charms in Malagasy Folktales', in *Charms, Charmers and Charming: International Research on Verbal Magic*, ed. Jonathan Roper (London, 2004), pp. 246–59.

64   *Slave* is the correct word. Slavery persisted longer in the Comoros (in a thinly disguised form under the French autocrat Léon Humblot) than in any other island of the region, as late as 1909: Jean Martin, *Comores: quatre îles entre pirates et planteurs* (Paris: L'Harmattan, 1983).

65   *La belle*, p. 372, n. 9.

66   'Several more or less direct relations can be grouped by the term *zama*, maternal uncle. Hence this very common expression, which avoids exactly stating the genealogical relation between the two relatives' (Gueunier, *La belle*, p. 372 n. 11). Matrilineal societies give special honor to maternal uncles.

67   This entire episode replaces a more rapid and linear ending in another version Gueunier summarizes, in which Farananomby's baby son vows he will grow up to marry a daughter of Creator. He succeeds.

68   *La belle*, pp. 334–74. Motifs: T131.1.2.4, Son refuses to marry father's choice; F636, Remarkable thrower; F642.8, Person sees enormous distance; F516, Person unusual as to his arms; F642, Person of remarkable sight; E52, Resuscitation by magic charm; T100, Marriage; K2252, Treacherous maid-servant; K1934, Impostor forces heroine to change places with her; S145, Abandonment on an island; D955, Magic leaf; D150, Transformation: man to bird; H12, Recognition by song; D211, Transformation: man to fruit; D451.3, Transformation: fruit to another object; R351, Fugitive discovered by reflection in water; H1212.4, Quest assigned because of longing of pregnant woman; S165, Mutilation: putting out eyes; R10.3, Children abducted; G440, Ogre abducts person; D1461.0.1, Tree with golden fruit; T68, Princess offered as prize; H509, Tests of cleverness or ability; D1654.4.1, Sword can be moved only by right person; H541, Riddle propounded with penalty for failure; Q461, Impalement as punishment; Q499, Other humiliating punishments; D475.1, Transformation: objects to gold; F785, Extraordinary throne; H12, Recognition by song; H162, Recognition of disguised princess by bee lighting on her.

      Three Malagasy texts are clear forerunners; one, classifiable as a version of The Three Oranges (ATU408), begins with the oft-told false bride motif and continues into repeated self-transformations by the real bride, while the false one reveals her identity by asking for insects to eat and then showing her *kaka* tail. The rest is as straightforward as this kind of storytelling can be. André Dandouau collected two Sakalava versions that resemble our tale very closely indeed, pp. 255–71. The differences are charming. The intermediary who offers to lead the hero's party demands a price: his foot sores (consequence of syphilis) must be cured; the girl's grandmother, having taken in the hero, suspects he is a king's son when he won't eat (H71, Marks of royalty). Food becomes important: he refuses food twice, then the third time, Farinañomby, cooking offstage, changes the menu to milk, rice, and coconut, and the grandmother herself serves it. Wanting to keep his face concealed, he asks her to leave the room; because she is unwilling, he has her cover the walls and windows and unveils his face, which causes the old lady to faint and knock over the food (H41, Recognition of royalty by personal characteristics or traits). Revived, the old woman tells Farinanomby, who invites him to dine with her family, but he refuses. At last Farinanomby is reinstated as the true bride, the chameleon false bride is killed in front of her, and she proceeds to the palace by walking first on the chameleon's body and then on a herd of oxen. Then the Sakalava narrator starts a new episode. Farinanomby gives birth to a son, so troublesome that she stops speaking until at last he forces her. Wanting to marry, he goes to Creator's house and asks for his youngest daughter. She must be chosen from among her identical sisters; the boy succeeds at that test and at three more tests Creator assigns him. So he marries this divine creature, and 'everything they asked for was granted them by Creator's daughter, to whom her father could not refuse anything'.

69   Jacques Derrida and Derek Attridge, *Acts of Literature* (London: Taylor & Francis, 1992)

70   Dady ny Saidy was brought out from Gueunier's anonymity in Blanchy's *La maison*, pp. 99–130. The tale belongs to type ATU327, The Children and the Ogre; two dozen versions of this 'supertype' were recorded in Madagascar in the nineteenth and twentieth centuries (*Malagasy Tale Index*, pp. 380–91).

71   *La Maison*, pp. 6–7.

72   Émile Birkeli, 'Folklore sakalava recueilli dans la région de Morondava', *Bulletin de l'Académie Malgache*, n. s. 6 (1922–1923), pp. 234–39. Renel 1: 243–46, 2: 35–36.

73   Tzvetan Todorov, *The Poetics of Prose*, trans. Richard Howard (Ithaca: Cornell University Press, 1977), p. 72.

74   *Le coq*, pp. 96–121. The tale was also published by Blanchy in *La Maison*, pp. 99–133, with the text transcribed in Arabic alphabet. Motifs: S301, Children abandoned; S321, Destitute parents abandon children; G406,

Lost person falls into ogre's power; G501, Stupid ogre; R311, Tree refuge; G512.3.2, Ogre burned in his own oven.

75   *Le Coq*, p. 121, n. 19. Anthropologists have observed, indeed have been part of, many such 'joking' relationships.

76   Roger D. Abrahams, *Deep Down in the Jungle: Negro Narrative Folklore from the Streets of Philadelphia* (Hatboro, PA: Folklore Associates, 1964), pp. 51–52. On this capacity for verbal ambiguity Henry Louis Gates, Jr., has built his compelling theory, *The Signifying Monkey: A Theory of Afro-American Literary Criticism* (New York: Oxford University Press, 1988).

77   Gérard Genette develops a major literary theory around this practice, without referring to the most obvious place where it occurs, oral narrating (*Palimpsests: Literature in the Second Degree* (Lincoln: University of Nebraska Press, 1997), pp. 24–30. An equally accurate term would be *pastiche*, in Proust's sense, if readers did not so often think it means collage.

78   *L'Oiseau*, p. xix. The birds' refusal to carry a message happens in a Betsimisaraka tale: Soafara's message to her parents is refused by the guineafowl, the umbrette, and the crow, because all have been insulted by her; the roller-bird accepts the errand and takes the message (Renel 1: 282–87).

79   *L'Oiseau*, p. xix.

80   *L'Oiseau*, pp. 208–15.

81   *L'Oiseau*, pp. 50–55. The myth is found in Jacques Faublée, *Récits bara* (Paris: Institut d'Ethnologie, 1947), pp. 257–59. Although the story bears some resemblance to ATU400, The Man on a Quest for His Lost Wife, it is a textbook example of the cyclic type of tale in which a man satisfies his hunger or gets a wife, only to lose her by violating a prohibition. Motifs: T543.1, Birth from tree; C31.2, Tabu: mentioning origin of supernatural wife; C952, Immediate return to other world because of broken tabu.

82   Serious parody, in fact, is recognized in musicology as a kind of novelty: '[I]n the 18th century "parody" was understood primarily as the fashioning of a new poem on the model of an extant one. It is now taken to mean the retexting of a vocal composition, and more generally *the production of a new vocal work* based on the music of another piece' (Daniel R. Melamed, 'Parody', in *J. S. Bach. Oxford Composer Companions*, ed. Malcolm Boyd (Oxford: Oxford University Press, 1999), pp. 356–57 (p. 356), emphasis LH. Bach's practice of reusing secular materials in sacred pieces is analogous to what oral storytellers do with the materials they have inherited, and also to Gérard Genette's subgenre of serious imitation.

83   Pierre Maranda, ed., *Mythology, Selected Readings* (Harmondsworth (England): Penguin Books, 1972), p. 8.

84   I take this brilliant phrase from Bengt Holbek, 'Games of the Powerless', *Unifol* 1976 (1977), 10–33.

85   *Le Coq*, p. xvii.

86   *Contes comoriens*, p. 4.

87   Barbara Kirshenblatt-Gimblett, 'Studying Immigrant and Ethnic Folklore', in *Handbook of American Folklore*, ed. Richard M. Dorson (Bloomington: Indiana University Press, 1983), pp. 39–47 (p. 40).

88   *L'Oiseau*, pp. 66–71. By honoring the locality, the piece reverses the values of motif C952, Immediate return to other world because of broken tabu.

89   Birkeli, pp. 198–203.

90   Ottino, *L'Étrangere intime*, p. 576.

91   I derive the idea of multiple presences from Stuart Hall, 'Créolité and the Process of Creolization', in *Créolité and Creolization. Documenta 11 Platform 3*, ed. Okwui Enwezor et al. (Ostfildern-Ruit (Germany): Hatje Cantz, 2015), pp. 27–41.

92   *L'Oiseau*, pp. 84–94.

93   *La Belle*, pp. 282–98.

94   Caryl Emerson and Gary Saul Morson, *Mikhail Bakhtin: Creation of a Prosaics* (Stanford, C.A.: Stanford University Press, 1990), p. 16. Richard Bauman, 'Conceptions of Folklore in the Development of Literary Semiotics', *Semiotica* 39 (1982), 1–20.

95   *Contes comoriens*, p. 8. Motif S211, Child sold to an ogre.

96   *Contes comoriens*, p. 151, n. 10.

97   Real lions do not require being sent out to pasture. This one is rather bovine.

98   This same narrator, in a second performance of this piece recorded six months later, here inserted a new episode: 'We have to understand that the king (the girls' father) had bet [the other king] two casks of gold that the boy would not succeed in taming the lion' (Gueunier, *Contes comoriens*, p. 165, n. 7).

99   First version recorded December 1977 (pp. 138–51), second version recorded May 1978 (pp. 152–65). Motifs: T465, Bestiality; S12.1.1, Treacherous mother and paramour plan son's death (Indian); S11, Cruel father.

100   Paulme, *La Statue*, p. 97.

101   Roland Barthes, 'The Death of the Author', in *The Rustle of Language*, trans. Richard Howard (New York: Hill and Wang, 1986), pp. 49–55 (p. 49).

102   'Salafi Muslims derogate these practices by calling them simply dances' (Noël Gueunier, personal communication). The narrator makes the *daira* setting part of Kôto's story.

103   *Contes comoriens*, pp. 16–79, quotation from p. 6. The performance was witnessed, recorded, and translated to French by Madjidhoubi Said; Noël Gueunier collaborated with him on the Kibushi transcription and the French translation. M. Gueunier notes, 'The name of the language, as its speakers know it, is Kibushi ('Malagasy'), or more accurately, Kibushi *kimaore* ('Mayotte Malagasy').' I am grateful to these colleagues for permission to translate the text and include their ethnographic information.

104   Translating his name as No-Ass is my most outrageous liberty, since *mpundra* means donkey. The image appears also in Gueunier's *fille* who insists on a husband who won't defecate for a week. This piece was recorded by Madjidhoubi Said the same night as Gueunier's #92 and #118. Here, the same narrator gives Kôto's adversary the titles *waziri* (vizier or minister to a king) and *ampanjaka* (king) indifferently. The latter term means something like *chief* of a village. A member of the audience asks if *Kana-mpundra* could really be his name; the narrator confirms, adding an attempt to enhance its realism, 'but I don't know that village, don't know if it's in Africa or some place else' *Contes comoriens*, pp. 316–17. The porters intervene at the point where a folktale hero encounters a donor. By getting him adopted, their action redirects his future more effectively than any magic object a donor might provide him. Motif T615, Supernatural growth.

105   *Contes comoriens*, pp. 316–23. Motif S22.1.1, Adopted son plots death of parents, usurps the throne.

106   *Contes comoriens*, pp. 6–7.

107   ATU950, Rhampsinitos, might even be of African origin, '[d]ocumented in the 5th century B.C.E. by Eugammon of Cyrene in northern Africa' (Uther *Types*, p. 589). William Hansen discusses its history and variant

forms, provides labels for the components, and calls the hero a 'charming sociopath': *Ariadne's Thread: A Guide to International Tales Found in Classical Literature* (Ithaca: Cornell University Press, 2002), pp. 363–71).

108   *Contes comoriens*, p. 76, n. 5.

109   'Serious imitation', Gérard Genette's term from literary study, denotes most folktale performances, such as the ones from Allibert's schoolboys. Most informants, making honest attempts to pass to the interviewer a narrative the informant has heard, are producing a serious imitation. In Genette's terms, the Hakoa narrator's additions produce a serious transformation (*Palimpsests*, pp. 24–30).

110   Paulme, *La Statue*, p. 95.

111   In African and Malagasy versions, trickster is holding up a rock. Examples: Gerhard Lindblom, *Kamba Folklore, with Linguistic, Ethnographical and Comparative Notes* (Leipzig: Harrassowitz, 1928–1935), p. 29; L[ars] Dahle and John Sims, *Anganon'ny Ntaolo* (Antananarivo: Trano Printy Loterana, 1971), pp. 49–50. African versions use animal characters, the Malagasy one uses the twin tricksters Ikotofetsy and Imahaka. Motif K1251, Holding up the rock.

112   Motifs: K130, Other worthless animals sold; H950, Task evaded by subterfuge; D1524, Magic object enables person to cross water.

113   *Bricolage* is the term promulgated by Claude Lévi-Strauss for 'the formation of fresh cultural forms from the ready-to-hand debris of old ones' Richard Werbner, 'Afterword', in *Syncretism/Anti-Syncretism: The Politics of Religious Synthesis*, ed. Charles Stewart and Rosalind Shaw (London: Routledge; 1994), p. 215. In poor countries *bricolage* often remodels imported commercial things, in effect making them traditional. What Lévi-Strauss sees as a habit of the universal mind has long been the practice in creole societies annexing the global or the foreign. Anyone can hear the result by calling up Mauritian or Jamaican music on YouTube. If a world language like English or French, translating island folklore, perpetuates colonial domination, then a creole language and the artistic use of it become instruments of counterhegemony. Through mediation and negotiation the global becomes local.

114   *Contes comoriens*, pp. 16–79. Motifs: I. J1113, Clever boy; K346, Thief trusted to guard goods; D1413, Magic object holds person fast; K730, Victim trapped; K365, Theft by confederate; N511.1, Treasure buried by men; K407.1, Thief has his companion cut off his head so that he may escape detection; J1142.4, Thief's corpse carried through street to see who will

weep for him; cf. K1875, Deception by sham blood; E752.10.1, Corpse must be watched carefully before burial; K355, Trickster pollutes house so that he is left in possession.

II. L101, Unpromising hero; K842, Dupe persuaded to take prisoner's place in sack; K1970, Sham miracles; K1919, Marital impostors, miscellaneous; L11, Lowly hero marries princess.

III. K1251, = ATU1530, Holding up the rock, ATU1737, The clergyman in the sack to heaven; K130, Sale of worthless animals; K1839, Other deceptions by disguise; K347, Cozening; K2030, Double dealers.

IV. T230, Faithlessness in marriage; Q241, Adultery punished; J494, Death and revenge preferred to life; P214.1, Wife commits suicide at husband's death.

115   Wes D. Gehring, *Handbook of American Film Genres* (New York: Greenwood Press, 1988), p. 66.

116   *Human Spirits*, p. 25.

117   Personal communication.

3. Giving an Account of Herself

Fig. 11 Twentieth-century women. Photo by Jacquier-roux, CC BY-SA 4.0, Wikimedia Commons, https://upload.wikimedia.org/wikipedia/commons/3/38/Mayotte_%287%29.jpg

How does a woman achieve recognition? Well before the tales in this book were collected and recorded, says a historian, '[w]omen play[ed] a more influential, even conspicuous role in public life [in Mayotte], for instance, than they [did] in the stricter Koranic paternalism of the other islands.'[1] In 1980s Grande Comore, perhaps also in Mayotte, women enjoyed 'particular respect and protection, as daughters — as sisters? — and as mothers, a deference sometimes justified by quotations from the Qur'an'.[2] Some achieve recognition by being artists of the word (some men do too). Before French TV invaded people's evening gatherings, an old lady in Kany Kely could draw on traditional narrative forms to dramatize the contradictions in male-dominated ideology. Maybe she still can. Noël Gueunier noticed older women enjoying a liberty of speaking about — well, delicate subjects. Sophie Blanchy found skilled *conteuses* commenting, through their stories, on the social system they live in. Her outstanding storytellers are women skilled in metaphor, irony, and ambiguity.[3] They understand that the aphorism of the American poet Kenneth Koch applies to them: 'There are a great many human

https://doi.org/10.11647/OBP.0315.03

relationships and a great many situations inside other relationships in which there is no communication without disguise...'.[4] Koch, a master of irony, would have appreciated their ingenuity. By combining protection with disclosure, these storytellers become not legislators, but mediators of Mayotte's culture. If they are unacknowledged outside, they receive plenty of acknowledgment from their audiences. Some of their pieces give a symbolic account of the narrator herself.

The tone of their social criticism is not always playful.

A Child Molester

Sometimes a girl in Wangani needs a tone subtler than parody. A bitter tale about child abuse reads like the sketch for a horror movie. A village teacher asks his pupils to bring him dry firewood from the forest every Monday and Thursday (not an exorbitant request: pupils of a Qur'an teacher are expected to serve him). In the forest they meet an old man, whose ceremonial dress of caftan, turban, and Arab-style fancy robe mirrors the suitor's disguise in *fille difficile* tales. From atop a rock he sings an incomprehensible song, directing them to answer in song and to dance (another clue to his identity: in a colony, pseudo-human beings who sing in a foreign tongue are all too familiar). Conventionally obedient, they comply; he comes down and dances with them, then pinches one boy. His big sister and then his elders refuse to believe that the old man keeps pinching the same boy, until someone in the village recognizes the children were deceived: 'THAT'S NO OLD MAN, IT'S A KAKA WANTING TO EAT YOU'. Aroused at last, the adults stop the children from going to the forest until the *kaka*, hungry by now, comes into the village. After Friday prayers, they all throw themselves on him and beat him to death.[5] In realistic detail, the young narrator, or her source, uses the *kaka* as a traditional symbol for allegorizing the relations of teacher and pupil, adult and child, *vazaha* (foreigner) and islander. It's the kind of unfunny story children learn from one another.

More vehement criticism comes in an equally unsubtle tale from Grande Comore, recorded from a man in the colonial 1930s. A certain king is so misogynistic that he forbids immigration by women and orders all girl children executed. Disguising as a man, the daughter of a neighboring king challenges him. Three times she avoids discovery;

before a fourth test, her dog sets fire to his village, she swims to her boat, and she shouts back, 'KING, YOU ARE A FOOL. I AM A WOMAN, A WOMAN WHO CAME TO PLAY ON YOUR STUPIDITY'.

In revenge, the king thinks to put her in her place by marrying her, not suspecting the stratagem she shares with other Comoran tricksters. In the wedding bed she puts a doll with a pot of honey as its head; she dons beautiful clothes and hides under the bed. The king slices the dummy, is pleased to see the goo oozing out, and victoriously runs away to his boat, only to hear her shout, 'MY LORD, DON'T REJOICE OVER YOUR BASE EXPLOITS. HAVE A LOOK AT THE BLADE OF YOUR SWORD AND TASTE WHAT IS STICKING ON IT.'

The roles are reversed when his people learn what has happened: they hang this misogynistic tyrant. 'THEN THEY WENT TO ASK THE PRINCESS-CAPTAIN TO COME REIGN OVER THEIR COUNTRY WHICH, THANKS TO THE EXTREMELY INTELLIGENT NEW QUEEN, WHO POSSESSED THE WISDOM OF SOLOMON, BECAME PEACEFUL AND PROSPEROUS.'[6]

Part of her intelligence is her verbal vigor, which may also have distinguished the several queens who ruled Grande Comore. It enables her to hit both men and hierarchy at the same time. A woman's tale, surely.

Men are not always the target. A scathing fable about a lazy wife was told to Gueunier by an old lady, Vavy Kombo Djabu, who probably learned it from a predecessor. This wife is so lazy that her husband must compromise his masculinity by cooking, drawing water, and pounding rice. After ten years of this upside-down version of marriage, he stages a feast, with help from his disapproving sisters. In preparation he teaches them an edifying song: he sings, WIFE, WIFE, GET WATER, and in chorus they must reply, I'M SICK, HUSBAND, I'M SICK. At the feast, the wife listens three times to the call-and-response. At last, she hides her head. At the beginning of the next rainy season, she has changed. She sends him out to clear land for rice, sweeps the house, goes to the river for water, and makes tea. Then she goes out to the bush and works all day, coming back at evening to make dinner. Reformed thenceforward, she does all the housework (except sowing the rice, which requires two people to work together). As her final gesture, she offers her husband that he repudiate her, in conformity with Muslim law, but he refuses, saying she was ill and he has cured her. Her family all confirm this idea and tell her to stay with him. 'AND I LEFT THEM THERE AND CAME TO SIT HERE WITH MY BABY ON MY KNEES,' concludes the narrator.[7] Nothing allegorical about that. Isn't it a social function of art to enforce correct behavior?

An Islamic Master

Islamic priests are not prominent in the tales collected in the 1980s, but in a twice-told tale, the aged Reny Daosy (remembering her sources) blends strong skepticism about Islam with the African theme of men's abuse of authority. The object of her censure is an epitome of hypocrisy: an Islamic master who fucks (*Fondy nikozany*).[8] Knowing that such a man should personify both religious and secular authority, she names him after the main Qur'anic teacher in her village. Her heroine, says Gueunier, 'is intelligent, being capable of exceeding her husband in casuistry, great master though he be. She brings off this feat by sleeping with him, doing only her wifely duty, while he, not recognizing her, commits in the same act the sin of fornication, the gravest possible since he is deflowering a virgin.' In the Comoros, deflowering is as offensive as rape in the West. By winning out over a *sheho* (sheikh), the young woman acts in the guileful spirit of Shakespeare's Helena in *All's Well That Ends Well*, whose innumerable counterparts are assembled in Wendy Doniger's fascinating book *The Bedtrick*. But none of her hundreds of bedtrick stories is a law case like this one.

At the outset Sheikh Said is quoting God. 'HE SAYS YOU MUST NOT COMMIT FORNICATION. YOU MUST NOT DEFLOWER ANYBODY'S DAUGHTER, THAT IS A SIN!' He overhears a woman saying, 'HUH! NOT ME.... SHOW ME A SCHOLAR WITH LEARNING UP TO HEAVEN, HE WON'T TEACH ME A THING'. Such defiance demands an arrogant response from an authoritative male. He goes into a dialogue with the woman's parents, who respond not quite as he expects.

> "MY GOOD WOMAN, AND YOU MY GOOD MAN, I'VE COME TO ASK FOR YOUR DAUGHTER HERE IN MARRIAGE."
>
> "AH, FATHER. ARE *YOU* THE MAN TO MARRY OUR DAUGHTER?"
>
> "WHY DO YOU ASK?"
>
> "WE ARE TOO POOR, WE CAN'T MAKE A PROPER HOUSE FOR THE MARRIAGE, WE CAN'T FIT OUT THE HOUSE FOR THE MARRIAGE, WE CAN'T AFFORD ANY EXPENSE."
>
> HE SAID, "ALL THAT, I CAN TAKE CARE OF IT."
>
> "OH NO, YOU ARE HERE ONLY TO SHAME US."
>
> HE SAID, "ALL THAT, I CAN TAKE CARE OF IT."

A member of the audience questions Reny Daosy about the sheikh's overbearing manner: 'What does that word *kotsombolia* mean?' The narrator replies he's pulling rank: It means if he comes and tells them 'If not to me, you'd never marry her off... I've done the whole thing'. As soon as the marriage is held, the sheikh violates custom but follows folktale tradition: he removes the woman from her parents' domicile and silences her on a little island just offshore, guarded by an old woman. He sends food. After that day he never went there again. (Audience member: 'Whew!')

From the beach the young woman can hear the *shigoma* (dance). One night she sends the old woman to bed, dresses up, walks over the reef to shore, and joins the dance. There she spots her husband wearing religious-ceremonial costume, which accentuates the sin of fornication he is about to commit.

> SHE ARRIVED, DRAPED IN HER VEIL, SMELLING SO SWEET! SHE CAME UP AND WENT BY AND DID LIKE THIS [TOUCHING HER HUSBAND WITH HER VEIL, AN INVITATION]. ("WHO, HER?" "THE YOUNG WOMAN, THE ONE HE'D MARRIED.") SHE DID LIKE THAT, AND WENT BY, AND WENT INSIDE. THE MAN GOT UP, THAT *SHEHO* — , BUT IT WASN'T *SHEHO* SAIDY.

Only at this point, Gueunier notes, 'does the narrator pretend to notice that it's insulting for her to meld together, as she has been doing up to this point, the village sheikh and the character in her story, who is about to commit a dreadful sin. One amusing point is that that honorable sheikh's own son is in the audience.' The man's hypocrisy is inseparable from his lust. He follows her into the shadows, and 'HE DEFLOWERED HER, HE DEFLOWERED SOMEONE ELSE'S DAUGHTER, NOT KNOWING THAT WAS HIS WIFE, THE ONE HE HAD MARRIED JUST SO...' After a second and third night she knows that by masquerading she has made the bedtrick into a rape, brought off a successful deception, and initiated the consummation of her marriage. She announces, 'I won't come back anymore.' Custom obliges him to award a compensatory gift to this seemingly compliant woman.

> "WHAT AM I GOING TO GIVE YOU?" HE TOOK OFF HIS TURBAN TO GIVE IT TO HER. "I DON'T WANT IT". HE TOOK OFF HIS BIG LOINCLOTH, WHICH HE WORE ON HIS LOINS. "I DON'T WANT IT". "THEN WHAT DO YOU WANT?" "I WANT THAT RING YOU HAVE THERE." NOW, THAT RING HAD HIS NAME ON IT. HE TOOK IT OFF AND GAVE IT TO HER.

And she returns to the island, pregnant (to the duenna's horror), and in time gives birth. The duenna goes crying to the boatmen, thus launching the necessary message to the sheikh (whom Reny Daosy now calls the king, targeting masculinity, Islam, and secular authority).

> HE CAME IN. "WHOSE BABY IS THIS?" SHE SAID, "ISN'T IT ME HOLDING HIM, SO THEY CAN SAY I'M HIDING HIM UNDER MY VEILS? LOOK AT HIM. WHOSE BABY IS HE?"....
>
> "AREN'T YOU GOING TO TELL ME WHOSE CHILD THIS IS?"
>
> "WELL," SHE SAID, "TAKE THIS MIRROR. WHEN YOU SEE THE IMAGE OF YOUR OWN BODY, YOU WILL SEE THIS CHILD".
>
> BUT HE WOULDN'T BELIEVE HER. SO, SHE SHOWED HIM HER RING, THE ONE HE'D GIVEN HER. "THIS RING, WASN'T IT ON YOUR FINGER?"
>
> "YES".

At this moment, an audience member says, 'HE WAS CAUGHT?' and the narrator replies, 'CAUGHT.'

The sheikh, saying nothing to acknowledge his disgrace, turns away to his men to give orders and distract himself, or perhaps the audience. The narrator inserts a song (part in Kibushi, part in Shimaore), teaching the children around her to repeat the refrain. Back home, the sheikh drives away his childless first wife, and a meeting ensues.

> SO — WHEN EVERYBODY WAS SEATED, THE WIFE SAID TO HER HUSBAND, "TELL ME, HOW LONG DID YOU THINK YOU WOULD LEAVE ME OUT THERE ON THAT ISLAND WITH THE OLD WOMAN? YOU WANTED TO TEST MY INTELLIGENCE?"... .
>
> "BUT I," SHE SAID, "I DID KNOW YOU WERE MY HUSBAND, AND THAT'S WHY I CAME TO FIND YOU. WHILE YOU — YOU DIDN'T RECOGNIZE ME. SO, YOU REALLY DID COMMIT FORNICATION, SINCE YOU DIDN'T KNOW I WAS YOUR WIFE, AND YOU DEFLOWERED ME. BY DEFLOWERING ME YOU TRULY COMMITTED FORNICATION. YOU COMMITTED ADULTERY. BUT I, I RECOGNIZED YOU. YOU WERE TAKING ME FOR AN IDIOT (MDJINGA). YOU WANTED TO LEAVE ME ALL ALONE OUT THERE. WELL, I WON'T STAY HERE." SHE TURNED AWAY FROM HIM. "I WON'T STAY HERE. I CAME ONLY TO HAVE YOU SEE WHAT YOU DID TO ME. I'M GOING BACK TO MY MOTHER", SHE SAID. AND SHE LEFT.

The sheikh admits to village notables that he's in the wrong, but she is resolute.

> "HE TOOK ME FOR AN IDIOT. BECAUSE HE SEEMS TO BE A SCHOLAR, WHILE I, I SAID, 'HIS KNOWLEDGE CAN GO UP TO THE SKIES, NOBODY WILL BE ABLE TO TOP ME FOR INTELLIGENCE.' AS FOR HIM, IT SEEMS HE WANTED TO KNOW IF I WAS

REALLY INTELLIGENT. BUT I AM MORE INTELLIGENT THAN HE. WHY DID HE COME AND DEFLOWER ME? WHY DID HE COME AND DRILL ME? HE DIDN'T NOTICE THAT IT WAS ME, HIS WIFE!"

HE WAS BEATEN. HE WAS COMPLETELY BEATEN. THE NOTABLES PLEADED WITH THE WIFE SO MUCH THAT THEN SHE WENT TO LIVE WITH HER HUSBAND, AND HE GAVE HER ALL HIS WEALTH, SO THAT SHE WOULD COME BACK AND LIVE WITH HIM. HE GAVE HER HIS STONE HOUSE. HE GAVE HER HIS GOLD, HE GAVE HER EVERYTHING SHE COULD WISH, SO MUCH THAT SHE CAME BACK TO LIVE WITH HIM. BUT SHE DID NOT WANT TO LIVE WITH HIM ALWAYS, BECAUSE HE'D REALLY TAKEN HER FOR AN IDIOT.

IT'S FINISHED.[9]

Is the target of the tale Islamic religion, or men in general? In it Gueunier finds

a kind of women's revenge. The storyteller's visible pleasure as she insists on the husband's shame and confusion of the husband leaves little doubt on this point... At the end of the account, the young woman's only way to show her superiority is to give her husband a legitimate child, although he has intended to prevent that by refusing to cohabit with her. The *maître* is at fault for wanting to challenge the woman's properly feminine privilege of childbearing. In short, a woman's 'intelligence' and virtue are first shown by her accomplishing this duty, if necessary against her own husband. Beyond the piquant aspect of the casuistic controversy lies a quite traditional moral, which even the most misogynistic of the learned would have difficulty disputing.[10]

The hearer is left free to choose how much this hypocrite represents Islamic religion or the male sex. Women's power shines out in the wife's passionate dialogue.

The Orphan Girl and Her Sisters

In a more positive vein is Sophie Blanchy's revelatory discovery: several women storytellers narrate pieces in which a young orphan girl is mistreated by another female character to the point of real or symbolic death, then is recognized and restored to her proper place through the intervention of her dead mother, or both parents, in supernatural form.[11] The plot pattern of this group can be illustrated from one prosaic version.

THERE WAS A GIRL WHO HAD NO MOTHER.

HER FATHER HAD TAKEN HER TO HER STEPMOTHER'S, WHO DIDN'T LOVE HER... DIDN'T GIVE HER THE SAME THINGS AS HER CHILDREN. SHE DIDN'T DRESS HER HAIR, SHE DIDN'T TAKE HER TO THE RIVER. THE CHILD GOT VERY THIN... ONE DAY THE CHILD WENT TO HER STEPMOTHER TO GIVE HER A PIECE OF POTTERY AND THE STEPMOTHER TOLD HER TO KILL HER MOTHER. "YOU ARE GOING TO WEEP AND SHE'S GOING TO ASK YOU WHY. SO, TELL HER THAT YOU WANT TO BATHE, BUT NOT IN THE RIVER WATER, NOT IN RAINWATER, BUT IN WATER FROM THE WELL." THE GIRL WAS TOO YOUNG TO KNOW WHAT SHE WAS GOING TO DO.

She endures a period of isolation outside society, a period of liminality or marginality. Finally, she achieves restoration and acceptance into the social world through the intervention of her dead mother.

ONE DAY THE CHILD SAW HER DEAD MOTHER. SHE INVITED HER TO GO TO HER TOMB TO GET *TCHIIRIS* [A KIND OF WATERMELON]. SHE FOUND THEM ON HER MOTHER'S TOMB, NEAR THE WAY FROM THE QUR'AN SCHOOL. SHE ATE SOME AND WENT BACK TO HER STEPMOTHER'S. EVERY DAY SHE WENT TO EAT AT HER MOTHER'S TOMB. THE GIRL BEGAN TO GAIN WEIGHT AND LOOK WELL. THE STEPMOTHER WANTED TO KNOW WHERE SHE WAS GETTING HER FOOD. SHE HAD HER CHILDREN FOLLOW HER. THE GIRL HID TO GO EAT.

Only in a folktale can a woman gain weight by eating watermelon. The narrator goes on.

THE CHILDREN FOUND OUT WHERE SHE WAS GOING. JUST WHEN SHE WAS EATING, HER PSEUDO SISTERS CAME AND ATE WITH HER. THEY ATE TOO MUCH AND COULDN'T CARRY WHOLE FRUITS BACK TO THEIR MOTHER. WHEN THEY GOT BACK, THEY TOLD THEIR MOTHER THAT THEY'D FOUND OUT THEIR SISTER'S SECRET, THEY GAVE THE GIRL'S STEPMOTHER A TASTE OF THE *TCHIIRI*. THE REAL, DEAD MOTHER WAS ANGRY. THE PLANT FADED, ONLY LITTLE FRUITS WERE LEFT. THE GIRL GOT MISERABLE AGAIN.

ANOTHER DAY SHE SAW HER MOTHER IN A DREAM. SHE TOLD HER THAT THERE WAS A BLACK AND WHITE COW IN HER FATHER'S HERD, WHICH WAS HERS. SHE TOLD HER SHE HAD TO SING, "PAPA'S AND MAMA'S COW, OPEN A WAY!" SO, THE COW WOULD OPEN HER MOUTH, SHE WOULD GO INSIDE, SHE WOULD BE HAPPY.

THE NEXT DAY HER FATHER TOOK HER TO HIS HERD. SHE SAW THE COW, SHE SANG. THE COW OPENED ITS MOUTH AND SHE WENT INSIDE. INSIDE THE COW'S STOMACH SHE FOUND WOMEN WHO GAVE HER FOOD, DRESSED HER HAIR AND GAVE HER CLEAN CLOTHES. THEN SHE CAME OUT.

THE STEPMOTHER ASKED HER WHAT HAPPENED, AND SHE SAID SHE'D GIVEN ALMS AND A FRIEND HELPED HER. THE GIRLS AGAIN WERE SENT TO SPY ON HER. THEY FOLLOWED HER AND SAW HER GO TOWARDS A COW. SO, ONE GIRL WENT UP TO THE COW AND SANG, BUT THE COW REFUSED TO OPEN HER MOUTH. THE

ORPHAN TOLD HER HOSTESS TO GIVE THE GIRLS FOOD. SO, THE WOMEN GAVE THE GIRLS A FEW CRUMBS, AND ONE OF THEM LICKED HER HAND SO MUCH IT MADE A WOUND. WHEN THE WOMEN SAW THE HOLE, THEY STOPPED IT WITH GOLD.

AT THE HOUSE, THE GIRL SHOWED HER HAND AND ACCUSED THE ORPHAN. THE [STEP]MOTHER WANTED TO KILL THE COW. SHE WENT AND FOUND A *FUNDI* [HEALER] AND ASKED HIM TO MAKE HER ILL AND SAY A COW HAD TO BE KILLED AS A SACRIFICE. SHE TOOK TO HER BED AND PRETENDED TO BE ILL. THE FATHER SAID TO GO SEE THE *FUNDI*; HE SAID WHAT HE WAS SUPPOSED TO SAY TO THE FATHER.

WHEN THE GIRL FOUND THAT OUT, SHE TOLD HER FATHER HE MUST NOT KILL THE COW. THE FATHER OBEYED THE STEPMOTHER. THE COW WAS KILLED. THE GIRL ASKED THE MEN NOT TO THROW AWAY THE COW'S BONES, BUT TO MAKE A PILE OF THEM. WHILE EVERYBODY WAS EATING, SHE THREW THEM INTO THE SEA.

A FEW DAYS LATER, THE BONES TRANSFORMED INTO JEWELS AND TURNED INTO A GOLDEN TREE. A FISHERMAN TRIED TO PICK THEM, BUT EVERY TIME HE PUT THEM IN HIS *PIROG*, THE JEWELS MELTED AWAY. THE FISHERMAN WENT AND TOLD THAT TO THE VILLAGE KING. THE KING WENT WITH HIM BUT HAD NO BETTER RESULTS. SO, HE ASKED THE VILLAGE WHO COULD PICK THEM. THE GIRL WANTED TO GO, BUT THE STEPMOTHER FORBADE HER. EVERYBODY TRIED, THEN THE GIRL WENT AND BROUGHT BACK THE TREE. THE KING MARRIED HER. THE STEPMOTHER'S DAUGHTERS BECAME HER SERVANTS.[12]

Being married, the girl eradicates her orphan status and vanishes into a kind of identity with her mother.

This plot encapsulates the ideology of women's tales in Mayotte. Marriage relations, which are negotiated by father and groom, are unstable, as we know from the *fille*. The mother-daughter relation is permanent and enduring: you inherit her house, she survives in the spirit world. Blanchy found that the initial fictional situation — the mother dying, the father remarrying, the stepmother's villainy — corresponded to real-life internal tensions in 1980s Mayotte. Thus, a narrator, consciously or unconsciously, invites her hearer to apply the tale broadly. Her relation to her mother is her weapon against change, which was impending then in real life. Try, for instance, to practice Islamic marriage under French law. The recurrent plot answers out of tradition: your mother, and everything she represents, will aid you. Thus, the plot pattern Blanchy discovered, preaching a woman's reliance on matrilineality, is as potent as the message about interdependence in the making-and-breaking of friendship pattern, or the *djinn* husband symbolizing the oppressor in the *fille* tale.

Naturally it undergoes ingenious variations by the best performers. The version quoted above is told in a bald, unornamented, anti-performed style, which doubtless resulted from the pupil-teacher interview situation. Blanchy's women are more engaging, being ready to modernize a traditional tale, The climactic moment in many of the pieces is an impassioned speech in which the heroine reclaims her place by giving an account of herself.

Fig. 12 Zebu. Photo by Christophe Laborderie, CC BY 2.0, Wikimedia Commons, https://upload. wikimedia.org/wikipedia/commons/8/8e/ Z%C3%A9bu-Mayotte.jpg

Her Parents' Cow

Fatima Maolida dictated her version, with her children nearby, to Sophie Blanchy in la Réunion in July 1984. She begins it at Qur'an school. The orphan is befriended by another girl, whose mother first feeds and takes care of her, then proposes that the widowed father marry her. He sees the danger, labeling this stepmother-to-be as a *mama kambo,* an artificial mother, but reluctantly he agrees. The sign of the stepmother's predictable hate is that after her own daughter has eaten her fill, SHE FED HER HUSBAND'S DAUGHTER *PANGU,* the hardened, tasteless rice that sticks to the edge of the pot. As the girl loses weight on these leftovers day after day, her real, dead mother comes to her in a dream. She directs her to go find the white-and-black mother cow in her father's herd, and teaches her the charm to say:

PAPA'S AND MAMA'S COW,
  OPEN, OPEN MY WAY IN!
PAPA AND MAMA'S COW,
  OPEN, OPEN MY WAY IN!

That works: the cow opens its mouth, in she goes, and inside the cow she finds her real mother, who feeds her, dresses her hair, and gives her jewelry and fine clothes. Back at home, the stepmother tears them off her, accusing her of theft. The quarrel repeats next day, but she is warned by her mother that if she doesn't allow the jewels and clothes to be torn off, her father will die. So, the stepmother returns her to wearing rags, and sends her own daughter to follow the girl. Stepsister overhears the charm, repeats it, and now both girls enter the cow. The narrator gives this stepsister more realistic, envy-filled dialogue: 'HEY, YOU KNOW THIS PLACE, YOU NEVER BROUGHT ME HERE, ALL THESE BEAUTIFUL THINGS, YOU DIDN'T TAKE ME TO YOUR MUM', claiming credit for a liberality she has never manifested.

When the stepmother hears this news, she is ready to lie and kill. Disregarding the bad luck that will come from killing the first cow of a herd, she finds an ally, an evil old-lady donor, who tells her to sham illness and instruct the healers that she will get well only if that cow is killed. The mother-in-the-cow, source of truth, tells her daughter to accept that, to eat only a tiny bit of the meat, and (with her father) to save the bones in a sack and throw them into the sea. 'YOU WON'T DIE', she says. Once the cow is killed and the bones have been thrown out, the stepmother gets well at the mere sight of all that meat, but as instructed, the girl refuses it.

After blending these naturalistic details of diet into the traditional opposition of good and bad mothers, Fatima (or her source) introduces an Islamic symbol of hope, which is the real mother's last incarnation and her own most startling innovation.

THEY WERE IN BED WHEN THEY SAW SOMETHING BRIGHT, A STRONG LIGHT ON THE WHOLE VILLAGE. EVERYBODY GOT UP TO SEE WHAT IT WAS. THE BONES HAD TRANSFORMED INTO A LUMINOUS MINARET RISING OUT OF THE WATER.

The king sets a suitor task, another element from tradition: whoever retrieves the minaret will have his daughter in marriage. All attempts are unsuccessful: always it recedes out of reach.

Now the king's cock, playing messenger and moving the plot ahead, reveals where to find the girl, as the one who can accomplish the task. Six times his servants go to the stepmother's house and are refused. They have to threaten her before the girl is brought out, taken to the king's house, washed, dressed, and made beautiful. Six times she calls to her transformed mother, 'Papa and mama's minaret, come ashore, come!' At last, it does, and all is quickly resolved. The girl is recognized, the king marries her, his first wife and the stepsister are made servants, and the girl's father becomes a king's minister. The dead mother has performed her principal function, to reinsert her daughter into the real world.

You may feel the plot should end there. Why doesn't Fatima Maolida stop? Evidently she has decided, or has learned from another storyteller, that there has to be a second part, into which she will bring more realistic details and justify inventing that otherworldly minaret. As transition she uses the punishment of the stepsister. Dressing the newlywed's hair (in her servant role), this unpleasant person violates a *miko* (taboo) not known before: she must not use *munyongo* (a sort of Q-tip for the hair).[13] She does that. Instantly the heroine transforms into a bird and goes to join her mother, now also in bird form. Listeners who remember false-bride stories can expect that having returned to a marginal state, the heroine will call for recognition in song. She sings to a new character, the king's gardener Makame, to ask for food.

She told him her name was Bibi. She flew around him and perched for a minute.

> MAKAME, MAKAME?
> GIVE ME SOME NUTMEG TO EAT!
> MAKAME SAID,
> EAT, BIBI, EAT!
> [SHE] GIVE ME SOME *HALUA* TO EAT!
> [HE] EAT, BIBI, EAT!
> [SHE] YOUR MASTER, WHERE'S HE GONE?
> [HE] GONE TO THE MOSQUE.
> [SHE] WHAT WILL HE DO AT THE MOSQUE?
> [HE] PRAY AND STUDY.
> [SHE] WHEN HE COMES BACK, GREET HIM FOR ME!
> SHE FLEW AWAY.

Now strictly, *halua* is that confection of crushed sesame seeds and honey, which Americans and Europeans can buy online, and which Mayotte inherited from long-ago Persians. But in the king's folktale orchard, it somehow grows among other sweet fruits. She knows the gardener will carry the message, and will allow her to live on the fruits in the meantime. Of course she will sing again.

But the king has returned home heavy-hearted; the minaret and even his multi-story house have disappeared. He hears his wife's story from Makame's recounting it. The two try to catch her by spreading birdlime on the branches, but she eludes capture as smoothly as the minaret did. Having learned from her bird mother that her father will die otherwise, she allows herself to be stuck, captured, and caged. The king, stroking her (the same motion as when her hair was being dressed, with the opposite effect), accidentally undoes the taboo, and she is retransformed. The minaret comes back, so does the king's house. Given a place to live, they have what no one will remember is their second *grand mariage*. The stepmother's punishment is to be thrown into a sack on the ground, where the heroine will trample her every day.[14]

Fatima Maolida, or her source, blends traditions with fidelity to the message about the mother-daughter connection. From Malagasy tradition Fatima draws characters (heroine, donor, king, stepmother), magic objects (the *munyongo* and the minaret), and incidents (a dead mother's helpful return, a person enclosed in an animal, bones that transform). With these elements she combines real-life details like nutmeg, coffee, *halua*, dates, and the *munyongo*. Her characters — the gardener, the evil donor woman, and the caustic stepsister — are original touches, but no one will miss the importance of the mother-daughter connection.[15] Only that second marriage, resulting from the two-part form she is inventing or repeating, presents a problem to the reader. It looks like a mistake. Narrators do sometimes make mistakes; they may get help from listeners, as Gueunier noticed several times. We can forgive that oddity from a narrator who is inventive enough, or recalls tradition well enough, to produce both a luminous minaret and an orchard where a woman can live on *halua* and nutmeg. Her blend is striking.

Performativity in Performances: Fatima Maolida and Anfiati Sufu

The principle of these women's narrating places them firmly in tradition. They confront the Mayotte they live in with plots and characters inherited from Africa and Madagascar. They enact, in their artistic communication, a dialectic between (old) tradition and (new) situation that distinguishes all folklore. For the anthropological folklorist Dell Hymes, that dialectic is the matrix for 'creativity in the senses of adaptation, re-creation, and the mark, I think, of true creativity within a tradition, innovation at need'.[16] Creativity like that minaret? Visualize Fatima Maolida in performance. The most subjective aspect of her performing is a kind of confession. Her heroine's narrating about herself is a narration about Fatima.

Then (after taking a breath) apply the abstract terms of a philosopher like Judith Butler, writing about confession. 'A certain performative production of the subject within established public conventions is required of the confessing subject and constitutes the aim of confession itself.'[17] Public convention makes Fatima Maolida a storyteller and gives her occasions to perform. She is an instance of Butler's performative production. As much as Emily Brontë or Zora Neale Hurston narrating in a novel, the Mahorais storyteller performatively produces herself as Woman. Her 'narrative capacity constitutes a precondition for giving an account of oneself and assuming responsibility for one's actions through that means'.[18] For a particular audience, she can select this story, which dramatizes the contradictions in male-dominated ideology and shows them to be unresolvable. That is the truth she tells; by narrating, she also tells the truth about herself.

Blanchy's outstanding performer, Anfiati Sufu, is a master of this technique. She is at her expansive best in one mother-daughter tale, which looks to be as much a Mayotte creation as Fatima's tale.

Grandmother Shark

Its character, plot, and texture are totally traditional; a cruel stepmother drives the heroine's persecution, and the familiar plot includes her adoption into a foster family, her quasi-death and resuscitation, and her marriage.

Anfiati Sufu obviously knows the standard repertoire of her sources, but her piece does not recapitulate any text previously recorded. Like many of her sisters-in-narrating, she keeps her tale close to home, emphasizing the sense of place by identifying herself explicitly as a mother.

As the tale begins, Shura is her father's only daughter, a bit spoiled. After she loses her mother and her father remarries, he rejects the protests of other family members and takes his daughter to his new wife's house, where he lives (remember, it's women who own the houses). There she undergoes malnourishment from her stepmother, who gives all the food to her own children. God keeps Shura alive until the stepmother murderously throws her into the water. Instead of drowning, she is taken up on the back of a foster mother. Grandmother Shark is several kinds of role model: donor, female ally, queen of the sharks, and reincarnation of her dead mother. At the bottom of the sea, she gives all her attention to restoring Shura to her proper station and helping her achieve recognition.

Fig. 13 Under water. Photo by VillageHero, CC BY-SA 2.0, Wikimedia Commons, https://upload. wikimedia.org/wikipedia/commons/7/76/ Snorkeling_at_Ngouja_Beach_1_%28Mayo tte%29_%2831371866746%29.jpg

Every night, Grandmother Shark takes her to the shore, where she sings her song.

> MISTRESS SHARK
> YOU HAVE NOT MISTREATED SHURA
> MISTRESS SHARK
> YOU HAVE NOT MISTREATED SHURA
> SHURA HAS NO FATHER, NO
> SHURA HAS NO FATHER, NO
> MAMA, WHERE DID SHURA GO?

> SHE WENT INTO THE WATER
> DIDN'T ASK FOR ANYTHING, ANYTHING!

Seeing her beauty, a bystander wonders if that's the drowned girl, but says nothing until he can confirm his hunch the next day by repeating her song to the king. At first, he is not believed, but when 'they' decide to catch her, Grandmother Shark suggests Shura allow herself to be caught. On shore, her radiance causes everybody to faint as she sings her song. She brings them all back to life by touching them with her garment (another female power). After the king too faints and is resuscitated, he takes her to a chamber high in his house, as a sign of her now-high rank. Having sung her song three times, she switches channels to claim recognition.

> "I WAS AN ONLY DAUGHTER" ('CAUSE THE SHARK TOLD HER WHO HER MOTHER AND FATHER WERE), "MY REAL MOTHER DIED, BUT I DON'T REMEMBER HER. MY FATHER WENT AND MARRIED ANOTHER WOMAN. THAT WOMAN CAUSED ME MUCH PAIN, AND ONE DAY SHE TOOK ME TO THE SEA WITH HER CHILDREN, SHE THREW ME INTO THE WATER, AND AS I FELL IN I FOUND SOMEONE WHO CAUGHT ME."
> "BUT WHO CAUGHT YOU?"
> "SOMEONE CALLED *PAPA DADI*, GRANDMOTHER SHARK, SHE BROUGHT ME UP TILL I WAS GROWN UP; THEN EVERY DAY AT *MAHARIBI* TIME [PRAYERS AT DUSK] SHE LED ME SAYING, 'I WANT YOU TO KNOW YOUR MOTHER AND FATHER, YOUR MOTHER IS NO MORE BUT YOU WILL KNOW YOUR FATHER.' SO THE DAY BEFORE YESTERDAY, WHEN SHE BROUGHT ME, I SAW TWO PEOPLE ON THE SHORE. SO WE WENT HOME AND TODAY MY MOTHER GRANDMOTHER SHARK SENT ME WITH ALL MY THINGS."
> "AND YOUR MOTHER, WHO WAS SHE?"
> "SHE WAS NAMED SOANDSO."
> "YOUR FATHER?"
> "MY FATHER WAS CALLED SOANDSO, AND HE IS STILL ALIVE."

One scrawny man matches that description; by telling his story, he too gains recognition.

> 'I and my wife had a daughter.' (The father had got very thin, he was nothing, he thought only of his daughter.) 'My wife died and left me with my daughter, then I married another woman, I took my child to her house. One day my wife took my daughter, supposedly to catch winkles, she took her, and until today I have never seen my child'.

When she appears, more visible than ever, she has to revive the fainting bystanders. Father and daughter are reunited, the stepmother and her children are decapitated, and Shura becomes the king's sole wife.

To make her final point, Anfiati Sufu asserts the primacy of the mother-daughter relationship over this new marriage. Shura asks only one thing of her royal husband. 'WHEN YOUR SERVANTS MAKE FOOD FOR ME, I ASK YOU TO HAVE THEM TAKE SOME OF IT AND GIVE IT TO MY MOTHER.' Knowing she is an orphan, the king asks, 'WHERE IS SHE?' 'OUT THERE, IN THE SEA.' Her mother, through the shark, has controlled every move in her life. Dependent as she must be on her new husband, she is even more so on that powerful mother-surrogate. Her embedded story tells the truth: to learn to be a woman, one must rehearse one's gender.[19] Her account of herself in song and narrative is the lesson for women in Mayotte, which Anfiati Sufu enacts through performing assertively: when a silenced woman speaks, everything changes. Shura, starting from a position of equilibrium or safety, is threatened with danger and must extricate herself. But unlike the silent wife in any *fille difficile* tale, who is similarly threatened, Shura speaks up. So does her narrator. The particularly feminine skill Shura exercises is narrating. As in certain Indian tales, 'the whole tale is the tale of her acquiring her story, making a person of her, making a silent person a speaking woman.'[20]

To perform such a loving account of persecution and rescue, to show self-revelation deferred and delayed yet ultimately successful and convincing, is to offer women the proof and manifestation of ideological truth. Telling such a story 'is a tacit project to renew one's cultural history in one's own terms.'[21] Or maybe, being entirely cast in words, it's not tacit. Maybe it invites women and men in the audience to dwell safely in an alternative reality, from which they can look at the constructed ideology of sex and gender around them. When Anfiati Sufu tells Shura's story to her audience, she is enacting women's power, representing herself and other women, and critiquing the gender system implied in these tales. What about intention? Does the message of the tale mean that this narrator, or any female narrator, must have an ideological slant? Does she deliberately choose this kind of story to send that message? In chapter 1, the choice of place legends seemed to result from the circumstance of being recorded. Perhaps Anfiati Sufu discerned Sophie Blanchy's interest in the subordination of women and performed accordingly. However that might be, the assertiveness of Shura and her other heroines, her vivid use of dialogue, and her loving attention to her audience all mark her artistry.

In a contrasting version, by the way, a young man of Mronabeja has more trouble with this plot, but he does give the heroine more ruinous words once she is recognized. After she forces the king to acknowledge that her baby is his — she shows him his own ring — he breaks down and offers to be stabbed, and she comes back with sarcasm: 'YOU TOOK ME FROM MY MOTHER'S AND FATHER'S SIDE TO GO AND ABANDON ME FAR AWAY ON AN ISLAND, SO TODAY IT'S FOR YOU TO KILL ME, SINCE YOU SAY YOU ARE THE KING, THAT YOU HAVE KNOWLEDGE, BUT I'M THE STUPID ONE, I'M A POOR MAN'S DAUGHTER.' He submits to her superior verbal power, but to restore the normal power relation, she remonstrates submissively and both say, 'SLAY ME!' But not wanting to kill off this young couple, the narrator hauls in an irrelevant punishment to finish his tale. 'THE KING WENT TO FIND HIS FIRST WIFE, TOOK HER AND PUT THE SWORD THROUGH HER, AND I LEFT THEM THERE AND CAME HERE. THAT'S ALL.'[22] That looks like a narrator's mistake, but the piece remains a woman's story.

Furukombe as Boeing

Another great performance by Anfiati Sufu is her version of the *fille* tale, the best told of all the Mayotte versions collected. To begin with, she is especially skilled with faithfully handling and elaborating folktale conventions, for instance in her quadruple opening formula and the conventional fixed phrases.

HALE HALELE	OLD-TIME STORY
VWUKA MUTRU NAKA MUTRU	THERE WAS A MAN AMONG MEN
VWUKA TADJIRI	THERE WAS A RICH MAN
VWUKA MASIKINI	THERE WAS A POOR MAN
VWUKA WAZIRI	THERE WAS A MINISTER
VWUKA MFALUME	THERE WAS A KING
ATA BARANI YA HADITHI, NDRANI!	TO THE LAND OF STORIES, INTO IT!
NDRANI, NDRANI!	INTO IT, INTO IT!
HAY, DZAHO, DZAHO!	YES, IN YOU, IN YOU!

WELL, THERE WAS A FATHER AND MOTHER — KINGS — THEY HAD SEVEN CHILDREN. THE SEVEN WERE GIRLS.

Six of the seven girls are quickly married off. Hadidja refuses all offers, saying, 'I know my husband will come'. She spies her husband-to-be arriving in his boat. 'He had to be an Arab, so shining, bi dzho bi dzho bi!' But of course 'Na lile djini', he was a *djinn*, and quickly the marriage is arranged. When Mari, her youngest sister, offers to accompany her, Hadidja's jealousy erupts: 'You want to come and spoil my marriage!' Instantly Anfiati Sufu speaks an aside (a device hardly any other Mayotte storyteller uses, but not a spoiler if you've heard the tale before): 'But it was Mari who would save Hadidja.' Of all Mahorais narrators of this piece, only Anfiati Sufu shows the cannibal digging a hole, dumping into it the human food he is offered, and gobbling up his preferred food of worms, snakes and snails, saying 'Yum' in Shimaore: 'Kowa ini yangu, ah, mm, nyoha ini yangu, These snails for me, ah, mmm, these snakes for me'. She also emphasizes how fast he resumes his disguise: 'Ah, sister-in-law, come and take back the plate, I'm finished eating'. This fast change enables Mari to spy his horn, teeth, eyes, and tail coming out. So, in another special touch, before they have even left the parents' house, Mari has recognized his real nature.

This *djinn* is remarkably human-seeming and verbal, well disguised. He explains to Mari the charm she will have to speak, to call his attention at lunchtime. The more he talks, the more his hunger transpires as avarice (he must be a portrait of one of the neighbors). If all husbands in Mayotte are *djinn*s, as many *fille* tales seem to say, their cannibalism symbolizes a husband's demand for the *shungu*, the meal or other celebration he must give to his relatives in celebration of marriage. This one even admits it in an aside: 'With the shungu I'm going to give them they won't complain about me.' On the long trip to his place, they pass through the village he has devoured. He explains all the empty houses in modern terms: he is the landlord and he made the tenants all leave. (In other versions we hear about but do not see his previous depredations.) Hadidja, searching in the refrigerators and freezers of these 1970s houses, finds nothing but the meat he is reserving for himself and the other *djinn*s. He boastfully shows her his herds of goats, sheep, beef cattle, ducks, and pigeons, and his plentiful vegetable gardens, including tomatoes. 'All this is yours! You get to decide what you want and don't want to eat'. 'All this' is more than we are shown by other narrators.

Eating and food, a big item for a cannibal *djinn*, reaches its peak after the naming-of-parts scene. In details only Anfiati Sufu or her sources give us, the wife must find her terrified way to the donor lady and tell her story. The old lady gives an account of herself, explaining the custom to the innocent:

> "MY GIRL, HE IS GOING TO GATHER HIS RELATIVES, BECAUSE HE OWES THEM A *SHUNGU*. HE HAS EATEN OTHERS' *SHUNGU* AND HAS NOT GIVEN BACK. HE CAME INTO THIS VILLAGE AND ATE ALL THE PEOPLE; I AM THE ONLY ONE WHO ESCAPED. I TOOK COVER IN THIS CAVE, AND HIM — EVERY MORNING HE COMES TO EAT ME, AND HE SHITS ME AT NOONTIME, AND IN THE AFTERNOON HE COMES BACK TO EAT ME AND AT EVENING HE SHITS ME!"

Is that what marriage feels like? No other donor in a *fille* tale takes part in the cannibal's alimentary cycle. This character, being past childbearing age and living outside society with magic powers, is still under male control.

This obliging lady, with Hadidja's help, deposits magic betel spittle in all corners of the house and calls the sparrowhawk to fly the girls home, but then rejects its call, as she does with all the other birds except the gigantic Furukombe.[23] (Anfiati Sufu need not describe a legendary bird her audience will recognize.) He must expect to be asked, 'ISN'T THAT MY WIFE YOU ARE CARRYING?' Only Furukombe gives the right answer, in a song that will be sung at least three times. He agrees to carry seven gourds of ground coconut, both girls, and all their possessions. 'HE GATHERED AND CARRIED, GATHERED AND CARRIED. THEY SAY BOEINGS GO FAST — JUST LIKE THAT!'

Special touches continue: for instance, he says his prayers — even a legendary bird can be a good Muslim — and takes off with his load. On the way, he meets the boats of pursuing, challenging *djinns*. Each time, the narrator names the island; each time he answers the *djinns* correctly and drops the gourds of coconut. Suddenly at their destination, bushes magically expand to block the *djinns'* passage, but they make their way to the house, expecting to find Hadidja and Mari. The answers from the betel spittle keep them outside until the husband arrives, says the charm, and finds the house emptied. Fearing to be eaten by his gang, he digs a hole and hides. Only his huge tooth sticks out. An infant *djinn* finds the tooth and says 'MAMA, TOY!', but she shuts him up. The *djinns* find their brother in the hole and throw him into the fire, but before being cooked and devoured, he has time to say, 'DON'T BREAK MY BONES!'

He won't completely die. They eat him up, leaving the bones; they dance around and sing their happiness at having eaten their brother; they get back into their dhows and leave. At every point Anfiati Sufu enlivens the conventions and keeps her audience engaged. Her version of an international tale type responds to her specific situation of performance and life. Her capacity of responding to the request to perform is the measure of both her traditionality and her innovativeness.[24]

A Laughing Palm and a Speaking Leaf

In the performance that most clearly reveals Anfiati Sufu's mastery, evil sisters accuse a king's wife of giving birth to a dog, then her children are banished, rescued, and after having adventures are finally restored. Characters and relationships are quite realistic, and touches by Anfiati Sufu bring the tale right into the village. Two of her leading characters are the *areca* palm and betel leaf, chewables the listeners know and taste. In the tale world of Mayotte, magic objects are not very fanciful.[25]

Fig. 14 Betel leaf. Photo by Wajira, CC BY-SA 4.0, Wikimedia Commons, https://upload.wikimedia.org/wikipedia/commons/2/27/Betel_leaf_%28In_ Sinhalese_-_Bulath_Kola%29.jpg

Anfiati Sufu asserts her connection to the listeners with a classic opening formula, a fixed phrase to which her audience must give an equally fixed response.

HALE HALELE [tale from old times]

The audience responds with the untranslatable 'GOMBE!'

THERE WAS A MAN AMONG MEN.
    WAKA [YES]!
    THERE WAS A MAN AND A WOMAN. YES. AND A CHILD, LIKE MY LITTLE MARIDJA HERE.

Maridja and her other two daughters are present; later she will link one of them to one of the lost babies; soon she will mention the mosque and the rest of the town. Anfiati Sufu is completely at ease with making each performance of a folktale, especially in a village community like Mtsapere, a tissue of references to things known to the audience. They probably know the folk etymology that derives the name of the village from the realistic legend about Musa, who was seeking a resting-place in Mayotte after being driven out of Madagascar. One of his two companions noticed his unadorned hand and uttered the phrase *Musa a latsa y péré*, Musa lost his ring. The loss nearly came to blows, but the phrase got shortened into a place name.[26] Details like naming the men make the legend believable, as do the details Anfiati Sufu supplies, things already known to an audience in Mtsapere: that Mbalamanga is the nobles' quarter of their town, around the grand mosque, and that Kavani is the poor folks' quarter, lying out at the other end of town. Between those quarters there is no contact.[27]

IN THAT VILLAGE THERE WAS A KING, WHO LIVED... LIKE, LET'S SAY IN MBALAMANGA, AND HER GRANDMOTHER WAS IN KAVANI. DO THE PEOPLE THERE EVEN KNOW THERE ARE PEOPLE HERE? AND THE ONES HERE, DO THEY KNOW THERE ARE PEOPLE OVER THERE?

Having established physical separation as the sign of rank, she can begin her story.

The heroine is being raised by grandparents, i. e. shamed without parents, and growing up ill, with sores or boils, but she is no ninny. What can she do besides wish for a husband? Speak up. She sets a mat out on the veranda, where by speaking to the king, she challenges their obvious class difference.

ONE DAY THE GIRL WAS LYING THERE ON HER MAT STRETCHED OUT ON THE
VERANDA, SHE SAW ONE OF "THEM" GOING BY, SHE HAD A CRAZY IDEA. SHE
TURNED AND CALLED OUT, "KING! KING!" HE TURNED AROUND. "WHY DON'T
YOU COME CURE MY SICKNESS, AND WHEN I'M CURED, YOU'LL MARRY ME, AND
I'LL GIVE YOU SEVEN CHILDREN — SIX BOYS AND THE SEVENTH ONE A GIRL".

Knowing the magic healing power of kings, the young woman calls him
as he passes by three more times. At first, he disregards her, keeping
her in her place; the second time, either compassionate or charmed, he
sends her healing milk that cures most of her sores. After she calls him
again (the call is repeated like the songs in other tales), he goes home to
fetch clothes for all three of the little family. NOW SHE HAD CLOTHES AND
FOOD, NO MORE PROBLEMS! SHE COULD SLEEP SOUNDLY. NOT LIKE ME! Uneasy
lies the head of the village storyteller, it seems. Finally, the proud king,
after three times disregarding this insistent woman's call, comes around:
he makes a formal proposal to her grandmother, whose poverty Anfiati
Sufu emphasizes by her living in a *banga* (hut) instead of a real house.
WHAT WERE THE GRANDPARENTS GOING TO SAY? THE GIRL HAD NOTHING,
THAT'S HOW THINGS GO WITH A KING. The narrator is quick to remind us, in
her asides, of her heroine's function in a king's eyes (and in an African
fairytale plot).

THAT KING HAD ONE WIFE ALREADY. SHE WAS CHILDLESS. (SEE, THAT'S WHERE
THE GIRL CAME IN, FOR A HAPPY ENDING.) CHILDLESS!

Yet that barren wife does give birth to a boy, at the same time that the
young wife bears the six boys and a girl she promised. This defeat goads
the first wife, aided by an old henchwoman, into throwing away the
children and putting stones in their place. To denote the degradation of
this recurrent character, folklorists say she is 'calumniated', a term you
have to love in order not to forget it. This calumniated wife, accused of
giving birth to stones, says not a word in protest, but is blindfolded and
never sees her children. Anfiati Sufu murmurs an aside: 'HOW COULD SHE
GIVE BIRTH TO A HUMAN CHILD AND NOT KNOW IT?' Her silence foreshadows
the verbal skill she will demonstrate later.

Here enters another *koko* (grandmother) figure, parallel to
Grandmother Shark, who will rescue and foster the children. The
stunning reduplications in Anfiati Sufu's sentence narrating the
rescue are better heard than translated. Try pronouncing the words:

AWARENGELEDZA, AWAHEDZA, AHISA, ARANDRUA-RANDRUA-RANDRUA MWANA

WA MASAMBI MACAMBA WAHE VALE, AWAVAMBIA-VAMBIA-VAMBIA AWALADZA. She cut the cord, she took care of them, washed them, then cut her loincloth up into pieces, wrapped each one, laid them down. Meanwhile the king, believing the first wife's calumny about the stones, resumes his earlier behavior: instead of staying with his young wife, he sends her rice.

Next Anfiati Sufu follows the usual plot of Golden Children tales. The children must be sent on a seemingly impossible quest by the henchwoman.

> Well, day after day, the old woman, the one from the birth, was going somewhere and stopped by the grandmother's house, saw that fine little girl, her eyes widened: just like the king! "Whose house is this?"
> "My mother's."
> "Your mother's?" She said yes. "So do you have any brothers?"
> "Yes, I have."
> "How many?"
> "Six," she said, "I'm the seventh."
> "And do your brothers love you?" The girl said yes.
> "They don't love you. If they loved you, they would go get you lion's milk." [That woman knew that] If the thing became known, she would lose her head. Don't lions eat people?

Against grandmother's protests, the girl convinces her brothers to go on the quest, with a big sugared *muhare* (pancake) to appease the *djinn* children they will meet. *Djinn*s love sweets. A bit of modernization shows when the boys meet up with *djinn* children: they are not a bit surprised at having to bribe them by sharing their pancake. The price is that the *djinn*s find lion's milk for them. 'OK, give it to us,' the *djinn* children say. 'The lion is our mother!' The quest has been successful.

For the boys' second adventure, Anfiati Sufu brings back the henchwoman, to repeat some Madagascar-style dialogue.

> "Where is your mother?"
>> "She went out to the country."
> "And your father?"
>> "Went to the country."
> "And your brothers?"
>> "Went to the country."
> "Do your brothers love you?"
>> "Sure they do, they went and got me lion's milk."

"WELL! BUT THAT'S NOT IT! THEY DON'T LOVE YOU, BECAUSE IF THEY DID, YOU'D TELL THEM TO GO GET YOU THE LAUGHING *ARECA* NUT AND THE SPEAKING BETEL!"[28]

Areca palm and betel nut are the two ingredients for *shileo*, the stimulating chew that Indian people know as *paan*. The areca and betel, they're the ones who are going to reveal the whole thing. These are real twentieth-century plants; they have magic speaking powers.

IT WORKED LIKE THE MOVIES. "HOW DO YOU MAKE IT WORK?" THEY [THE *DJINN* BOYS] SAID, "I'LL TELL YOU. GO HOME, PUT IT DOWN LIKE THIS, YOU'LL HEAR ONE OF THEM LAUGHING AND THE OTHER SAYING 'WHAT ARE YOU LAUGHING AT?'"
'REALLY?'
'YEAH.'

The magic plants are gendered: the areca, more articulate than the betel, is female. Next day at lunchtime they lay out a mat and put the areca and betel on it.

THEN AS SOON AS THEY PUT IT THERE, THEY HEARD "HA, HA, HA, HA, HA, HA." IT WAS THE ARECA. THE BETEL ASKED, "WHY ARE YOU LAUGHING? WHAT ARE YOU LAUGHING AT, ARECA?"
IT ANSWERED, "AMAZING! LET ME LAUGH..."

The areca palm can do a lot more than laugh. She now becomes an embedded narrator, no less skilled than Anfiati Sufu herself, and recycles the whole story from the top, framing dialogue into her treatment. She even starts with a formula. 'LONG AGO [*HALE HALE*] THERE WAS AN OLD WOMAN AND AN OLD MAN... A WOMAN AND A MAN, THEY HAD A DAUGHTER.' Anfiati Sufu comments, IT WAS REALLY LIKE THE MOVIES, but it is more like a live storytelling session. By embedding the recapitulation into the areca's reported speech, Anfiati Sufu hides and reveals herself, even implying that her audiences ought to pay for what she's giving them.

The climax will require another recapitulation, repeating the previous events and performing a known story. The boys — you have to love their cunning — charge a woman passerby the fat sum of two thousand *riali* for the show. Noticing the strong family resemblance, she carries the message to the king, who comes to hear the whole story in hiding while his courtier pays the boys' admission charge. Quickly the king rushes in; to avoid being seen, the girl retreats into the house, re-enacting her banishment. The boys charge the king ten thousand *riali*, and then

ONE OF THEM SAID, "OK, THERE'S ONE MORE CHILD. A SEPARATE ONE."
"WHO'S THAT?"
"WE HAVE A SISTER. THIS IS JUST OUR SHARE."
"HOW MUCH?"
"ANOTHER TEN THOUSAND."

The boys turn the total of 20,000 over to the grandparents, but they don't let the king see the girl until he hears the betel speak. That causes him to faint; of course, she has to come out and revive him.

The king stages the climactic recognition scene at the Anjouannais mosque in Mtsapere, a place well known to the audience (see Fig. 4 in Chapter 1). For that occasion the six boys demand royal clothes and a *pousse-pousse* (rickshaw) to transport them. With some ceremonious setting up of ten chairs, the next recapitulation begins only after they've squeezed another forty thousand out of the king. (It must be clear by now that in these tales, a king is realistically a local chief and symbolically a Frenchified civil servant.) Then the cinema-areca tells the whole story again, at last conferring public recognition on the young woman. Narrators do love narrating.

Now that she has embedded the two scenes of recounting, Anfiati Sufu moves fast to the dénouement. The first wife's son confirms the recognition ('ALMIGHTY GOD HAS GIVEN ME MY BROTHERS AND SISTER'); he orders his mother and her henchwoman beheaded. The king gives away his royal turban and puts the six brothers in command. His restored wife is installed in a modern apartment with all her possessions, and is later given a new house. All are rich. The closing formula, TSIWALISHI VAVO NA USHONGA WAO [I LEFT THEM THERE, THEM AND THEIR SILLINESS] carries out its conventional functions, to help the audience make a transition from fiction to real life and to distance her vivid narration from her spirited self. I LEFT THEM THERE, THEM AND THEIR SILLINESS, I TOOK MY MOVIE THING AND ALL THOSE STORIES, I CAME HOME, I RAISE MY RICE TO EAT, AND I MIND MY BUSINESS.

This elegant narrative was one of the eleven pieces with which Anfiati Sufu responded after Sophie Blanchy and Zaharia Soilihi asked her for stories. The three that they translated, probably the others too, blend her recall of the shared traditions of Madagascar and Mayotte with her skill in translating them into twentieth-century terms. She blends the *djinn*s of Islamic Mayotte into the lions whose milk must be fetched. She transforms the magic laughing plant into a movie projector, her audience's gateway to the world of fantasy. All the while, knowing her audience will follow, she faithfully honors the underlying themes of the *fille* tale: the vulnerability of a marriageable girl, the necessity of her marrying, the essential saving role of her birth family, and her liberation from the calumniated-wife status into a rich marriage. This capacity for innovation is part of the African-Malagasy-Mahorais tradition, shared by who knows how many predecessors. The form of The Laughing Areca, drawn from 'one of the eight or ten best known plots in the world',[29] allows her to dominate her tale with its female characters, while she absorbs and transforms the gender system of Mayotte into parallels between her audience's life situation and the symbols of the story. The language of her performance is built on ordinary talk; already known from a listener's experience are the incidents of the tale. Yet her performing sets the two worlds apart. Her piece is unique because her innovations are in classic style. Her remodeling process is an essential component of creole narrative poetics, which takes ideology and makes it aesthetic. As Terry Eagleton says;

> the problem-solving process of the text is never merely a matter of its reference outwards to certain pre-existent ideological cruxes. It is, rather, a matter of the 'ideological' presenting itself in the form of the 'aesthetic' and *vice versa*.... Every phrase, every image of the text... is at once an 'answer' and a 'question,' mobilising new possibilities of conflict in the very moment of taking the weight of a provisional 'solution.'[30]

'Isn't it possible that 'such coded messages may ultimately help to empower a community and hence to effect change... '?[31]

Her Mother, Her House

A storyteller like Anfiati Sufu is a cultural mediator. By managing plot, language and dialect, she reminds women of their power. If a patriarchal ideology teaches women 'to think as men, to identify with a male point of view, and to accept as normal and legitimate a male system of values...,'[32] her stories teach women to think outside the system. Oral narration is hence a kind of 'women's writing'. Just at the time these tales were being collected, the French critic Hélène Cixous was decreeing, 'Woman must write her self... Woman must put herself into the text — as into the world and into history — by her own movement'.[33] For an audience of Comoran women, female-oriented folktales give powerful voice to deep, abiding present concerns by speaking the inherited language of metaphor. Their storytellers create in verbal art their own ways of resistance and protest. They act for themselves; they represent themselves; the word is their weapon.

In this group of tales, a woman ends her banishment by telling her own story. The outstanding performance is by Aïsha Hussein, known as Ma Sula, from Sada village on Mayotte's west coast in July 1984 (the same place and time as Fatima Maolida). To begin her tale, she uses formulas that echo centuries of African and Malagasy verbal artists.

> A TALE OF OLD TIMES.
> THERE WAS A RICH MAN
>   THERE WAS A POOR MAN
>   THERE WAS A *WAZIRI* [MINISTER]
>   THERE WAS AN OLD *DZINAFIKI*[34]
>   THERE WAS A MAN.

Ma Sula's orphan girl comes right out of that world. She is being raised by a *kadhi* [foster father], a figure of the 'real' world. Knowing what property she will bring to a future husband, he intends her for his son. After he shows her the contents of her mother's house, the audacious girl spies where he keeps the key; thereafter she goes to the house sometimes with her friends, to raid it for sweets, biscuits, and Cokes (it's 1984 in Mayotte). She took some clothes too, and gave them to them. All those children got into the habit of going to her place and looting, over and over — . behavior not found in most old-time tales, but believable enough in twentieth-century Mayotte or anywhere else.

The girl falls under the influence of a seemingly kind neighbor lady — poor, predatory, with several daughters, a would-be stepmother figure.[35] As if offering her a pseudo-family to replace her dead parent, she prompts the girl to steal more of her mother's goods and bring them to her. She empties her mother's house and gets some boys to pick all the coconuts and mangoes nearby. Noting that she's nearing marriageable age, the *kadhi* discovers the thefts and intervenes to retrieve everything. She admits having given it all away, the *kadhi* demands their restoration, and already the pseudo-stepmother is plotting to kill the girl. The abstract stylization of folktale doesn't require this motivation; Ma Sula supplies it as part of her (or her sources') remodeling. The daughters take the girl fishing the next day. Firstly, they pick *uruba*, a plant used to line a fishing basket in the water; as the audience knows, the infusion of the plant narcotizes and inebriates the fish, and perhaps an innocent human as well.[36] But they don't succeed in drowning her: she is saved much as Shura was, by a little *djinn*. He is both grouper fish and a human-like only child, who rejoices,

> "MAMA, I FOUND MYSELF A SISTER!"
> "YOU FOUND YOURSELF A SISTER?"
> "YES."
> "WHERE?"
> "IT'S A HUMAN."
> "A HUMAN?"
> "YES."
> "WHAT HAPPENED?"
> HE SAID, "I SAW SOME HUMANS PUTTING OUT *URUBA*, I WENT TO GET HIGH, JUST THEN I SAW HUMANS PUSH THAT GIRL IN, AND I CAUGHT HER."

Being under water presents no more threat to this girl than it did to Shura. More realism: his motherly mother, queen of the *djinns*, notices that she is a good Muslim who has to avoid certain foods and directs her son to take correct food to her. As she grows up, the care these fish-foster-parents give her is realistic — they will make all provision for a marriageable girl — but they also sequester her where she may never be found, a regular incident both in tales of a mistreated heroine and in the life of a marriageable girl.

Ma Sula continues her realistic blending. At the age of seventeen, she observes that the girl 'LOOKED FINE, WITH NICE ARMS, NICE LEGS'. At twenty-five she has to be married. The humanlike *djinns* know the marriage rules: she can't marry one of them. Being helpful fish from the folktale world, they have no trouble buying real-world objects like beds, sheets, plates, and pots (imported from France); they put her on an island, where she sings her plight. Sequestration builds suspense. A friendly fisherman hears her song, with its riddle-like words no one can understand. If she was to be sequestered, she would use verbal art, posing a riddle only she could solve. When the fisherman has tipped off the king and the villagers come to persuade her, she begins recovering her social place. The fisherman is rewarded with riches but not promoted. The king welcomes her and marries her to his son. In this quasi-conclusive moment of order, she finds her new husband to be another helper. He will allow her to show her own mastery of language, to explain the riddle, and to show her gratitude for the generous treatment from the *djinn* fish.

Fig. 15 Jackfruit. Photo by Augustus Binu, CC BY-SA 3.0, Wikimedia Commons, https://upload.wikimedia.org/wikipedia/commons/b/ba/Jackfruit_hanging.JPG

A month goes by before she plays storyteller, framing her life as a local anecdote: 'BACK HOME, LONG AGO, I HEARD A STORY ABOUT A GIRL FROM HERE,' an orphan girl, ten years before, whose fortune was consumed and who was then killed. She takes her husband to the site of her mother's house, where she removes her quite realistic modern brassiere, and puts it around the trunk of a quite realistic *jacquier* (jackfruit tree). Thus does she identify the tree with herself: jackfruit are big and round and grow in pairs. The wood of the tree will be transformed into the replacement for her mother's house, which will be her own. Now when she repeats her riddle-like song, her husband says;

'WHY DON'T YOU WANT TO TELL ME WHAT YOUR SONG MEANS? I WANT TO KNOW.'
'NO, NO, IT'S ONLY A SONG. EVERY TIME YOU HEAR IT, YOU WANT TO KNOW THE MEANING? WHY DON'T YOU ASK ME THE MEANING OF ALL THE OTHER THINGS YOU HAVE HEARD?'

But she keeps the secret of her strange behavior. Repeatedly she refuses to explain the song or translate the riddle. Next day at sundown, they see that her mysterious song is somehow effecting a gradual rebuilding of her mother's house by the *djinn*s. In place of her bra, she buries a *dzivudzi* there — perhaps a skin or a feather. That provision from the folktale donor, her *djinn* mother, will help her gain her object of search, the house. On the third, fourth, and fifth day, they see the mother's house being realistically if magically reconstructed; on the seventh day it is finished. King and husband are equally mystified, but among the villagers, the young people guess, Maybe the owner is coming back and building the house. The king, being a modern landowner, wants to find out who is building in this unauthorized manner. This sort of updating, says Blanchy, is necessary for the tale to remain pertinent and evolve at the lexical level.[37]

Now, in a storytelling flourish by Ma Sula or from her sources, the husband takes a turn at narrating what he knows to his father the king, embedding his wife's story in his own.

"ONE DAY MY WIFE ASKED ME QUESTIONS ABOUT A GIRL WHOSE PARENTS WERE DEAD, WHOSE FORTUNE HAD BEEN SWALLOWED UP, AND WHO GOT KILLED WHEN SHE COMPLAINED. I SAID OK, BUT SHE ASKED ME TO GO WITH HER TO SEE THAT GIRL'S MOTHER'S PLACE. THEN I SAW HER DO WEIRD THINGS I DIDN'T LIKE, AS IF... AS IF SHE WERE NOT HUMAN. SHE LEFT SOME THINGS THERE, AND THE NEXT DAY WE FOUND THE HOUSE HAD BEEN BUILT, AND FINALLY THE ROOF WAS ON AND IT WAS ALL DONE."
"AND CAN'T YOU SPEAK TO YOUR WIFE?"
"YES, OF COURSE I CAN."
"SO WHY HAVEN'T YOU ASKED HER ABOUT HOW THAT HOUSE GOT BUILT?"
"I DID ASK HER, BUT SHE WOULDN'T TELL ME."

He suspects she is a *djinn*; trying again to get the explanation, he arouses his father's anger when he fails. Inserting his bit of storytelling may be Ma Sula's special touch, but modernizing has probably always been part of narrating style in Mayotte. The woman takes charge.

> WELL, AT SUNDOWN HIS WIFE SAID, "LET'S GO [THERE]", AND WHEN THEY GOT THERE SHE OPENED THE DOOR AND SAW THE BEDS, AND ALL THE THINGS IN THE HOUSE HAD BEEN PUT THERE. IN THE KITCHEN SHE FOUND HER POTS, HER TINS, THE TRIVET FOR THE FIRE. IT WAS ALL IN ORDER AS IF SHE ALREADY LIVED THERE. SHE SAID, "YOU CAN COME IN TOMORROW."
>
> BUT HER HUSBAND SAID, "YOU'RE NOT COMING BACK INTO THIS HOUSE UNTIL YOU EXPLAIN. I WANT US TO BE FRANK WITH EACH OTHER, YOU AND ME. OR ELSE TELL ME TO LEAVE!"
>
> "ALL RIGHT, I'LL TELL YOU EVERYTHING ABOUT THIS HOUSE, BUT YOU HAVE TO GET THE DRUM BEATEN AND EVERYBODY COMES TOGETHER".

As the story moves to its close, the evil forces are left behind and the untranslatable words of the song are translated, her performance of herself as herself is enough to close both the embedded narrative and its frame.

> SHE WENT TO WHERE SHE WAS BORN, HER MOTHER'S HOUSE, TO WORK THE MEDICINES SHE'D GIVEN HER. THAT'S HOW HER PARENTS CAME TO BUILD HER HOUSE AND GAVE HER EVERYTHING NEEDED FOR INSIDE IT. AND THAT GIRL'S FATHER IS *UMIE MUZAWAGE*, HER MOTHER IS *MAMAE SHIZAWAGA; NANA HINDI BALI MAGAZA* IS HER SISTER, *AMIA SHO FII IHA YOSA* IS HERSELF.
>
> I LEFT THEM THERE AND WENT ON MY WAY.

Her climactic answer to the riddle, as the last line of the piece, points to the identity of mother and daughter with the house, which, says Blanchy, is;

> the place of all material and psychological security. Although in Mayotte everyone belongs as much to his or her father's family as to the mother's, it is only the mother's side that represents rooting, security. The orphan girl, deprived of her maternal house by a neighbor's malignity, is at last restored to her heritage thanks to the providential help of a fish mother. Now, like any respectable woman, she has her own house, where a husband — a king's son, of course — will come to join her.[38]

The heroine's interest is any woman's interest: recovering her inheritance, regaining the house that is rightfully hers, installing a proper husband in it, preserving the kinship rules. The symbolism of her ritual of fastening her bra to the tree, then removing it and burying a skin there, is not so mysterious after all: she acts to identify herself with her parents. Most emphasized is the ideological point: a woman knows she is entitled to help from her dead mother, and knows how to assert her identity by telling her story.

What about Ma Sula's own story? Given her delight in embedding, she could have invented this one on the traditional models. For a narrator to embed storytelling, says Barbara Johnson of Mallarmé, is to question how a story comes into existence and what that means.[39] Folklorists have evaded that question by attributing the origin of a present performance to a mystified something of the past called 'oral tradition.' As more knowledge accumulates about African and Malagasy storytelling, and about the diverse languages and cultures converging in Mayotte, the ways in which a present performer preserves and modifies what she remembers from her predecessors will become clearer. To examine and critique the patriarchal system of Mayotte in the 1980s was the artistic form of women's resistance to male domination, as their ownership of property is the material form of that resistance. When this character's narration reveals her previously hidden identity, gender becomes part of poetics. If the audience for Ma Sula's performance perceives the thematic relationship between the framed and the framing narrative, the nature of a woman's mistreatment will have been revealed to both audiences. Her moment of recognition is all-important. Only by singing the song or telling her story will the heroine be recognized. This moment is what Aristotle, writing about effects in tragedy, calls a shift from ignorance to awareness. Formally it is recognition, *anagnorisis*, as much as it is *peripeteia*, a shift of direction. As in Attic tragedy, the 'reversal brought about in the realm of knowledge (an enigma is resolved, a false accusation disproved, a fallacious interpretation corrected) completes and closes the narrative movement'.[40] Formal analysis identifies this as the most moving moment in the piece. The plot requires it. The *hale* loves its resolution as much as tragedy does.

Tales like Her Mother's House embody the contradiction Michelle Rosaldo noted: 'The very symbolic and social approaches that appear to set women apart and to circumscribe their activities may be used by women as a basis for female solidarity and worth'.[41] Tellers and audiences of repeated performances have the advantage of the repetition. As

Butler says, 'it is only within the practices of repetitive signifying that a subversion of identity becomes possible.'[42] For the performer to sing the same song five times in the voice of her character is literal repetitive signifying. When both find their voice, both become real. 'To embody the norms that govern speakability in one's speech [says Butler] is to consummate one's status as a subject of speech,'[43] and one's status as a speaker.

Narrating in Mayotte critiques gender as part of the social order the storyteller and her audience live in. Performing what a woman can 'be,' as Butler says (drawing on Foucault);

> is constrained in advance by a regime of truth that decides what will and will not be a recognizable form of being. Although the regime of truth decides in advance what form recognition can take, it does not fully constrain this form. Indeed, decide may be too strong a word, since the regime of truth offers a framework for the scene of recognition, delineating who will qualify as a subject of recognition and offering available norms for the act of recognition... His point, however, is not only that there is always a relation to such norms, but that any relation to the regime of truth will at the same time be a relation to myself.[44]

It is left to the reader or hearer to draw a conclusion that the dominant ideology has to suppress.[45] As they maintain the oral-literary matrilineage, the women's narrating becomes a tool for 1980s modernization by honoring ambiguity, presenting their alternative social vision.

Incidentally, an animal mother, in a contrasting Mayotte story collected by Gueunier, has magic powers. A woman is rescued from the forest by a prince, an encounter that looks promising until she refuses to marry him. Her mother, she tells him, is a fierce, powerful cow. In some versions, she is born from an egg and the cow is foster mother. Either way she is alien, unsuitable for human marriage. So fierce, in fact, is this bovine mother (in some versions a stepmother), and so determined to assert the primacy of the birth family, that when the prince takes the girl, she goes in pursuit, removes her daughter's eyes, takes them home, and sets them over her hearth. Each time the girl weeps — which she does a lot, because she is ceaselessly tormented by the prince's other wives — the mother sees the eyes fill with tears. At the end she relents: she restores the eyes, thus enabling her daughter to triumph over her rivals and become the prince's sole wife.[46] A mother's power, then, can cause her daughter both pain and happiness. What will the female listener take from the story?

What Is Your Mother's Name?

These tales share with Propp's donor sequence (formal analysis again) a kind of allegory. A woman's reality, her true nature or identity, is tested by being suppressed by male authority; she reacts within her oppressed circumstances, for instance by the permitted art of singing, sometimes acquiring female allies, until she reveals it by the art of narrating. One of the most powerful stories recorded in Mayotte, The Dog's Daughters, follows this sequence, combines it with the all-important mother-daughter relationship, and poses the question 'Where do babies come from?' The model comes from Madagascar.

> A jealous co-wife spreads the story that a wife, whom we know to be innocent, has given birth to an old broom (a human implement), the jawbone of an ox (detritus from the animal world), and a stone (from the natural world). In other versions of the slander, jealous co-wives remove her real children and put a broom and mallet in their place. Sometimes her sisters remove the babies and replace them with a cat and rat. Or if there are six babies, the wife's sisters replace them with pebbles, rags (human waste), brooms (human implements), ox's jaws (human discard from the animal world), gourds (vegetable objects of human use). In some versions these conspirators even convince the mother herself that their lie is true. Their slander, having been loudly announced to the people, must be disproved at the end of the tale by a recognition scene.[47]

Distantly the tale is traceable to the Malagasy legend of descent from a woman from under sea or out of the river (the Ranoro story in chapter 1). Its triggering point is the dog mother's insistent presence.

The dog, both detested and honored, is an ambivalent symbol. 'Everyone knows' that dogs are despised in Islamic societies; in Mayotte and Islamic parts of Madagascar, dogs are not allowed into villages. 'This animal [says one historian] appears there as especially impure; the tiniest contact with it entails immediate and scrupulous ablutions'. Yet Malagasy people do raise dogs outside their village. They need them to hunt the *tenrec*, the hedgehog used for meat.[48] Some Malagasy, such as the Bara in the south, have affection for a dog as a dependent: 'The greatest dishonor, the Bara still say, is to see the dog who has chosen to follow you die of hunger.' One can still hear people there describe an unprovided man as having 'No DOG, NO OX' [*TSY AMBOA TSY LAMBO*].[49] In the tale, the fictional dog is both despised and honored, blending Malagasy tolerance with Islamic scorn for man's best and most impure friend. Creole ambivalence loves contradiction. Throughout the tale, two sisters — that beloved folktale pair, the kind and unkind girls — are confronted by the necessity of deception and driven by the fear of shame.[50] Gueunier recorded two versions four years apart, one told sparely in plain style in 1977, by a woman of Poroani, the other much richer, by a young woman originally from Kany Kely, living in Mwamoju when he recorded her in 1981. Her version is a Mayotte original.

The Poroani Version

The Poroani narrator (or her source) poses the paradox of parentage right at the outset: 'WELL, THERE WAS SOMEONE, IT WAS A DOG, SHE GAVE BIRTH TO HUMAN CHILDREN, IN THE FOREST — THERE, AT THE FOOT OF A TREE'. The birth of twins is not unusual, but the image of a dog mother takes the audience instantly into an alternative world not too distant from the real one. Descent from a dog in any world is more mundane and unsavory than descent from a woman from under sea. So shameful is the birth of these babies from an animal that it must be kept secret; the question of what family a girl comes from is the primary consideration for her future marriage.[51] At that same moment, the king's wife, barren until now, gives birth to a daughter — how? The Kany Kely narrator answers: an old woman provided a magic remedy, a mango. The king's wife obediently eats it, but forgets the wise woman's requirement that the peelings must not be eaten by an animal. A dog eats the peels. After nine months, the dog bears twin human girls and the wife gives birth to a little girl. Immediately she commands secrecy: 'WELL, LOOK, WHAT TO DO, WE'LL TAKE THOSE TWO BABIES AND WE'LL PUT THEM WITH THIS ONE, AND IN THE MORNING, WHEN PEOPLE COME TO ASK IF THE KING'S WIFE HAS GIVEN BIRTH, WE'LL TELL THEM "YES, SHE HAD TRIPLETS".' How quick the ruling class is to steal and conceal.

As the twins grow up, in both versions they quickly polarize into a treacherous sister, who despises her dog mother and ultimately kills her, and a dutiful sister-daughter, who reveres her mother and acts accordingly. The thinly told Poroani version plays up the themes of secrecy and shame. The girls grow up and marry. The dog mother, having taken refuge at her kind daughter's house, dies. 'WHEN SHE DIED,' the narrator says unemotionally, 'HER DAUGHTER TOOK HER AND WRAPPED HER IN A SHROUD, JUST LIKE A PERSON. SHE BURIED HER'. When her husband demands that they follow convention by visiting her mother, she lies: her mother, she says, lives in the neighboring island, Anjouan. So they must go there. They load a boat with gifts; on the way, shame impels her to lie again. WHEN THEY'D GOT, UH, PRETTY FAR OFF, THE WIFE SAID, 'HAVE THEM STOP THE BOAT, I'M GOING TO GO DO *MAUDHURI*'. It is a woman's regular practice to go to defecate on the beach, knowing her husband won't follow her there. In fact, she is resolved to drown herself. On the beach she meets a *Biby* (monster snake) and asks it to devour her, so ashamed is she. But the *Biby* is a donor, who refuses to eat her, as she has received her mother's blessing. He tells her how to pass for a king's lost daughter. She goes on to Anjouan and succeeds in the deception. Much excitement; her *grand mariage* temporarily creates a society of the spectacle, and excites the envy of her sister. Both versions end in an unsuccessful imitation by that treacherous sister. The Poroani narrator uses the reporting style of Allibert's narrators: the unkind sister meets the *Biby*, repeats her sister's account, says, 'Eat me!', and obligingly the snake does just that.

The Mwamoju Version

The 1981 narrator makes more of that, and of every scene leading up to it. Firstly, she elicits sympathy by delaying the women's marriage until they have left home. Their canine mother's affection for them incites catcalls from their human sister: 'ZANAKA NY FANDRÔKA! [THE BITCH'S DAUGHTERS!]' They are so humiliated that they leave ('WE ARE TOO SHAMED') and find their way to an unknown village. Then men's abuse of power comes in, personified by a *kadhi*, an arrogant civil servant whose duties consist of sitting in an office and looking out at what is happening in the road. His dialogue with the girls gets him an impossible and honest answer that blends truth and secrecy.

> "WHAT'S YOUR MOTHER'S NAME?"
> "WE DON'T KNOW."

"WHAT'S YOUR FATHER'S NAME?"

"WE DON'T KNOW."

"AH, BUT WHERE ARE YOU COMING FROM?"

"WE JUST LEFT, WE DON'T KNOW WHERE OUR MOTHER IS, WE ARE LOST, WE JUST WENT STRAIGHT AHEAD OF US." IN FACT THEY KNEW PERFECTLY WELL, BUT THEY DIDN'T WANT TO TELL HIM.

How skillfully these women's verbal prowess controls a man through fiction. The *kadhi* and his deputy take and marry (appropriate) the girls. In the phrase of the poet L. S. Asekoff, 'rescue = kidnap; kidnap = rescue'.[52] If the dog mother were not still offstage, the story could end right there, with the girls safely married, but as the shame of their birth is not yet cleared, the Mwamoju narrator continues.

Their dog mother has followed them. No other dog would dare come into the village. From their house the women recognize their mother's voice. The elder one said, 'THAT AWFUL DOG! SHE'S REALLY AWFUL, THAT DOG! HOW DID SHE GET HERE TO EMBARRASS US SO?' SHE QUICKLY SAID TO HER SERVANTS, 'GO AFTER THAT DOG THAT'S BARKING, CATCH HER, KILL HER AND THROW AWAY HER BODY.' But the younger sister is bereft at the loss of her mother. The narrator's solicitude for making sure the audience doesn't miss anything is reflected in her habit of stringing together clauses, quite discernible in translation: THEY BROUGHT IT, THE WOMAN PICKED IT RIGHT UP, SHE WENT TO BUY A BEAUTIFUL WHITE SHROUD, SHE WRAPPED THE DOG VERY PRETTILY, HER HUSBAND HAD A NICE BIG TRUNK, SHE TOOK HER HUSBAND'S CLOTHES AND PUT THEM SOMEPLACE ELSE, SHE TOOK THE DOG, SHE WRAPPED HER IN THE SHROUD VERY PRETTILY, AND SHE PUT IT IN HER HUSBAND'S TRUNK AND PUT A COVER OVER IT. What will her husband think when the odor reveals the decaying carcass? But instead of smelling bad, the trunk gives off a paradisal fragrance, which causes her husband to open it. He discovers treasure, which he takes to be a pile of gifts. When questioned, the younger sister can only stammer, 'THAT ALL COMES FROM MY MOTHER.' Some hearers will recognize that smell from the many tales in which a royal corpse, instead of beginning to stink, gives off a magical odor. All will catch the larger meaning, that all valuable things come from your mother. They pack their bags, mount horses, and set out.[53] When she meets the snake and must answer his question, the narrator frames in her life story.

SHE SAID, "OH — I WAS BROUGHT INTO THE WORLD BY A DOG, AND THAT DOG
FOLLOWED US EVERYWHERE, I WAS ASHAMED, 'CAUSE PEOPLE SAID I WAS A DOG'S
DAUGHTER. WE WERE ASHAMED, SO WE FLED, ME AND MY BIG SISTER, AND WE
GOT TO A PLACE WHERE WE FOUND MEN WHO TOOK US AS WIVES. BUT AFTER,
THE DOG CAME, AND MY SISTER'S SERVANTS KILLED IT. I TOOK IT AND PUT IT INTO
A SUITCASE [*VALIZY*], AND THE DAY MY HUSBAND OPENED IT, IT HAD BECOME
PERFUMES AND GOLD AND SILVER. THEN HE SAID WE WOULD GO SEE MY MOTHER.
BUT I DON'T EVEN KNOW WHERE MY MOTHER IS; MY MOTHER REALLY IS THAT
DOG. SO HE SAID WE WOULD GO SEE HER NOW, AND I'M ASHAMED. SO, EAT ME",
SHE SAID TO THE SNAKE.

But the snake is no threat; rather he is an agent of her transformation. He
helps her pass for the lost daughter of a king and queen who lost their
daughter long ago. He even disguises her with a *noro*, 'the mysterious
light [that] marks the face of a woman blessed by God for filial love, just
as it marked the face of the Prophet.'[54] The *noro* will eclipse her secret.
But before that king can give her the expected magnificent reception,
an old busybody tips him off and claims credit for the *noro*, in return
for a meal. 'I FOUND YOUR DAUGHTER, I FOUND YOUR DAUGHTER, AND I PUT A
LIGHT [ON HER FACE]. SHE'S HERE, SHE IS COMING, COME SEE HER.' The king
recognizes that light; she tells him her true story, which reveals that she
is ready for marrying him. Happy ending.

When her unkind sister learns what has happened, she must launch
an unsuccessful imitation:

"NOW THAT YOU, YOU GOT ALL THESE BEAUTIFUL THINGS, YOU DON'T WANT ME
TO HAVE MY SHARE, YOU DON'T WANT TO LET ME GO THERE."
SHE SAID TO HER, "WELL, GO AHEAD THEN, BUT IF YOU GO, I HAVE A FEELING
YOU WILL DIE."
SHE ANSWERED, "I'LL GO EVEN IF I MUST DIE FROM IT." SO NOW IT'S HER
TURN TO RECOUNT THE LIFE STORY, A TRUE ACCOUNT OF HERSELF AND HER KIND
SISTER.
"ME — MY MOTHER — WE DIDN'T HAVE ANY MOTHER, WE WERE BROUGHT
INTO THE WORLD BY A DOG, AND THAT DOG, WE STAYED WITH OUR MOTHER SO
LONG THAT THAT DOG FOLLOWED US EVERYWHERE WE WENT, AND WE WERE
ASHAMED. WE RAN AWAY, AND WE GOT TO A PLACE NEAR MTSAPERE, WHERE WE
FOUND MEN WHO MARRIED US. THE DOG FOLLOWED US AND I SENT SERVANTS TO
KILL THAT DOG, AND SHE'S DEAD."
SHE EXPLAINED EVERYTHING SHE'D DONE, AND THE SNAKE ANSWERED,
"WELL, I WAS SENT TO LOOK FOR PEOPLE WHO WEREN'T BLESSED BY THEIR
MOTHER, TO KILL THEM. WELL, YOU WEREN'T BLESSED BY YOUR MOTHER. YOU

KILLED YOUR MOTHER, YOUR MOTHER THE DOG." SHE WANTED TO RUN AWAY, BUT
THE SNAKE CAUGHT HER, BIT HER, SWALLOWED HER INTO HIS STOMACH. SHE DIED.

The husband returns and reports his loss. AND I LEFT THEM THERE AND
CAME HERE.[55]

That young woman of Mwamoju knows how to vivify her story;
whoever her mentor was, she learned well. Plentiful dialogue and ironic
touches, like that colonial Frenchman in caricature, convey respect for
her two women characters. The climactic device in all these tales is to
resolve the tension between shame and secrecy by having the oppressed
woman tell the truth. This device (in Tzvetan Todorov's words) 'is
an articulation of the most essential property of all narrative. For the
embedding narrative is the *narrative of a narrative*.' For characters (and
their narrators) to live, 'they must narrate.'[56] The framed-in life story
makes the whole piece into what Roland Barthes calls 'that type of
message which takes as its object not its content but its own form'.[57]
Yet beyond that resolution lies ambivalence. Riches, acceptance, and
a royal husband are awarded to a woman who has disguised herself.
Concealing her secret and telling her story brings her power.

Questions of Interpretation

One way to read this piece assumes that folklore is about the past. Then
it is a historical legend of long-ago Madagascar, preserved in Mayotte's
folk memory. Its theme, says the historian Jean-Pierre Domenichini,
is native resistance by Malagasy to foreign usurpation. He hears the
earlier, Poroani version speaking out of a Madagascar untouched
by Arab influence, and the later version speaking for the time after
Islamic conversion. Hence it 'presents both a profession of faith and a
political analysis of the situation', and it declares that though people
are conventionally Muslim, fundamentally they are Malagasy.[58] Noël
Gueunier, while agreeing that the tale speaks to deep concerns about
invasion, reads its theme as not resistance but convergence. The *oaziry*
(ministers), for example, are owners of the land under Muslim law.
Being of local origin, they have tended to resist the new law and uphold
the older Mahorais tradition of matrilineal power. The story shows the
two systems converging in a view of history: 'Marriage between the
Arab and the *oazir*'s daughter produces the ideal heir to the kingdom,

carrying legitimacy from both sides'.[59] Readers of the *fille difficile* will wonder how marrying an Arab can make a happy ending. But both scholars place the story firmly in Madagascar's past.

An alternative reading would ask why such a tale would be told in Mayotte in the 1980s. Around the same time, Sophie Blanchy collected a Shimaore version from Salima Djindani, of Bandrele. What keeps it current is that it speaks to 'the great fear of everyone in Mayotte..., being publicly shamed'.[60] The dog's daughters are motivated by shame, which (disguised in secrecy) prevails until marriage ends the tale. The function of the narrative, in Lévi-Straussian terms, is to resolve such a contradiction. The authority figures commendably rescue the two young women from being out in the world on their own, but because they also appropriate the women, they are branded as dictatorial; juxtaposition of opposites constitutes a blend. With the Malagasy passion for secrecy the tale combines the houseowner role for women, a belittling of men, and a declaration that only a woman's mother will save her. Its contradictions speak to enduring gender and family tensions in Mahorais society. In the terms of creolization theory, the function of the narrative is to allow those contradictions — which suggests that the dog mother story must be a new and hybrid creation in and of Mayotte.[61]

What These Women Are Particularly Good At

The plot of The Dog's Daughters shows the Malagasy habit of secrecy as inseparable from its opposite, a woman's drive towards recognition. Judith Butler speaks to the contradiction for a female narrator: 'That my agency is riven with paradox does not mean it is impossible. It means only that paradox is the condition of its possibility. As a result, the "I" that I am finds itself at once constituted by norms and dependent on them...'[62] The narrator role makes it possible to show how dependent she is on social norms and empowers her to question them. In an era of global cultural flows, secrecy and masking are the cherished qualities for a quasi-colony to practice. No tale expresses more poignantly the concern of Mahorais women for legitimizing themselves, or their reliance on narrative to that end. No vehicle for expressing such concerns is more sophisticated or effectual than these narratives.[63]

Listening to this tale, at the time when Mayotte was asserting its independence, what effect could scenes of the construction of a self have on women? To a western observer, it might seem that a woman of a long-neglected colony must have been 'in fact trapped within a discourse [she] has no power to evade or to alter'; that a storyteller's performing, which looks so much like agency, 'is merely yet another effect of the law disguised as something different'.[64] But it's equally possible that some narrators are using narrative discourse to criticize the law. Their texts suggest that. Observing Mauritius, another formerly colonized island in the region, anthropologist Patrick Eisenlohr sees acts of performance both creating and claiming identities.[65] Beyond the Indian Ocean, in the Caribbean or Peru for example, new folklore always results from cultural convergence. Nor is that re-creation confined to creole societies: the social subordination of immigrant populations in the United States and Britain encourages them to create new folklore. All societies engage in cultural renegotiation in their own ways.

Blanchy's women narrators are especially attentive to their listeners. Anfiati Sufu, beginning The Laughing Areca, locates the king character in the familiar ground of the social scene they share with her characters. When the girl's grandparents die, she says something her usual audience doesn't need to be told: a girl without parents is alone.[66] Referring in this way to something listeners or readers will recognize is familiar in literature under the name of allusion. Oral narrators continually refer to things familiar to their audience, as poets do everywhere. African tales and proverbs often allude to each other in a way only the in-group will fully enjoy. Not all Mahorais storytellers rely on allusion as much as these women do, but all of them appeal to community standards, and the use of allusion is a force for cohesion. Performance of folktales is one of Foucault's 'practices that systematically form the objects of which they speak'.[67] When they perform, Anfiati Sufu, Fatima Maolida and the rest (re)create tradition, combining the motifs from Africa and Madagascar with the cultural and local emphases of Mayotte. Of course, that's just part of the job, but these women are especially skilled at handling the dialectic between tradition and the performing situation.

Tradition in Mayotte is obviously multiple, being an agglomeration of discourses that began in the 13th century. Audiences probably expect something that feels traditional, like the *fille* story. A narrator's creativity may consist in reproducing a heard performance closely. The tales we read today are reproduced verbatim by their collectors, but orally they have been creatively remodeled by tellers like these women. Probably some of Claude Allibert's schoolboy narrators did that with trickster tales. Some of Gueunier's narrators seem to be doing that without remembering their sources very well. Tradition does not equal blind repetition. It is more traditional, in a society of mixed heritages, to recontextualize or adapt an old story like the *fille* to its new setting. That's why the handsome husband is a *djinn*. Creole societies excel in a third kind of creativity, coining a new tale like The Dog's Daughters in the pattern Blanchy identified. All these kinds of feminine creativity draw energy from a social context that the storyteller and the hearer use to interpret the tale. Part of that context, says Blanchy, is that a woman is in a position of solidarity with her house, her mother, and her daughter, and of rivalry with women of all other houses. If she must avoid isolation, she must also steer clear of the spontaneity and frankness so much valued by some westerners.[68] That caution may help to account for the spare style of some texts. Anonymity is impossible in Mayotte, as fieldworkers have discovered. Communication takes place through the use of significant linguistic symbols, which are a great aid to simultaneously hiding and revealing oneself. The tales that have been collected and translated by our three collectors are a congeries of those symbols, artistically arranged.

In Closing

Once folktales from Mayotte are translated, how much can a reader at a distance expect to appreciate them? Readability depends on emphases in that reader's culture, which differ as much the difference between Kibushi and English or French. 'In light of contingency and embeddedness, it seems untenable to claim transcultural, transhistorical literary value', writes one critic (about Shakespeare, by the way).[69] Really? Does embeddedness mean anything more than that performance takes place in an identifiable social setting? Think of the performance of *Macbeth* before James I in 1606. Publication is a variety of performance: think of the publication of *Bleak House* in nineteen numbers of Dickens's periodical *Household Words* in 1852–53, or the posthumous publication of three volumes of *À la recherche du temps perdu* in 1923–27. The reception of those three works is part of their performance. Their embeddedness also means their reception. Similarly, the translations and commentaries of our three collectors enable a reader to imagine folktale performance and understand how it fits, in one network of human communication. The contingency of the tales — their reference to the past, or to present concerns — is a question to be investigated, like Shakespeare's topical reference to bad weather embedded in the second act of *A Midsummer Night's Dream*.

In this book I practice on Mahorais narrators the literary-critical approach called Theory of Mind, which its advocates call 'our ability to explain people's behavior in terms of their thoughts, feelings, beliefs, and desires'.[70] Imagine being asked to tell stories (*hale* or *angano*) by a person you more or less know. You agree. You have to think and decide what you will tell the collector; maybe you will think back to occasions when you heard stories being told, and recall one that stands out, but the present occasion is distinct from that one. Most of what gives form to your individual style is a result of selection among pre-existing cultural ideas.[71] Your sources, like your mental spaces, are realized in 'a variety of sources — traditional, functional, technological, innovative...'.[72] They are the cultural equivalent of the conceptual metaphors studied by cognitive linguists. In print, you will be seen both calling up the past and recreating and renegotiating your culture. Your collector will bring experience of his or her past and translate your words for a prospective audience. Few of the tales in this book dive into history. If their derivation, say from Madagascar, meant that they were primarily 'about' Mayotte's past, only a few specialized readers would care about them, and no one would claim they had transcultural, transhistorical literary value. In fact, however, the tales in this book became available to the memory of their tellers and the notebooks of the collectors because they meant something about the concerns of the 1970s–80s. Concepts like mixing, adaptation, re-creation, remodeling, parody, and creolization help to answer the universal question how storytellers use the past help the present. They produce knowledge.

This book has been based on the principle that blending formal and historical analysis investigates 'the historical conditions of possibility of specific forms...'.[73] Some other principles follow.

- All cultures have and use equal powers of expression and channels for communication.

- Creativity is universal. So is storytelling.

- 'Creativity may consist in the use of an old sentence [or tale] in a new setting just as much as in the use of a new sentence [or tale] in an old setting'.[74]

- 'Stories are not difficult to make up. If you have understood life, it's easy to make stories' (Sydney Joseph, Mauritian storyteller).

- Heard melodies are sweet, but those yet unheard may turn out to be sweeter.

- Cultures are never isolated from one another; they continually 'borrow', translate, and appropriate cultural elements.

- People in situations of unequal power renegotiate their cultures and thereby create new folklore. 'The production and consumption of art... is socially organized'.[75]

- 'Paradoxically enough, elements and structures of folktales can present a surprising formal similarity across the most diverse ethnicities and cultures. But analysis shows that the signification arising from them, or permeating them, is altogether different, for each culture they are part of employs them with its own motivation and perspective'.[76]

- 'Our ordinary conceptual system, in terms of which we both think and act, is fundamentally metaphorical in nature'.[77]

- 'The metaphoric innovations of poets... consist not in the totally new creation of metaphoric thought but in the marshalling of already existing forms of metaphoric thought to form new extensions and combinations of old metaphorical mappings'.[78]

- 'The blended space contains information which has been partially selected from each of the input spaces in a way that a new structure emerges, resulting from a new arrangement of pieces of information present in the inputs'.[79]

- 'A successful work of art is not one which resolves objective contradictions in a spurious harmony, but one which expresses the idea of harmony negatively by embodying the contradictions, pure and uncompromised, in its innermost structure.'[80]

- 'If a lion could talk, we wouldn't be able to understand it'.[81]

Endnotes

1   Philip M. Allen, *Security and Nationalism in the Indian Ocean: Lessons from the Latin Quarter Islands* (London: Routledge, 2019), p. 128.

2   Sophie Blanchy, *Maisons des femmes, cités des hommes. Filiation, âge et pouvoir à Ngazidja (Comores)* (Nanterre: Société d'Ethnologie, 2010), pp. 22–24.

3   The storytellers Blanchy names are Fatima Maolida, Hafuswati Abdallah, Anfiati Sufu, Salima Djindani, Salama Yankubu, Mariamu Atumani, Camille Abdillahi, Aïsha Useni, and Anfiati Sufu. She recorded many others. Dady ny Saidy, Reny Daosy, and Vavy imbo Djabu were recorded by Noël Gueunier. The names, villages, and stories are tabulated in the index. Blanchy's collaborators in the research were Zaharia Soilihi and Ramlati Ahmed.

4   Quoted in Richard Howard, *Alone with America: Essays on the Art of Poetry in the United States since 1950* (New York: Atheneum, 1980), p. 285.

5   *L'oiseau*, pp. 374–77. Motifs: G10, Cannibalism; G303.3.1.2, The devil as a well-dressed gentleman; G512.8, Ogre killed by striking.

6   Maurice Fontoynont and Raomandahy, 'La grande Comore', *Mémoires de l'Académie Malgache* (1937), pp. 77–79. The tale, from deep colonial times, has been collected only in Grande Comore. Raomandahy was Dr. Fontoynont's Malagasy collaborator, perhaps the teller of this one, unless, as Sophie Blanchy advises me, their article was drawn from notes made by the district chief, M. Pechmarty, who lived for several years in Grande Comore. Motif K525.1, Substituted object left in bed while victim escapes; P16, End of king's reign.

7   *L'oiseau*, pp. 174–83; Blanchy et al., *La maison*, pp. 159–73. Motifs: W111.3, The lazy wife; D1781, Magic results from singing; Q321, Laziness punished. The baby represents real life.

8   *L'oiseau*, pp. 132–56. The second version was recorded in January 1983, seven and a half years after the first (July 1975).

9   *L'oiseau*, pp. 132–35. Motifs: N455.4, King overhears girl's boast as to what she should do as queen; S411, Wife banished; N711.6, Prince sees heroine at ball and is enamored; T160, Consummation of marriage; H86, Inscribed name on article as token of ownership; H94, Identification by ring; S411.3, Barren wife sent away; Q288, Punishment for mockery.

10   *L'oiseau*, p. xii.

11   She reports her discovery in her 1986 thesis, *Lignée féminine*. The quotations are from 'Histoire de l'orpheline élevée par une marâtre', Allibert, *Contes mahorais*, pp. 29–30. Also following the pattern is Fatima Said Achirafi's tale (*Contes mahorais*, pp. 71–73), in which the heroine is named for the narrator, Fatima. She is so innocent that she has no fear of a stepmother; she urges her father to take another wife, and so on.

12   *Contes mahorais*, pp. 29–30.

13   'The little stick is made out of the central vein of the leaflet of the coconut palm... used to part the hair'. Sophie Blanchy and Zakaria Soilihi, *Furukombe et autres contes de Mayotte* (Paris: Éditions Caribéennes, 1991), p. 42, n. 9.

14   *Furukombe*, pp. 13–43. Motifs: L111.4.2, Orphan heroine; S31, Cruel stepmother; E323.2, Dead mother returns to aid persecuted children; E323.3, Dead mother called up from grave to give her son a charm; ± D1552.2, Life of helpful animal demanded as cure for feigned sickness; H355, Suitor test: finding an extraordinary object; H12, Recognition through song; Q482, punishment, noble person must do menial service; B335.2, Life of helpful animal demanded as cure for feigned sickness; D1162, Magic light; H355, Suitor test: finding an extraordinary object; D150, Transformation: man to bird; D720, Disenchantment; Q450, Cruel punishments. This may be the only Indian Ocean tale in which a king's suitor task leads back to his own marrying.

15   *Lignée féminine*, p. 44.

16   'Folklore's Nature', p. 356.

17   Judith Butler, *Giving an Account of Oneself* (New York: Fordham University Press, 2005), p. 113.

18   'Giving an Account', p. 12.

19   *La maison*, pp. 45–62. The word *Mwenye* in the song, which I translate as Mistress, can also mean someone authoritative like a landlord (Sophie Blanchy, personal communication). Relevant is Butler's quotation of Michel Foucault: 'It is the confession, the verbal act of confession, which comes last and which makes appear, in a certain sense, by its own mechanics, the truth, the reality of what has happened. The verbal act of confession is the proof, is the manifestation, of truth', in 'Giving an Account,' p. 113.

20   A. K. Ramanujan, 'Toward a Counter-System: Women's Tales', in *Gender, Genre, and Power in South Asian Expressive Traditions*, ed. Arjun Appadurai, Frank J. Korom, and Margaret A. Mills (Philadelphia: University of Pennsylvania Press, 1991), p. 42.

21   Butler, 'Variations on Sex and Gender: Beauvoir, Wittig, and Foucault', in *Feminism as a Critique: On the Politics of Gender*, ed. Seyla Benhabib and Drucilla Cornell (Minneapolis: University of Minnesota Press, 1987), p. 131. Also, as Sophie Blanchy has suggested to me, and as Christiane Seydou has said about the *fille*, Shura's tale is a way of seeing marriage as an initiation that changes a girl into a woman; male heroes have a corresponding initiation.

22   *L'oiseau*, pp. 158–72.

23   The series of rejected bird calls happens in a Merina tale (Madagascar), in which the birds choose a king by its good speaking voice (Renel 2:233–34). The role of messenger or transporter is more often played in tales by the roller, *Leptosomus discolor* (Gueunier, *La belle*, p. 161, n. 3).

24   Another version of it, almost as well told, was recorded a few years before by Noël Gueunier. The narrators (both female) are careful to make the *djinn* disgusting and to emphasize (perhaps realistically) the force of the wife's jealousy of her well-behaved sister (*La belle*, pp. 138–61).

25   Afiati Sufu's Laughing Areca (*La maison*, pp. 64–97) is a version of The Three Golden Children (ATU707), which shows up in the Arabian Nights, in the classic Italian collection by Straparola in 1550, and in Grimm as tale number 96, The Three Little Birds. In Madagascar versions, a woman is accused of having given birth to animals or objects (motif K2115). Elsewhere in the Indian Ocean the animal birth slander has been told in the island of Réunion. Motifs: P292.1, Grandmother as foster mother; S351.1, Abandoned child cared for by grandmother. D2161, Magic healing power; D1711.7, King as magician. M262, Person promises to have but one consort if he is cured; N210, Wish for exalted husband realized. F950, Marvelous cures; L162, Lowly heroine marries king; T121.8, King weds common girl; N201, Wish for exalted husband realized; D2161.3.11, Barrenness

magically cured; K2222, Treacherous co-wife; K2251.1, Treacherous slave-girl. S185.1, Co-wife cruel to pregnant woman. K2110.1, Calumniated wife. K525, Escape by use of substituted object; S322, Children abandoned by hostile relative; S301, Children exposed; W26, Patience; W31, Obedience; P272, Foster (grand)mother: S351.1, Abandoned child cared for by (foster) grandmother; N856.1, Forester as foster father; H911.1, Task (quest) assigned at suggestion of jealous co-wife; H1361, Quest for lion's milk; D1619.3, Fruits that laugh or cry; D1617, Magic laughing object; H1333.2, Quest for extraordinary plant; H71, Marks of royalty; H20, Recognition by resemblance; E52, Resuscitation by magic charm; K1911.3, Reinstatement of true bride; S451, Outcast wife at last united with husband and children. Objective criticism can hardly go farther than a dry list like this.

26   *Contes mahorais*, pp. 117–18.

27   *La maison*, p. 97, n. 3. As anthropologists have long known, all folklore alludes to bits of the economy, technology, religion, and social organization of the people. In Africa, says Isidore Okpewho, to name known people and places and disregard any boundary between fiction and fact is 'accepted practice in oral narrative performance'; it represents a 'peculiar intersection of aesthetic and pragmatic imperatives,' some of which are political (Isidore Okpewho, *African Oral Literature: Backgrounds, Character, and Continuity* (Bloomington: Indiana University Press, 1992), p. 225). A less explicit form of the allusive device is what Claude Lévi-Strauss finds in South American mythology: unconscious interconnections among hundreds of myths.

28   The girl's impertinent answers recall the smart-ass replies of a clever lad to a king, incorporated in Madagascar versions of type ATU921, The King and the Farmer's Son (Dandouau, pp. 302–13). The term for these one-line dialogic exchanges, stichomythia, was first used for Greek tragedy. The device is often used by folktale narrators.

29   Stith Thompson, *The Folktale* (New York: Holt, Rinehart, and Winston, 1946), p. 121.

30   Terry Eagleton, *Criticism and Ideology: A Study in Marxist Literary Theory* (London, 1978), pp. 88–89.

31   Joan N. Radner and Susan S. Lanser, 'Strategies of Coding in Women's Cultures', in *Feminist Messages: Coding in Women's Folk Culture* (Urbana: University of Illinois Press, 1993), p. 4.

32   Judith Fetterley, *The Resisting Reader: A Feminist Approach to American Fiction* (Bloomington: Indiana University Press, 1978), p. 304.

33   Hélène Cixous, 'The Laugh of the Medusa', in *New French Feminisms, an Anthology*, ed. Elaine Marks and Isabelle de Courtivron (New York: Schocken Books, 1981), p. 245.

34   The old woman trusted to verify a bride's virginity and defloration (*Lignée féminine*, p. 164, n. 3). Recorded around the same time, Dady ny Saidy of Poroani used a very similar formula. Other tellers often omitted opening formulas, probably for lack of their usual audience. Being easily recognized, an opening formula calls for listening mode and announces the fictional genre of *angano*. Imaginatively it transports the hearer into the world of *ny taloha*, former times.

35   Note that she does not marry the heroine's father. In a tale similar to Grandmother Shark, such a stepmother pushes the girl into the water, then presents her daughter to the kin, who first marries her, then drives her away after discovering the imposture. The girl, undersea, is found and cared for by a *djinn* who takes care of her, the later discovered and married to the king. Of course the stepmother and her daughter are punished. More realistically, some Mahorais acknowledge a negative attitude between mothers-in-law and daughters-in-law (who may not be from the same village community that they are), and sometimes the young women have to woo them with gifts, patience, and submission (*Lignée féminine*, p. 30).

36   *La maison*, p. 43.

37   *Lignée féminine*, p. 45.

38   *La maison*, p. 6.

39   Barbara Johnson, *The Critical Difference: Essays in the Contemporary Rhetoric of Reading* (Baltimore, 1981), p. 54.

40   Terence Cave, *Recognitions* (Oxford: Clarendon Press, 1988), p. 200.

41   Michelle Zimbalist Rosaldo, *Woman, Culture, and Society* (Redwood City: Stanford University Press, 1974), p. 39.

42   Butler, *Gender Trouble: Feminism and the Subversion of Identity* (New York: Routledge, 1990), p. 145.

43   Butler, *Excitable Speech: A Politics of the Performative* (New York: Routledge, 1997), p. 133.

44   Butler, *Giving an Account of Oneself* (New York: Fordham University Press, 2005), p. 22.

45   I draw on Paul De Man, *Blindness and Insight: Essays in the Rhetoric of Contemporary Criticism* (Minneapolis: University of Minnesota Press, 1983), p. 104.

46   *Le coq*, pp. 174–83.

47   Summarized from the versions in *Malagasy Tale Index*, pp. 416–21.

48   Jean-Pierre Domenichini, 'Un aspect de la résistance de l'ancienne culture malgache à l'influence arabe', *Omaly Sy Anio*, 25–26 (1987), p. 86. I make extensive use of this great historian's thinking in my comments.

49   Bakoly Domenichini-Ramiaramanana, *Du ohabolana au hainteny. Langue, littérature et politique à Madagascar* (Paris: Karthala, 1983), pp. 490–91, n. 139.

50   The tale was told by both a woman narrator in Poroani and a young woman of Mwamoju, originally from Kany Kely (*L'oiseau*, pp. 20–49). The piece is distantly related to European tales such as The Three Birds (Grimm no. 96). Motifs, Poroani version: B754.7, Unusual parturition of animal (reversal of T554, Woman gives birth to animal); Q2, Kind and unkind; K2212, Treacherous sister; ±T111.3, Marriage of man with woman who has come from an egg (Indian); Q65, Filial duty rewarded; Q261, Treachery punished. The Kany Kely version: B754.6.1, Unusual impregnation of animal; D1925.1, Barrenness cured by eating; T511.1.3, Conception from eating mango; T589.7, Simultaneous conception and births; B754.7, Unusual parturition of animal; B535.0.4, Dog as nurse for child; K2110.1, Calumniated wife; cf. R169.7, Royal minister rescues abandoned queen (Indian); T100, Marriage; H79.3, Recognition by voice (Indian); B332, Too watchful dog killed; V222.4, Saint's house filled with fragrance; D2167, Corpse magically saved from corruption; Q111, Riches as reward; Q65, Filial duty rewarded; E323, Dead mother's friendly return; E373, Ghosts bestow gifts on living; E363.5, Dead provide material aid to living; B491.1, Helpful serpent (transformation of swallowing monster); H71.1, Star on forehead as sign of royalty; D1860, Magic beautification; Q411, Death as punishment; Q211.2, Matricide punished; Q281.1.2, Girl cruel to her mother is slain by God. Mwamoju version: B754.6.1, Unusual impregnation of animal; D1925.1, Barrenness cured by eating; T511.1.3, Conception from eating mango; T589.7, Simultaneous conception and births; B754.7, Unusual parturition of animal; T670, Adoption of children; cf. T676, Childless couple adopt animal as substitute for child; B535.0.4, Dog as nurse for child; T100, Marriage; H79.3, Recognition by voice; B332, Too watchful dog killed; D422.2, Transformation: dog to object; V222.4, Saint's house filled with fragrance; D2167, Corpse magically saved from corruption; Q111, Riches as reward; Q65, Filial duty rewarded; E323, Dead

mother's friendly return; E373, Ghosts bestow gifts on living; E363.5, Dead provide material aid to living; B491.1, Helpful serpent; H71.1, Star on forehead as sign of royalty; Q411, Death as punishment, Q211.2, Matricide punished, Q281.1.2, Girl cruel to her mother is slain.

51   Being born at the foot of a tree recalls Malagasy myths of the origin of woman, and Comoran tales in which a supernatural girl emerges from a tree-trunk (Renel 3:39–41, *L'oiseau*, p. 25, n. 2).

52   L. S. Asekoff, *Freedom Hill, a Poem* (Evanston (IL) TriQuarterly Books, Northwestern University Press, 2011), p. 42.

53   Horses (*farasy*) don't exist in Mayotte except in these stories.

54   *Le coq*, p. 49, n. 18.

55   *L'oiseau*, pp. 26–91.

56   Tzvetan Todorov, *The Poetics of Prose*, trans. Richard Howard (Ithaca: Cornell University Press, 1977), pp. 72, 76.

57   Roland Barthes, *The Rustle of Language*, trans. Richard Howard (New York, 1986), p. 411.

58   Jean-Pierre Domenichini, 'Un aspect de la résistance de l'ancienne culture malgache à l'influence arabe', *Omaly Sy Anio*, 25–26 (1987), pp. 91–92.

59   *L'oiseau*, pp. xxi-xxii.

60   Sophie Blanchy-Daurel, *La vie quotidienne à Mayotte* (Paris: L'Harmattan, 1993), p. 128.

61   Evidently the story has enduring appeal for the descendants of Malagasy, or for other Comorans. Other versions are in Veronika Görög-Karady, *L'enfant dans les contes africains* (Paris: C I L F, 1988), pp. 153–60 and Abdallah Daoud, *Zamani. Hale za shikomori, hadisi za kikomori* (Moroni: CNDRS, 1983), pp. 57–90.

62   Butler, *Undoing Gender* (New York: Routledge, 2004), p. 4.

63   Framing in a narrative doesn't always require a female voice, as we saw in The Laughing Areca. In a reversal of the *fille difficile* plot, told by a female narrator, the male character proclaims in song that a boar-wife is ethnically unsuitable. Mahorais versions of the international tales The Clever Precepts (ATU910) and The Treasure Finders Who Murder One Another (ATU763) include a scene of recognition through narration (*Contes comoriens*, pp. 442–50, 480–85). In the complex *fille* story of Kalevola, told by an old

woman, the mother character, betrayed into the power of a cannibal ogre who then devoured their child, produces a second daughter as the heroine. Hidden by female protectors, found, devoured, resuscitated, sent far away, displaced by her servant, sent to the fields, and recognized, she is finally adopted and married off by a benevolent king. During these adventures the song is sung again and again. After the fifth repetition, she still has to explain it in speech, like a Los Angeles folksinger singing in Serbian. Her recognition through performance unlocks the mystery. Narrators' reliance on a scene of recognition through narration or song indicates its traditional status, at least for Mayotte.

64   I use words of Sara Salih, *Judith Butler* (London: Taylor & Francis, 2002), p. 67.

65   Patrick Eisenlohr, *Little India: Diaspora, Time, and Ethnolinguistic Belonging in Hindu Mauritius* (Berkeley: University of California Press, 2006), p. 112.

66   *La maison*, p. 97, n. 6.

67   Michel Foucault, *The Archaeology of Knowledge and the Discourse on Language*, trans. A. M. Sheridan Smith (New York: Pantheon Books, 1972), p. 49.

68   *La vie quotidienne*, p. 67.

69   A. E. B. Coldiron, 'Canons and Cultures: Is Shakespeare Universal?' in *How to Do Things with Shakespeare: New Approaches, New Essays*, ed. Laurie Maguire (Oxford: Blackwell, 2008), p. 248.

70   Lisa Zunshine, *Why We Read Fiction: Theory of Mind and the Novel* (Columbus: Ohio State University Press, 2006), p. 6.

71   Munro S. Edmonson, *Lore: An Introduction to the Science of Folklore and Literature* (New York: Holt, Rinehart and Winston, 1971), p. 200.

72   James Deetz, *Invitation to Archaeology* (New York: American Museum of Natural History, 1967), p. 83.

73   Fredric Jameson, *Postmodernism, or, the Cultural Logic of Late Capitalism* (Durham: Duke University Press, 1991), p. 298.

74   Dell Hymes, 'The Contribution of Folklore to Sociolinguistic Research', in *Toward New Perspectives in Folklore*, ed. Américo Paredes and Richard Bauman (Austin: University of Texas Press, 1972), p. 49.

75   Peter Uwe Hohendahl, *Prismatic Thought: Theodor W. Adorno* (Lincoln: University of Nebraska Press, 1995), p. 160.

76 Christiane Seydou, 'Un conte breton: "Petit-Louis, fils d'un charbonnier et filleul du Roi de France". Essai d'analyse et d'étude comparative'. *Cahiers d'Études Africaines* 12, 45 (1972), p. 130.

77 George Lakoff and Mark Johnson, *Metaphors We Live By* (Chicago: University of Chicago Press, 1980), p. 3.

78 Lakoff & Johnson, p. 267.

79 Ralf Schneider and Marcus Hartner, *Blending and the Study of Narrative: Approaches and Applications* (Berlin: De Gruyter, 2012), p. 6.

80 Theodor W. Adorno, *Prisms* (Cambridge, MA: MIT Press, 1981), p. 32.

81 Ludwig Wittgenstein, *Philosophische Untersuchungen* = *Philosophical Investigations* (Berlin: Suhrkamp, 2009), p. 235.

Works Cited

Abdallah Daoud, and Amina Kassim Bashrahii, *Zamani. Hale za shikomori. Hadisi za kikomori*. Moroni (Comoros): Centre National de Documentation et Recherche Scientifique, 1983

Abdallah Paune, Kamaroudine, *Cultural Traditions in Comoro Islands*, master's thesis (mémoire de maîtrise d'anglais), Université de Paris III, 1977

Abrahams, Roger D., *Deep Down in the Jungle: Negro Narrative Folklore from the Streets of Philadelphia* (Hatboro, PA: Folklore Associates, 1964)

____, *The Man-of-Words in the West Indies* (Baltimore, MD: Johns Hopkins University Press, 1983)

____, 'Proverbs and Proverbial Expressions', in *Folklore and Folklife, an Introduction*, ed. Richard M. Dorson (Chicago: University of Chicago Press, 1972), pp. 117–27

Adorno, Theodor W., *Prisms* (Cambridge, MA: MIT Press, 1981)

Allen, Philip M. *Security and Nationalism in the Indian Ocean: Lessons from the Latin Quarter Islands* (London: Routledge, 2019)

Allibert, Claude, *Contes mahorais*, Archives orales mahoraises (Paris: Académie des Sciences d'Outre-Mer, 1977)

____, *Mayotte: plaque tournante et microcosme de l'océan indien occidental* (Paris: Éditions Anthropos, 1984)

Baissac, Charles, *Folklore de l'île Maurice* (Paris: G. P. Maisonneuve et Larose, 1887)

Barthes, Roland, 'The Death of the Author', in *The Rustle of Language*, trans. Richard Howard (New York: Hill and Wang, 1986), pp. 49–55

Bascom, William R., *African Dilemma Tales* (The Hague: Mouton, 1975)

Bateman, George W. *Zanzibar tales told by natives of the east coast of Africa* (Chicago: A. C. McClurg, 1901)

Bauman, Richard, 'Conceptions of Folklore in the Development of Literary Semiotics', *Semiotica*, 39 (1982), 1–20

Beaujard, Philippe, *Mythe et société à Madagascar (Tanala de l'Ikongo): le chasseur d'oiseaux et la princesse du ciel*, preface by Georges Condominas (Paris: L'Harmattan, 1991)

Bird, Charles, 'The Heroic Songs of the Mande Hunters', in *African Folklore*, ed. Richard M. Dorson (Garden City, NY: Doubleday, 1972)

Birkeli, Émile, 'Folklore sakalava recueilli dans la région de Morondava', *Bulletin de l'Académie Malgache*, n. s. 6 (1922–1923), 185–417

Blandenet, Yves, 'La diaspora des contes africains dans les mythologies de l'Océan Indien', *Notre Librairie*, 72 (1983), 21–31

Blanchy, Sophie, 'Changement social à Mayotte: transformations, tensions, ruptures', *Études Océan Indien*, 33–34 (2002), 165–95

____, 'Lignée féminine et valeurs islamiques à travers quelques contes de Mayotte (Comores)' (Saint-Denis: Université de la Réunion, 1986)

____, *Maisons des femmes, cités des hommes. Filiation, âge et pouvoir à Ngazidja (Comores)* (Nanterre: Société d'Ethnologie, 2010)

____, 'Proverbes Mahorais', *ASEMI*, 12, 3–4 (1981), 109–32

____, *La vie quotidienne à Mayotte* (Paris: L'Harmattan, 1993)

____, and Zakaria Soilihi, *Furukombe et autres contes de Mayotte* (Paris: Éditions Caribéennes, 1991)

____, and Zakaria Soilihi, 'Le tambour', *L'Espoir* (Réunion), 2 (August 1989), 20–31

____, and Zakaria Soilihi, Noël Jacques Gueunier, and Madjidhoubi Said, *La maison de la mère: contes de l'île de Mayotte* (Paris: L'Harmattan, 1993)

Blandenet, Yves, 'La diaspora des contes africains dans les mythologies de l'Océan Indien', *Notre Librairie*, 72 (1983), 21–31

Boyd, Raymond, and Richard Fardon, 'La fille difficile tchamba, sauvée par un chanson (Nord-Cameroun)', in *La fille difficile, un conte-type africain*, ed. Veronika Görög-Karady and Christiane Seydou (Paris: CNRS Éditions, 2001), pp. 139–66

Burton, Richard F., translator, *The Book of the Thousand Nights and a Night, a Plain and Literal Translation of the Arabian Nights Entertainments* (n. p.; n. d.)

Bushnaq, Inea, *Arab Folktales* (New York: Pantheon, 1986)

Butler, Judith, *Excitable Speech: A Politics of the Performative* (New York: Routledge, 1997)

____, *Gender Trouble: Feminism and the Subversion of Identity* (New York: Routledge, 1990)

____, *Giving an Account of Oneself* (New York: Fordham University Press, 2005)

____, *Undoing Gender* (New York: Routledge, 2004)

_____, 'Variations on Sex and Gender: Beauvoir, Wittig, and Foucault', in *Feminism as a Critique: On the Politics of Gender*, ed. Seyla Benhabib and Drucilla Cornell (Minneapolis: University of Minnesota Press, 1987)

Callet, R. P., *Tantaran'ny andriana*, trans. G.-S. Chapus and E. Ratsimba (Antananarivo: Librairie de Madagascar, 1958)

Cancel, Robert, *Allegorical Speculation in an Oral Society: The Tabwa Narrative Tradition* (Berkeley: University of California Press, 1989)

Cave, Terence, *Recognitions* (Oxford: Clarendon Press, 1988)

Cixous, Hélène, 'The Laugh of the Medusa', in *New French Feminisms, an Anthology*, ed. Elaine Marks and Isabelle de Courtivron (New York: Schocken Books, 1981)

Coldiron, A. E. B. 'Canons and Cultures: Is Shakespeare Universal?', in *How to Do Things with Shakespeare: New Approaches, New Essays*, ed. Laurie Maguire (Oxford: Blackwell, 2008), pp. 255–79

Dahle, L[ars], *Specimens of Malagasy Folk-lore* (Antananarivo: A. Kingdon, 1877)

_____, and John Sims, *Anganon'ny Ntaolo* (Antananarivo: Trano Printy Loterana, 1971)

Deetz, James, *Invitation to Archaeology* (New York: American Museum of Natural History, 1967)

Dégh, Linda, *Narratives in Society, a Performer-Centered Study of Narration* (Bloomington: Indiana University Press, 1995)

Delarue, Paul, and Marie-Louise Tenèze, *Le conte populaire français: catalogue raisonné des versions de France* (Paris: G. P. Maisonneuve et Larose, 1976–2002)

Deleuze, Gilles, and Félix Guattari, *A Thousand Plateaus: Capitalism and Schizophrenia*, trans. Brian Massumi (Minneapolis: University of Minnesota Press, 1987)

De Man, Paul, *Blindness and Insight: Essays in the Rhetoric of Contemporary Criticism* (Minneapolis: University of Minnesota Press, 1983)

Djoumoi, Ali M'madi, 'Transmission traditionnelle des savoirs et des savoir-f aire à Ndzaoudze, M'Vouni', master's thesis (M'vouni, Grande Comore, 1989)

Domenichini, Jean-Pierre, 'Un aspect de la résistance de l'ancienne culture malgache à l'influence arabe', *Omaly Sy Anio*, 25–26 (1987), 81–98

Domenichini-Ramiaramanana, Bakoly, *Du ohabolana au hainteny. Langue, littérature et politique à Madagascar* (Paris: Karthala, 1983)

Ducrot, Oswald, and Tzvetan Todorov, *Dictionnaire encyclopédique des sciences du langage* (Paris: Éditions du Seuil, 1972)

Dundes, Alan. 'The Making and Breaking of Friendship as a Structural Frame in African Folk Tales,' in *Structural Analysis of Oral Tradition*, edited by

Pierre Maranda and Elli Köngäs Maranda (Philadelphia: University of Pennsylvania Press, 1971), 171–85

Eagleton, Terry, *Criticism and Ideology: A Study in Marxist Literary Theory* (London: Verso, 1978)

Edmonson, Munro S., *Lore: An Introduction to the Science of Folklore and Literature* (New York: Holt, Rinehart and Winston, 1971)

Eisenlohr, Patrick, *Little India: Diaspora, Time, and Ethnolinguistic Belonging in Hindu Mauritius* (Berkeley: University of California Press, 2006)

El-Shamy, Hasan, *Folktales of Egypt* (Chicago: University of Chicago Press, 1980).

Emerson, Caryl, and Gary Saul Morson, *Mikhail Bakhtin: Creation of a Prosaics* (Stanford, CA: Stanford University Press, 1990)

Faublée, Jacques, *Récits bara* (Paris: Institut d'Ethnologie, 1947)

Feintuch, Burt, editor, *Eight Words for the Study of Expressive Culture* (Urbana, IL: University of Illinois Press, 2003)

Ferry, Marie-Paule, 'Telling Folktales — Why?', trans. Lee Haring, *Southwest Folklore* 6, 1 (1986), 1–16

Fetterley, Judith, *The Resisting Reader: A Feminist Approach to American Fiction* (Bloomington: Indiana University Press, 1978)

Fontoynont, Maurice, and Raomandahy, 'La grande Comore', *Mémoires de l'Académie Malgache* (1937)

Foucault, Michel, *The Archaeology of Knowledge and the Discourse on Language*, trans. A. M. Sheridan Smith (New York: Pantheon Books, 1972)

Gates, Henry Louis, *The Signifying Monkey: A Theory of Afro-American Literary Criticism* (New York: Oxford University Press, 1988)

Gecau, Rose, *Kikuyu Folktales* (Nairobi: East African Literature Bureau, 1970)

Gehring, Wes D., *Handbook of American Film Genres* (New York: Greenwood Press, 1988)

Genette, Gérard, *Narrative Discourse: An Essay in Method*, trans. Jane E. Lewin (Ithaca: Cornell University Press, 1980)

____, *Palimpsests: Literature in the Second Degree*, trans. Channa Newman and Claude Doubinsky (Lincoln: University of Nebraska Press, 1997)

Glassie, Henry, 'Tradition', in Burt Feintuch, ed., *Eight Words for the Study of Expressive Culture* (Urbana, IL: University of Illinois Press, 2003)

Görög-Karady, Veronika, and Christiane Seydou, ed., *La fille difficile, un conte-type africain* (Paris: CNRS Éditions, 2001)

Gueunier, Noël J., *La belle ne se marie point: contes comoriens en dialecte malgache de l'île de Mayotte* (Paris: Peeters, 1990)

_____, *Le coq du roi: contes comoriens en dialecte malgache de l'île de Mayotte* (Paris: Peeters, 2001)

_____, *L'oiseau chagrin: contes comoriens en dialecte malgache de l'île de Mayotte* (Paris: Peeters, 1994)

_____, and Madjidhoubi Saïd, *Contes comoriens en dialecte malgache de l'île de Mayotte. La Quête de la sagesse* (Paris: Éditions Karthala, 2011).

Hall, Stuart, 'Créolité and the Process of Creolization', in *Créolité and Creolization. Documenta 11 Platform 3*, ed. Okwui Enwezor et al. (Ostfildern-Ruit (Germany): Hatje Cantz, 2015), pp. 27–41

Hansen, William, *Ariadne's Thread: A Guide to International Tales Found in Classical Literature* (Ithaca: Cornell University Press, 2002)

Haring, Lee, 'A Characteristic African Folktale Pattern', in *African Folklore*, ed. Richard M. Dorson (Garden City, NY: Doubleday, 1972), pp. 165–79

_____, 'Interpreters of Indian Ocean Tales', *Fabula* 44 (2003), 98–116

_____, *Malagasy Tale Index*, FF Communications 231(Helsinki: Suomalainen Tiedeakatemia, 1982)

_____, 'Parody and Imitation in Western Indian Ocean Oral Literature', *Journal of Folklore Research*, 29, 3 (1992), 199–224

_____, 'Performing for the Interviewer: A Study of the Structure of Context', *Southern Folklore Quarterly*, 36 (1972), 383–98

_____, *Stars and Keys: Folktales and Creolization in the Indian Ocean* (Bloomington: Indiana University Press, 2007)

_____, 'Verbal Charms in Malagasy Folktales', in *Charms, Charmers and Charming: International Research on Verbal Magic*, ed. Jonathan Roper (London, 2004), pp. 246–59

Harris, Joel Chandler, *Nights with Uncle Remus: Myths and Legends of the Old Plantation* (Boston: Houghton Mifflin, 1883)

Hohendahl, Peter Uwe, *Prismatic Thought: Theodor W. Adorno* (Lincoln: University of Nebraska Press, 1995)

Holbek, Bengt, 'Games of the Powerless', *Unifol*, 1976 (1977), 10–33

Howard, Richard, *Alone with America: Essays on the Art of Poetry in the United States since 1950* (New York: Atheneum, 1980)

Hymes, Dell, 'The Contribution of Folklore to Sociolinguistic Research', in *Toward New Perspectives in Folklore*, ed. Américo Paredes and Richard Bauman (Austin: University of Texas Press, 1972), pp. 42–50

_____, 'Folklore's Nature and the Sun's Myth', *Journal of American Folklore*, 88, 350 (1975), 346–69

Jacobs, Melville, *The Content and Style of an Oral Literature: Clackamas Chinook Myths and Tales* (Chicago: University of Chicago Press, 1959)

Jameson, Fredric, *The Political Unconscious: Narrative as a Socially Symbolic Act* (Ithaca: Cornell University Press, 1981)

____, *Postmodernism, or, the Cultural Logic of Late Capitalism* (Durham: Duke University Press, 1991)

Johnson, Barbara, *The Critical Difference: Essays in the Contemporary Rhetoric of Reading* (Baltimore, 1981)

Kirshenblatt-Gimblett, Barbara, 'Studying Immigrant and Ethnic Folklore', in *Handbook of American Folklore*, ed. Richard M. Dorson (Bloomington: Indiana University Press, 1983), pp. 39–47

Knappert, Jan, *Myths and Legends of the Swahili* (Nairobi: Heinemann Educational Books, 1970)

Kristeva, Julia, *Desire in Language: A Semiotic Approach to Literature and Art*, ed. Leon S. Roudiez (New York: Columbia University Press, 1980)

Lakoff, George and Mark Johnson, *Metaphors We Live By* (Chicago: University of Chicago Press, 1980)

Lambek, Michael, *Human Spirits: A Cultural Account of Trance in Mayotte* (Cambridge: Cambridge University Press, 1981)

____, *Island in the Stream: An Ethnographic History of Mayotte* (Toronto: University of Toronto Press, 2018)

Levine, Caroline, *Forms: Whole, Rhythm, Hierarchy, Network* (Princeton: Princeton University Press, 2015)

Lévi-Strauss, Claude, *Wild Thought: A New Translation of 'La Pensée Sauvage'*, trans. Jeffrey Mehlman and John Leavitt (Chicago: University of Chicago Press, 2021). https://doi.org/10.7208/chicago/9780226413112.001.0001

Lindblom, Gerhard, *Kamba Folklore, with Linguistic, Ethnographical and Comparative Notes* (Leipzig: Harrassowitz, 1928–1935)

Lord, Albert B., *The Singer of Tales* (Cambridge: Harvard University Press, 1960)

Lüthi, Max, *The European Folktale: Form and Nature*, trans. John D. Niles (Bloomington: Indiana University Press, 1986)

Maranda, Pierre, ed. *Mythology, Selected Readings* (Harmondsworth: Penguin Books, 1972)

Martin, Jean, *Comores: quatre îles entre pirates et planteurs* (Paris: L'Harmattan, 1983)

Melamed, Daniel R., 'Parody', in *J. S. Bach. Oxford Composer Companions*, ed. Malcolm Boyd (Oxford, 1999), pp. 356–57

Mills, Margaret A., *Rhetoric and Politics in Afghan Traditional Storytelling* (Philadelphia: University of Pennsylvania Press, 1991)

Mintz, Sidney W., and Richard Price, *An Anthropological Approach to the Afro-American Past: A Caribbean Perspective* (Philadelphia: University of Pennsylvania Press, 1976)

Njururi, Ngumbu, *Agikuyu Folk Tales* (Nairobi: Oxford University Press, 1966)

Okpewho, Isidore, *African Oral Literature: Backgrounds, Character, and Continuity* (Bloomington: Indiana University Press, 1992)

Olrik, Axel, *Principles for Oral Narrative Research*, trans. Kirsten Wolf and Jody Jensen (Bloomington: Indiana University Press, 1992)

Ottino, Paul, *L'étrangère intime: essai d'anthropologie de la civilisation de l'ancien Madagascar* (Paris: Éditions des Archives Contemporains, 1986)

____, 'Un procédé littéraire malayo-polynésien: de l'ambigüité à la plurisignification', *L'Homme*, 6, 4 (October-December 1966), 5–34

____, 'Le thème du monstre dévorant dans les domaines malgache et bantou', *ASEMI* 8, 3–4 (1977), 219–51

Paulme, Denise. *La statue du commandeur: essais d'ethnologie* (Paris: Le Sycomore, 1984)

____, 'Morphologie du conte africain', *Cahiers d'Études Africaines,* 12, 45 (1972), 131–63

Radner, Joan N., and Susan S. Lanser, 'Strategies of Coding in Women's Cultures', in *Feminist Messages: Coding in Women's Folk Culture* (Urbana: University of Illinois Press, 1993), 1–29

Ramanujan, A. K. 'Toward a Counter-System: Women's Tales', in *Gender, Genre, and Power in South Asian Expressive Traditions*, ed. Arjun Appadurai, Frank J. Korom, and Margaret A. Mills (Philadelphia: University of Pennsylvania Press, 1991)

Renel, Charles, *Contes de Madagascar* (Paris: Ernest Leroux, 1910)

Rosaldo, Michelle Zimbalist, *Woman, Culture, and Society* (Redwood City: Stanford University Press, 1974)

Roubaud, Jacques, 'Introduction: The *Oulipo* and Combinatorial Art', in *Oulipo Compendium*, ed. Harry Mathews and Alastair Brotchie (London: Atlas Press, 1998), pp. 37–44

Nina Sahraoui, 'Constructions of Undeservingness around the Figure of the Undocumented Pregnant Woman in the French Department of Mayotte'. *Social Policy and Society*, 20, 3 (July 2021), 475–486. https://doi.org/10.1017/S1474746421000038.

Salih, Sara, *Judith Butler* (London: Taylor & Francis, 2002)

Schimmel, Annemarie, *Islam: An Introduction* (Albany: State University of New York Press, 1992)

Schneider, Ralf, and Marcus Hartner, *Blending and the Study of Narrative: Approaches and Applications* (Berlin: De Gruyter, 2012). https://doi. org/10.1515/9783110291230

Seydou, Christiane, 'Un conte breton: "Petit-Louis, fils d'un charbonnier et filleul du Roi de France". Essai d'analyse et d'étude comparative'. *Cahiers d'Études Africaines*, 12, 45 (1972): 109–30

Storch, Anne, *Secret Manipulations: Language and Context in Africa* (New York: Oxford University Press, 2011)

Thompson, Stith, *The Folktale* (New York: Holt, Rinehart, and Winston, 1946)

———, *Motif-Index of Folk-Literature; a Classification of Narrative Elements in Folktales, Ballads, Myths, Fables, Mediaeval Romances, Exempla, Fabliaux, Jest-Books, and Local Legends* (Bloomington: Indiana University Press, 1955–58), https:// archive.org/details/Thompson2016MotifIndex/page/n7/mode/2up

———, and Jonas Balys, *The Oral Tales of India* (Westport, CT: Greenwood Press, 1958)

Uther, Hans-Jörg, *The Types of International Folktales: A Classification and Bibliography*, editorial staff Sabine Dinslage, Sigrid Fährmann, Christine Goldberg, and Gudrun Schwibbe, *FF Communications*, 285 (Helsinki: Suomalainen Tiedeakatemia, 2004)

Vérin, Pierre, *The History of Civilisation in North Madagascar* (Rotterdam: A. A. Balkema, 1986)

Werbner, Richard, 'Afterword', in *Syncretism/Anti-Syncretism: The Politics of Religious Synthesis*, ed. Charles Stewart, and Rosalind Shaw (London: Routledge, 1994), pp. 212–15

Wittgenstein, Ludwig, *Philosophische Untersuchungen = Philosophical Investigations* (Berlin: Suhrkamp, 2009)

Zunshine, Lisa, *Why We Read Fiction: Theory of Mind and the Novel* (Columbus: Ohio State University Press, 2006)

List of Illustrations

Index

About the Team

Alessandra Tosi was the managing editor for this book.

Lucy Barnes and Peio Pinuaga Arriaga performed the copy-editing and proofreading.

Margarita Louka designed the cover. The cover was produced in InDesign using the Fontin font.

Maria Teresa Renzi-Sepe wrote the Alt-text.

Jeremy Bowman typeset the book in InDesign and produced the paperback and hardback editions. The text font is Tex Gyre Pagella; the heading font is Californian FB.

Cameron Craig produced the EPUB, PDF, HTML, and XML editions. The conversion was made with open-source software such as pandoc (https://pandoc.org/), created by John MacFarlane, and other tools freely available on our GitHub page (https://github.com/OpenBookPublishers).

This book has been anonymously peer-reviewed by experts in their field. We thank them for their invaluable help.

This book need not end here...

Share

All our books — including the one you have just read — are free to access online so that students, researchers and members of the public who can't afford a printed edition will have access to the same ideas. This title will be accessed online by hundreds of readers each month across the globe: why not share the link so that someone you know is one of them?

This book and additional content is available at:

https://doi.org/10.11647/OBP.0315

Donate

Open Book Publishers is an award-winning, scholar-led, not-for-profit press making knowledge freely available one book at a time. We don't charge authors to publish with us: instead, our work is supported by our library members and by donations from people who believe that research shouldn't be locked behind paywalls.

Why not join them in freeing knowledge by supporting us:
https://www.openbookpublishers.com/support-us

Follow @OpenBookPublish

Read more at the Open Book Publishers BLOG

You may also be interested in:

Oral Literature in Africa
Ruth Finnegan

https://doi.org/10.11647/OBP.0025

How to Read a Folktale
The 'Ibonia' Epic from Madagascar
Lee Haring

https://doi.org/10.11647/OBP.0034

Storytelling in Northern Zambia
Theory, Method, Practice and Other Necessary Fictions
Robert Cancel

https://doi.org/10.11647/OBP.0033

Milton Keynes UK
Ingram Content Group UK Ltd.
UKHW020653310524
443422UK00002B/4